FRANKIE MANNING

FRANKIE MANNING

Ambassador of Lindy Hop

FRANKIE MANNING AND CYNTHIA R. MILLMAN

TEMPLE UNIVERSITY PRESS
PHILADELPHIA

Temple University Press
Philadelphia, Pennsylvania, 19122
www.temple.edu/tempress

Copyright © 2007 by Frankie Manning and Cynthia R. Millman
All rights reserved
Published 2007
Printed in the United States of America

Design by BTDnyc / Beth Tondreau

♾ The paper used in this publication meets the requirements of the American
National Standard for Information Sciences—Permanence of Paper for
Printed Library Materials, ANSI Z39.48-1992

Library of Congress Cataloging-in-Publication Data

Manning, Frankie.
  Frankie Manning : ambassador of lindy hop / Frankie Manning, Cynthia R. Millman.
    p. cm.
  Includes bibliographical references and index.
  ISBN-13: 978-1-59213-563-9   ISBN-10: 1-59213-563-3 (cloth : alk. paper)
  1. Manning, Frankie.   2. Dancers—United States—Biography.   3. Choreographers—
  United States—Biography.   4. Lindy (Dance)   I. Millman, Cynthia   II. Title.
  GV1785.M36A3 2007
  792.8092—dc22
  [B]   2006036174

  ISBN 978-1-59213-564-6 (paper : alk. paper)

Frontispiece: Frankie Manning arriving in Sydney Harbor, fall 1938 (detail). Courtesy of
Frankie Manning.

Last printed page: Frankie Manning celebrating his ninetieth birthday in New York City,
spring 2004. Photograph by Beth Tondreau. Courtesy of Beth Tondreau.

All reasonable attempts were made to locate the copyright owners of the materials contained
in this book. If you believe you have a copyright interest in any of these materials, please
contact the Rights and Permissions Manager, Temple University Press, 1601 N. Broad
Street, Philadelphia PA 19122.

6   8   9   7

To Herbert "Whitey" White, and
dancers around the world.

—F. M.

To my father, Lester Joshua Millman, and
his father, Jacob,
my first two dance partners.

—C. M.

CONTENTS

Illustrations follow pages 64, 128, and 192

FOREWORD

MERCEDES ELLINGTON

This may be one of the shortest forewords ever, for reasons that will become apparent as soon as you start to read this book—if you haven't done so already. It's a hard book to put down. Even the chapter headings are intriguing.

You feel the energy popping off of each page. When you jump right into the way Frankie Manning performs on the dance floor, there's no turning back, unless you want a chance to catch your breath before jumping back in again.

Frankie recounts his life's journey with warmth, spirit, and humor, and with insight from a long career and rich life experience. He also chronicles a plethora of important information, highlighting many people and events that have been overlooked or given only brief attention. Frankie's book is a great gift not only to the music and dance world but also to historians of the times. It is a prime example of the realization of the old African proverb: "Until the lions have their own historians, tales of the hunt shall always glorify the hunter."

Frankie's no-nonsense approach in his dancing is reflected in these pages. His decades of seeking the ultimate technical challenges, refining his craft, and inadvertently creating one of America's most treasured art forms eventually established him as a legend. It is noteworthy that, like most other trailblazers, he did not begin with the goal of attaining legendary status, which so many current reality television programs would have you believe is so easy and so automatic to achieve. His mission was simply to utilize his talent for and fascination with the dance to create the most outstanding routines on the ballroom floor.

By the time I became a young Apollo Theater denizen, Frankie had long left that scene. My maternal grandmother, who raised me, would deposit me into the hands of my father, Mercer, at the stage door on 126th Street, and he would in turn deposit me in a seat in the orchestra section of the audience with some of the band members' wives. There I'd sit in rapture all day and into the night, watching the Duke Ellington Orchestra alternate sets with some current movie (standard format for most theaters of the day). Between munching on bags of popcorn and other forbidden treats while watching the shows, and sharing in the food brought in by the orchestra wives, I felt like the luckiest kid alive.

I discovered Frankie years later at a family-run restaurant not far from the Apollo called Well's, where a most fabulous eighteen-piece band, The Harlem Renaissance Band, played every Monday night. I was doing research for a Broadway show I'd been commissioned to choreograph, and Ernie Smith steered me to this hub of the jumpin' jive. I ended up asking Frankie to be a consultant on the show (*Play On!*, conceived and directed by Sheldon Epps with musical arrangements of Duke Ellington's music by Luther Henderson, a longtime collaborator and arranger for the Duke Ellington Orchestra). Thus I experienced firsthand some of the energy, creativity, and inspiration conveyed in this story about "swingin' in time."

Frankie's life and times unfold chapter by chapter, interweaving subplots carved out of the historical context. With incredible clarity, Frankie sets the record straight about many events and credits others responsible for contributing to the creation of this dance form we call swing, or jitterbug, or Lindy hop. This particular aspect of the book is especially important to our youth, some of whom are currently mired in rootless anger, all of whom need to know more about the proud heritage Frankie has helped to create.

There is scarcely a place in this world that has not been visited and touched by Frankie's hand. I was invited to Stockholm, Sweden during a tribute to my grandfather. There was a program of music and dance in the great hall where the Nobel Prizes were awarded. As I sat there watching the local dancers meticulously executing some familiar routines, I said: "Frankie was here!"

With the help of this book, Frankie will continue to be here, there, and everywhere in the minds and hearts—and feet—of the world.

FRANKIE MANNING: AN APPRECIATION

CYNTHIA R. MILLMAN

Dancing Through the Decades

Like the enchanted heroine of the ballet *The Red Shoes*, Frankie Manning just keeps on dancing. Now an astonishingly youthful ninety-two, he has had a phenomenal dance career spanning more than seven decades. Frankie began social dancing as a teenager in the 1920s. During the 1930s and 1940s, he was one of the people most responsible for developing and disseminating the sensationally popular Lindy hop. Almost a half century later, he helped nurture an international swing dance revival. Today, with boundless energy and constant activity, he continues to lead and inspire Lindy hoppers the world over.

The swing era is the only time in United States history that jazz dominated popular tastes in music. As American youth gave physical expression to their beloved big band music, the Lindy hop became one of the hottest dance crazes of the twentieth century. The toe-tapping rhythms of swing music and exuberant movements of swing dancing provided just the right social restorative for Americans in need of escape from the miseries of the depression and World War II. Frankie Manning was a young man doing what he loved when he found himself at the center of a cultural storm that swept the country onto its feet and came to symbolize an entire generation. While they jitterbugged in local ballrooms or in overseas dance halls, few people knew how much they owed a young Harlemite who just had to dance.

From the moment his mother got his moxie up by disparaging his dancing at age twelve, Frankie's path swerved sharply toward that of the Lindy. For the next thirty years, his universe consisted of the Savoy Ballroom, fellow Lindy hoppers, swinging jazz bands, Herbert "Whitey" White, Harlem and the world beyond that clamored for black entertainment, and always the dance that was his truest soul mate.

Based at Harlem's Savoy Ballroom, the epicenter of swing culture, Whitey's Lindy Hoppers reigned as the greatest Lindy hop troupe in the land from the mid-1930s to the mid-1940s. Their spectacular exhibitions across the country and around the world—in ballrooms, nightclubs, theaters, and films—helped define and spread this major American dance. As chief choreographer and one of the lead dancers, Frankie was responsible for a number of seismically influential choreographic and stylistic innovations that permanently changed the content, aesthetics, and dynamics of the Lindy hop. His audience-pleasing inventions helped catapult the Lindy from the social dance floor to stage and screen by highlighting a series of formal dance elements.

By bending forward diagonally from the hips when he danced, Frankie transformed the upright ballroom posture of the earliest swing dances into a more energized stance that simulated a sense of flight. When he and his partner introduced Savoy Ballroom patrons to the first Lindy air step, he heightened the excitement of Lindy hop performances with gravity-defying, acrobatic movements. His use of synchronized ensemble choreography within Lindy routines exploited the powerful stage tool of unison movement. His addition of slow-motion sections into the whirlwind activity of the Lindy provided intriguing kinetic polarity. Inserting "stops" (brief freezes in the action) supplied satisfying rhythmic contrast to the propulsive energy of swing music.

Frankie also contributed specific steps to the Lindy vocabulary and nurtured the creativity of other Lindy hoppers by helping them develop new movements. Almost all of his artistic contributions are alive today, still performed around the world.

Except for four years in the military during World War II, Frankie and the Lindy journeyed together from 1926 until 1955, at which point the forty-one-year-old dancer went to work in the post office, where he remained for thirty years while the dance went into a period of decline. Frankie's personal grace and good-naturedness as he watched his career dissolve, struggled to support his family, and went on with life without dance is as inspiring as his thrilling years with Whitey's Lindy Hoppers and his postwar dance company, the Congaroos.

Dance and dancer met again at a cultural crossroads in the early 1980s. After a last hurrah to early rock 'n' roll, followed by twenty years during which nontouch dances reigned supreme on the disco floor, partner dancing had begun to make a comeback. By 1982, the Lindy hop (kept alive in part by the efforts of ex-Whitey's Lindy Hoppers Al Minns, Leon James, Norma Miller, and Pepsi Bethel; Savoy hostess Mama Lu Parks and her dance troupe; historians Marshall Stearns and Ernie Smith; and filmmaker Mura Dehn) was slowly starting to gain a new following rooted in various urban centers such as New York City, Los Angeles, London, and Stockholm. In 1984, Norma Miller enticed Frankie to come out dancing at Smalls' Paradise, a resuscitated 1930s Harlem hotspot that had recently instituted weekly swing dances. By May 1985, the New York Swing Dance Society, formed by a group of young devotees, started holding bimonthly big band dances at an East Village club. Work schedule permitting, Frankie began attending these Sunday night soirées.

Frankie and the Lindy hop soon linked arms and sallied forth to once again galvanize dancers around the world. The impetus came in 1986 from California dancers Erin Stevens and Steven Mitchell, who coaxed him into sharing his know-how. When word got out about Frankie, young swing dancers clamored to study with the master, commission his choreography, see him perform, and watch him social dance. Thus, at the age of seventy-two, Frankie began a new chapter in his illustrious and remarkably enduring career.

Today, Frankie flies to some distant point almost every week to teach Lindy hoppers eager to study with the acknowledged authority on the subject. He is as beloved for his dazzling personality and generous spirit as he is for his spellbinding anecdotes and intimate knowledge of the history of swing music and dance.

The last twenty years have been a glorious time in the life of Frankie Manning. He has lived to see the dance he helped define enjoy a worldwide resurgence in popularity, received international acclaim for his critical contributions to the evolution of this important American cultural form, and been summoned continually to dispense his expertise. Since retiring from the post office in 1987, Frankie has earned a Tony Award for his choreography in *Black and Blue*; choreographed for the Alvin Ailey American Dance Theater; consulted on and performed in Spike Lee's *Malcolm X* and Debbie Allen's made-for-TV movie, *Stompin' at the Savoy*; served as historic consultant to Mercedes Ellington's Broadway production of *Play On!*; been interviewed for numerous documentaries, including a *20/20* profile and Ken Burns's *Jazz*; received dozens of honors and awards; lectured internationally; and been written about in hundreds of newspaper and magazine articles and a number of books.

As much as Frankie appreciates the newfound recognition of his talent and accomplishments, by far his greatest pleasure comes from the opportunity to share the dance he loves so much with a new generation of enthusiasts, old and young.

The First Time I Saw Frankie Dance

Although I began attending NYSDS dances soon after they started, Frankie didn't enter my field of vision until a year later, in 1986, which is a testament to how low a profile he kept in the early days of the swing revival. The North River Bar, a small lounge in Tribeca, had begun holding dances every Wednesday night. This funky downtown nightspot and the Cat Club were the only two regular swing dance events in the city in those days, and we would crowd in, relieved and happy to get our midweek swing fix.

One evening, I was standing on the sidelines checking out the scene with NYSDS board member Michael Clancey, who was intently eying an older man dancing just in front of us. He seemed vaguely familiar from Smalls' Paradise, or perhaps the Cat Club. Overcome with admiration, my friend explained that this was Frankie Manning, one of the original Savoy Ballroom dancers, a member of Whitey's Lindy Hoppers, and a prime innovator of the Lindy.

Every single thing he said was news to me. Despite a master's degree in dance and dance education, which included a semester of dance history, I knew nothing about the background of the art form with which I was rapidly becoming obsessed. It wasn't my professor's fault; there just wasn't much information circulating out there. As of 1986, the Lindy hop had received little coverage in most dance histories, which generally focused on classical ballet and modern dance. Many works omitted it completely. Although a plethora of historical materials on the Lindy has since been brought to light, at the time these were unknown to me, as much information languished in specialized libraries and personal collections. Most of the original dancers, long out of the public eye, were either working day jobs or deceased. This was before videotape had become commonplace, so there weren't many of the accessible re-releases of historical films that we're so lucky to have today (although some dancers had started taping Lindy hop scenes from old movies off television). The Internet's far-reaching delivery of information was yet to come. And at that point, the swing revival was still a grassroots phenomenon of small clubs and private parties, too underground to have garnered significant media coverage or extensive scholarly research, other than Marshall and Jean Stearns's *Jazz Dance*, which was out of print and relatively obscure.

So there I stood, watching Frankie Manning do the Lindy hop. It would make a good story to say that his dancing electrified me in a way that turned my life around. Instead, I witnessed an individual who appeared to be in his fifties (he was seventy-two), dressed in a nondescript fashion, dancing differently from any swing dancer I had ever seen. He didn't just move his feet and legs; rather, his entire body and even his face were involved in every action as he responded to the rush of music coming from the bandstand. All of his joints seemed to be bending constantly and articulating rhythmically, an orchestra of moving parts. In addition, the actual physical pictures he was making with his body were unlike any within my aesthetic experience, and there was a hip nonchalance to his style.

It was a dance of great beauty and grace, intensely musical, with roots that delved deep into African American culture, but Frankie's subtlety was beyond me at the time. My eyes and ears had become so attuned to whitewashed, commercialized versions of the Lindy hop as depicted on television, on Broadway, and in films that I couldn't appreciate the real thing. What made it even more difficult to value this encounter with authenticity was that Frankie wasn't doing the acrobatic, flying-through-the-air-with-the-greatest-of-ease, performance-style Lindy that he had evolved and perfected in the mid-1930s. That daredevilish choreography thrilled audiences and contributed to the mass popularity of swing dancing in the late 1930s and early 1940s.

In fact, it was a reconstruction of this type of dancing by the Mama Lu Parks Dancers at the Brooklyn Academy of Music in 1983 that first inspired me to learn to Lindy hop. After their athletic and riveting performance as part of *Sweet Saturday Night*, a program celebrating three centuries of black dance, my boyfriend and I rushed home and attempted as many of the air steps as we could remember, gleefully bungling them all. Significantly, we didn't try any of the understated, albeit complex, footwork that forms the core of the Lindy. As the uninitiated, we gravitated to the showiest part of the dance.

At the North River Bar, Frankie adhered to the unspoken rules of a crowded social dance floor, shunning flashy performance steps and keeping his movements small and within his personal space. In fact, those diminutive actions were bursting with rhythm, joy, sensuality, humor, character, and the blues. Since that night, I've had many opportunities to watch Frankie dance and, as I've become more attuned to the nuances of swing dance and music, I've grown to appreciate his stunning and enchanting artistry. When he performs professionally, I'm dazzled by the explosive energy that he *chooses* to and, amazingly, still can inject into his Lindy hopping.

Later that evening, my friend Gabby Winkel introduced me to Frankie, and we spoke briefly. I took it as a precedent for chatting with him at future gatherings about his role in Lindy history, and found him as accessible to younger dancers then as he is now.

Categories

In 1990, I joined the Big Apple Lindy Hoppers, a semiprofessional troupe of swing dance performers founded in 1986 by two members of the NYSDS. Frankie was the group's chief coach and choreographer. Today, they are largely self-reliant, although they remain devoted to preserving and presenting Frankie's choreography and style of dance.

Membership in this dance company included a standing invitation for margaritas and Mexican food every Friday night after rehearsal. During my first evening out with the group, someone told a story about getting in trouble with the law as a kid for a minor infraction. It turned out that we all had similar accounts. One by one, we went around the table telling our tales of youthful indiscretion, which were transformed from shame into comedy thanks to the alchemy of time. Everyone agreed that we had stumbled upon a good party game, which we named "Categories." We called our first category "Brushes with the Law," and I've always remembered Frankie's poignant childhood tale as my initial window into his inner life.

Over the next several years, we entertained ourselves splendidly with increasingly hilarious topics. The BALH loved hearing stories about the personal life of the man who was a hero, star, and still largely unknown phenomenon to us, and these convivial evenings began the germination process for this book. Over time, bit by bit, Frankie divulged his amazing dance history, along with some of his personal background and several appalling incidents of bigotry. His skilled raconteurship and our enthrallment with his stories inspired a narrative to begin forming in my head that begged to be shared.

Book Him

In 1987, while I was interviewing Frankie at his home for a neighborhood newspaper article about the swing dance revival,[1] he allowed me to peruse his scrapbooks from the 1930s and 1940s. Brittle newspaper and magazine clippings were carefully glued down, along with silvery press photos of Frankie and other performers, fragile candids of family and friends, and dog-eared theater programs. As I read a remarkable 1936 gossip column that affectionately discussed the kids who were dancing up a storm at the Savoy Ballroom (including a whiz named Frankie), the past came to life.[2] I wanted to learn more about this special person.

About six months after I'd joined the BALH and had the joy of partnering with Frankie for my first several performances, he borrowed a video on social dances of the ragtime era. When he returned it a week later, I jumped at the chance to have a conversation with the leading luminary of the local swing dance scene. I was already interested in Lindy history and Frankie's role in it. As I questioned him, his desire to tell the truth about his career and aversion to bragging about his unique accomplishments soon became evident. Everyone notices it. It's one of the reasons he's so beloved in the swing community, a part of his "gorgeous personality."[3] Dance critic Tobi Tobias noted this characteristic in a review of a presentation given by Frankie and Norma Miller at the New York Public Library for the Performing Arts: "In the talk stretches of the show, Manning wove disarmingly egoless autobiography into the history of what is considered our sole made-in-America dance form."[4]

Frankie's commitment to accuracy was further demonstrated when I asked if he had invented *all* of the air steps. Now, this was too early in the swing dance resurgence for more than the broadest outlines of the Lindy's history to have emerged into general knowledge. He could easily have snowballed me with his answer, let me think that he had created all of the air steps and, knowing that I might never learn the truth, impressed the heck out of me, which I was clearly poised for him to do.

Frankie did impress me, tremendously so, but not because of what he said he had done. Rather, I admired his forthrightness about what he hadn't done. He proceeded to explain exactly which air steps he had made up, then listed those on which he had collaborated. Finally, he mentioned some of the many air steps that had been created by other Lindy hoppers who, he admitted only reluctantly, may have been inspired by his innovation. I was struck by what a reliable and honest source Frankie was.

Whenever possible, Frankie names those who deserve credit for their contributions. It's part of his code of ethics. He knows that, like a child raised by a village, the development of the Lindy hop was influenced by many, many people, from Savoy dancers to swing musicians to agents and managers to the general public. Remember, he was there. In fact, one of the hardest aspects of writing this book was convincing him to objectively define and evaluate his own role in the development of the Lindy. I'm grateful that he eventually accepted the importance of this task.

I also urged Frankie to remember his story in as much detail as possible. Although he was in his eighties and nineties during our thirteen-year interview and research process, his memory was surprisingly precise, and his willingness to plumb the depths of it was rewarding. He sometimes apologized for coming up short. For example, to my amusement, he once begged pardon for not being able to tell me the exact month something happened seventy years ago. I was thrilled that he could even give the year.

Of course, despite his best efforts, there were gaps in Frankie's recollections. We both especially regret the times when he could not recall a dancer's name. There were also moments when Frankie's memory contradicted fact. When I pointed these out, his lack of defensiveness and ability to adapt to new information was remarkable.

In 1993 (after I had coauthored a large research project while pursuing a master's degree in library science and curated an extensive exhibit, both on the history of swing dancing), at my behest, Frankie and I began presenting lecture/demonstrations that detailed the highlights of his life and career against a larger backdrop of the story of swing dance and music. His ability to keep an audience in rapt attention is quite astounding—even in 95-degree weather with no air conditioning, facing bouncy schoolkids or jaded teenagers, or amid a roomful of sleep-deprived swing maniacs who danced until dawn the night before. With each retelling, it became increasingly clear that Frankie's chronicle merited a full written treatment.

A word on the sidebars: These brief popular histories reflect areas of inquiry that I thought would enhance Frankie's narrative and be informative to the reader, and about which I wished to know more. Clearly, there are many other topics related to swing dance history that might have been included but could not be for a variety of reasons. I hope others will further explore these themes, and am delighted to know that some of this research is already under way.

Although bits and pieces of his history have been widely reported in various media, until now Frankie's complete story has never been documented, and no other work exists in which he serves as the main source. For the dancer he is, and the person he is, Frankie's memoir deserves to join the pantheon of dance history. I'm grateful to have been given the opportunity to work with this talented body and gracious soul on such an important project. Getting to know him has been a highlight of my life, a thrill equivalent to working with Bill Robinson for a hoofer, Isadora Duncan for a modern dancer, or George Balanchine for a ballerina.

Here, the man himself recounts all of his relevant dance experiences and shares much of his inner spirit. This autobiography is our way of presenting Frankie Manning's world, both professional and personal, directly from him to you.

ACKNOWLEDGMENTS

FRANKIE MANNING

Man! There are so many people out there who have helped me through all these many years that I have lived and performed, it would take until next Juvember to name them all. But I will try. For those I don't mention (and there will be many), please know that I thank you all.

I would really like to thank my mother for bringing me up the way she did; for letting me know that no matter how good you are, you can always get better.

MY THANKS TO:

Herbert "Whitey" White for recognizing my ability and giving me a chance to explore it.

The greats in show business, like Basie, Cab, Duke, Billy Eckstein, Nat King Cole, Sammy Davis Jr., Ella Fitzgerald, and Sarah Vaughan.

Ethel Waters, who taught the Lindy hoppers a lot about performing on stage. She used to tell us that you did your best at all times, whether there were two hundred people in the audience, or two.

All of the people who got together and sent me and my son, Chazz, to Africa.

My good friend Norma Miller, for many wonderful memories.

Erin Stevens and Steven Mitchell for helping to add a new chapter to my life.

Ryan Francois and Jenny Thomas.

The Mama Lou Parks Dancers for keeping the dance alive.

The Jiving Lindy Hoppers.

The Rhythm Hotshots (and now the Harlem Hotshots).

The New York Swing Dance Society, for helping to keep swing music alive by hiring big bands to play for their dances.

Sylvia Sykes and Jonathan Bixby.

Pasadena Ballroom Dance Association.

•

Mickey Davidson for helping to keep the Lindy alive during the poor years.

Pat Cannon of the Foot & Fiddle Dance Company for procuring an NEA Choreographers' Fellowship for me.

Larry Schulz and Sandra Cameron for their good deeds in helping to expose their students to the raw style of Savoy Ballroom dancers like Al Minns and myself. Neither Al nor I knew anything about teaching, but we learned, and I am still learning.

Scotty, my main man, my fifty-year friend. He was in my corner all the way encouraging me and pushing me to be better. He loved dancing as much as I did and knew all the people I knew. I miss him. Thanks, man.

My good friend Ernie Smith, collector of films and videos. He, Scotty, and I became the Three Musketeers, and would go dancing and listening to jazz anywhere it was being played.

My family for encouraging me to follow my dream and my love for dancing. Special thanks to my son, Chazz, who is also my best friend.

Judy Pritchett, my girlfriend, for her patience, support, friendship, and for helping me to keep my head on my shoulders instead of in the air. She encouraged me to write a book about my life. Thank you for being there for me. Love you.

Cynthia Millman, who after hearing some of my experiences with the Lindy hoppers, encouraged me to share my life story, and collaborated with me on writing it.

All you dancers, no matter what kind of swing you do. I hope you enjoy reading this book about my life as much as I have enjoyed living it.

—FRANKIE "MUSCLEHEAD" MANNING

ACKNOWLEDGMENTS

CYNTHIA R. MILLMAN

So many people supported the writing of Frankie's story in so many ways that I could happily devote an entire chapter to thanking them. The following acknowledgments only hint at their invaluable contributions.

Four people helped nurture this project from its very inception thirteen years ago. Warmest thanks to Robert P. Crease for allowing us to draw on his extensive interview with Frankie and his fine articles on original Lindy hoppers; to Donald Gardiner for guiding me to many superb resources and interviewees; to Lance Benishek for sharing his expertise on the history of the big apple and jazz dances of the 1920s; and to Monica Coe for research assistance, feedback, and ongoing encouragement.

I am indebted to three people who became deeply involved in bringing the book to fruition during the last year of writing. Judy Pritchett's familiarity with Frankie's life and Lindy history, as well as her connection to the swing dance community, made her an ideal advisor whose contributions added immeasurably to the book. Terry Monaghan generously shared aspects of his research on the Savoy Ballroom, pointed me toward resources, and gave many helpful editorial suggestions. Professional writer and swing dance teacher Linda Freeman combined her talents by offering extensive editorial feedback on the manuscript.

The generous support of the following people allowed Frankie and me to increase the quantity and quality of the illustrations: our deepest appreciation to Elliott Donnelly, his grandmothers, Jane Matteson and Ann S. Hardy, and the rest of the Donnelly and Matteson families; Buddy Steves, Rowena Young, and the Houston Swing Dance Society; the Northern California Lindy Society and Patrick Poon; and Judy Pritchett.

Paul Armstrong, Lance Benishek, Amy Bizjak, Frank Driggs, Hazel Hankin, Joyce Hansen, Rich Hansen, Mel Howard, Ed Kashi, David Lee, Stuart Math, Dianne Nilsen (Center for Creative Photography, University of AZ), Don Peterson, Anita and Steve Shevett, Kathryn Schuessler (Center for Creative Photography, University of AZ), and Kevin Smith kindly made photographs accessible for use in this book.

ACKNOWLEDGMENTS

Ernie Smith was instrumental in developing this project in its earliest stages, and in providing a window into swing dance history through his archival film work.

Jacqui Malone contributed much thoughtful feedback on the manuscript from her perspective as a scholar and author in the arena of American vernacular dance.

Phil Schaap shared his expertise on jazz music, helping to clarify historical background and musical points.

Larry Schulz's memories, notes, and records of the swing dance revival in New York City proved invaluable.

Researcher Kristine Krueger, of the Margaret Herrick Library of the Academy of Motion Picture Arts and Sciences, unearthed rare materials about Frankie's film work.

Thanks to the Archives Center, National Museum of American History, Smithsonian Institution for permission to use *Frankie Manning Interview*, Jazz Oral History Program Collection, and to Wendy Shay, Audio-Visual Archivist/Deputy Chair, Archives Center, NMAH for facilitating this use.

A salute to Frank Shirer, Military Historian, U.S. Army Retired, for his expert review of the Army chapter.

Pepsi Bethel, Eunice Callen, Jack Carey, Martha Charles, Elnora Dyson, Edward Ellington Jr., Ryan Francois, Martha Hickson, Gloria Manning, Peter Loggins, Lawrence Lucie, Frank Manning Jr., Steven Mitchell, George Reed, Ruthie Rheingold, Midge Simone, Hazel Smith, Erin Stevens, Sylvia Sykes, Eleanor Watson, Lennart Westerlund, Richard Yarde, and Chazz Young kindly shared their dance, music, and/or personal histories as they intersected with Frankie's.

Adam Nadler, Judy Gitenstein, and Harris Green made editing recommendations on portions of the manuscript either during the book's earliest incarnation as a biography or in its later autobiographical format. Thea Austen, Mitch Baranowski, Caroline Franklin Berry, Kathleen Finneran, Chester Freeman, Rick Perlman, Rosetta Reitz, Rudy Shur, and Alan Sugarman read various sections and versions of the book, and provided valuable observations that shaped its development.

Thanks to Mercedes Ellington for an eloquent foreword; to Leslie Kriesel for sensitive and sensible copyediting; and to Beth Tondreau for a stunning jacket and book design.

For responding to a variety of requests with assistance, information, and resources, many thanks to Cholly Atkins, Margaret Batiuchok, Emily Belt, Marlene Charnizon, Tommy Ciaccio, Jehudith Cohen, Charlotte Darrow, D. Daniel Dawson, Kevin Delaney, Frank Dellario, Theda Detlor, Bryant

Dupré, Jodi Fleischman, Rusty Frank, Malikia Gabay, Ralph Gabriner, Karen Goldstein, Lynn Gonen, Dawn Hampton, John Hasse, Annie Hirsch, Dr. Gregory Hodge, Keith Hughes, Fred Hunt, Elena Iannucci, Michael Ingbar, Delilah Jackson, Laura Jeffers, Paul Kelly, Sig Libowitz, Sing Lim, Tom Lisanti, Yvonne Marceau, Jun Maruta, Alice McInerney, Charlie Meade, Binnie Meltzer, Beckie Menckhoff, Linda Micale, Norma Miller, Dan Multer, Fayard Nicholas, Kenneth and Helena Norbelie, Julie Oram, Mark Ormsby, Rik Panganiban, Jeanne M. Petschauer, Murray Pfeiffer, Alice Pifer, Terry M. Prior (Curator, Oswego County Historical Society), Don Rayno, Rebecca Reitz, Hazel Riddick, Shelley Roth, Christine Sampson, Odella Schattin, Lianne Schoenwiesner, Dena Schutzer, Suzie Schwartz, Samuel Scott, Simon Selmon, Manu Smith, Vernon Smith, Jim Snedeker, Alex Soudah, Delores Spencer, Timothy Swiecicki, Robert Farris Thompson, Lana Turner, Rob Van Haaren, Leslie Willis, Janice Wilson, Gabby Winkel, Baerbl Kaufer, Marcus Koch, Carol Teten, and Jenny Thomas.

Eugene Corey of Brave New Words transcribed my interviews with Frankie and others with the greatest of care and respect for the interviewees.

My gratitude to Leon Pender, Calle Johansson, and Noel Brandel for their speedy responses to technology SOSs.

Much appreciation for the enthusiasm and support of my colleagues at The Town School, including Head of School Chris Marblo; librarians Maria Leston, Sarah Pennachio, Carrie Schindele, and Pam Pryor; and William Walsh, Al Doyle, Moe Amara, and Reshan Richards in the Technology Department.

Tony and Aurelie Tye provided a forum for exploring Frankie's history with annual invitations for us to lecture at their Beantown Lindy Hop Summer Camp.

Kudos to past and present board members of the New York Swing Dance Society and the folks at Yehoodi.com for building a swing dance scene in New York and beyond.

I will always appreciate the support of my family for this project.

Eternal thanks to Editor in Chief Janet Francendese, and everyone at Temple University Press for making the idea of this book a reality.

And, of course, I will be forever grateful to Frankie for giving me the opportunity to collaborate with him on his marvelous history. Thanks for living such an inspiring life.

—CYNTHIA R. MILLMAN

PROLOGUE • TOO STIFF

House Rent Parties

From the time I was about eight, my mother, who adored dancing, used to take me with her to social events in Harlem so she wouldn't have to leave me with a babysitter. We often went to house rent parties, which were a way for people to raise money to help pay their landlord. They were held right in someone's apartment, and you'd pay 25 cents to get in. Once you were inside, you'd have someone playing stride piano and blues for food and tips, pig's feet and potato salad to eat, bathtub gin for 10 cents a mug . . . and dancing.[1]

At first, my mother would leave me in a bedroom along with the coats so I could go to sleep, but I used to peek out through the door to watch the festivities. I was intrigued with the atmosphere. It was just so jolly, so full of life, so much fun. People would be telling jokes that I didn't understand, but I'd be laughing because everybody else was. It seemed like they were enjoying themselves so much. Folks would be chitchatting in the bedrooms and, of course, lots of people would be congregated in the kitchen because that's where the food was. But the living room was where they did the dancing. That's what I liked best. I loved watching my mother and her friends dance because it seemed like they were having such a good time out there on the crowded floor.

You haven't seen slow dancing until you've been to a house rent party. When people wanted to get funky, they'd do the black bottom, the mess-around, and slow drags—honky-tonk dances, what they did to slower music. If it was a blues number, everybody would be out there shakin' butt. You'd hear someone say, "Turn the lights down low and let the party get started!" Or, as Fats Waller used to say, "Put out the lights and call the law." These were private dances, so they didn't need much space.

When they played hot music—fast music, ragtime or Charleston-type music—if someone started getting a little wilder than everybody else, the crowd would back up and form a circle. Everybody would stand around clapping for the people in the middle, who would start shining, what we called "showing off." In those days, dancing could be very individual at times, particularly at private parties. I know that I saw a lot of Charleston steps, but I don't remember exactly what everyone was doing. They were out there by themselves, so they did whatever they were in the mood for. It might be one person or a couple, but they were improvising, so they needed more room.

To me, the dancing was what it was all about. It had a tremendous impact on me. But I wasn't thinking, *I've got to learn this* . . . yet.

After a couple of years, by about age ten, as the dancing became more fascinating to me, I began to venture out among the partygoers. I used to push people aside or lie down on the floor to look through their legs in order to see what was going on. I began going home and trying to move exactly like they did. Hearing the music with that rhythm and being able to move to it just got under my skin. That's when I started dancing.

Too Stiff

By the time I turned twelve, my mother had started taking me to parties that were sponsored by her social club. In October 1926, the Jolly Flapperettes were planning a Halloween dance at the Renaissance Ballroom. My mother was on the decorating committee, and when she told me that if I helped her decorate the hall she would let me go to the dance, I jumped at the chance. Most of those affairs took place on the weekend. On our way to decorate the ballroom, I saw some of my friends playing in the street. Now, you know how kids are. When I told them I was going to the dance tonight with my mom, they said, "Man, you ain't going nowhere. You just jivin'."

We spent the afternoon putting up cornstalks, pumpkins, lanterns, and autumn decorations with other club members, then went home to get ourselves ready. I got all dressed up, not in a costume, but in knickers, long stockings, shoes, a cap, a jacket with loops for a belt, and a bow tie. I thought I looked great. I was so anxious to go that I said, "Mama, I'm ready." "Frankie, it's only seven o'clock," she told me. "The dance isn't until nine." It seemed like I had to wait for days while my mother got herself dressed.

At about nine o'clock, we *finally* left for the dance. I was so sharp that I strutted by all the cats hanging around outside. Naturally, they asked, "Where you going, Frankie?" I said, "You guys didn't believe me when I said I was going to a dance tonight with my mama. Well, that's where I'm going."

The house band for the Renaissance, Vernon Andrade (I'm pretty sure), was playing and they were a very good, swinging band. People were doing different kinds of dances, mostly ballroom stuff like the foxtrot, the peabody, and the waltz, but also the Charleston, mess-around, and slow drag.

My mother's club had a box in the balcony, and I was the youngest thing in the hall sitting up there with all the big folks. I was just listening to the music and watching everybody out on the floor, when my mother came up and asked if I wanted to dance. I was so happy that I was bouncing along beside her as she led me by the hand onto this big ballroom floor. I put my arm around her waist, then tried doing the dances that I saw everybody else doing. I was just carrying on.

As soon as the music was over, my mother grabbed me by the hand and started walking off the floor, shaking her head. When I asked her what was the matter, she said, "Frankie, you'll never be a dancer. You're too stiff."

PART I
FIRST STEPS
(1914—Circa 1933)

....

1 • JAZZ BABY

Frankie's Great Migration

My mother was a party lady. She used to tell me that while she was carrying me, she could feel me kicking in time to the beat when she was dancing. She said that when I was born and the doctor held me upside down and slapped me, I started crying like this: "Uh-h-h . . . uh, uh." So I guess I was just born with rhythm.

Lucille Hadley Manning gave birth to me on May 26, 1914 in Jacksonville, Florida. She was fifteen. She and my father, Jerry (Jerome) Manning, who was ten years older, named me Frank Benjamin. Jacksonville was a good-sized city even then, but Campbell Hill, the neighborhood where I spent my first three years, had a small-town feel. Our house, which was very modest, was on a dirt road and had three little bedrooms, a kitchen, a living room, and an outhouse. Of course it was in a black section. This was 1914.

My parents had one child before me, but she died when I was two, so for all intents and purposes I was an only child. They never spoke about it, but I think she came down with pneumonia. My parents separated in 1917 and eventually divorced. In 1936, my mother had a second son by another man, who she never married. I was twenty-two when Vincent Manning was born, but I never got to know my half-brother well because of our age difference.

Other than my sister's passing, I had a pretty happy childhood. My mother worked as a chambermaid, then a laundress in a white section of town, my father in a lumber mill. They didn't have a lot of money, but we got by. Grandmother Hadley lived next door. She took care of me and my two female cousins, who would watch over me as I went back and forth between the two houses. We often stayed overnight at our grandmother's; she fixed all of our family meals, serving up plenty of Southern food.

My father was Methodist and my mother a Baptist. I rarely went to church with him, but I did attend her congregation, where she was a prominent member, every Sunday. It was her preacher who baptized me in the St. John's River, ducking my head under the cold water. My mother's church used to put on what they called Tom Thumb weddings. I was always the groom and this one little girl was usually the bride. My mother, who was a very good seamstress, made me a little tuxedo, and I would walk down the aisle in my little tie and tails to get married. Whenever I'd look over at my mother, she was beaming at me.

When I was three, my mother went to New York for an extended visit, leaving me in the care of my father and grandmother. She returned home about six months later, but left again immediately, this time taking me and her closest friend, Marie Robinson (Aunt Marie, to me), who was like her sister, along. She just left my father like that. Evidently it wasn't a happy marriage. I don't remember any fighting between them, but she wanted to go to New York and I guess he wasn't ready to make that move.

I think the main reason my mother came to New York was economic. But it was also because of a good friend of hers who worked as a cook for the Cunard Line, a very nice fellow named Robert Hightower. At the time, a lot of ships went back and forth between the South and the North. I think he persuaded her to leave Florida and helped us book passage for the trip up the coast. Eventually she started going with him.

I remember how I used to like to stare at the ocean through the ship's railing because the boat made waves as it passed through the water, and it seemed to me that the waves were making little patterns. It looked like one wave would dip underneath the next wave, then come up over the top of it, making a little circle. Then the waves would curl into each other. They looked like they were playing together, and I thought it was a heck of a game. I got so fascinated that I couldn't wait to run up on deck each day and see what the waves were doing. I used to say to myself, *I'm going to learn the little game those waves are playing so I can teach it to the kids up in New York*. I was engraving it in my mind so I could do my own interpretation of it.

New York, New York

New York took some getting used to. In the South, we had dirt roads, horses, wagons, and one-story houses. Here, the sidewalks were paved, and there were apartments with a whole gang of people living on top of each other. And I remember seeing a lot of uniformed soldiers walking around who had returned from fighting in World War I. Most of all, I was overwhelmed by the tall buildings. My apartment house was only five stories high, but that was huge to me. Everybody used to say, "You think this is tall, wait until you see the Woolworth Building." I used to walk around all the time with my head in the air, looking up.

When we first got to New York, we rented two rooms in the apartment of this lady named Mrs. Brooks at 109 West 138th Street, between Lenox and Seventh avenues. My Aunt Marie rented a room in another apartment in the same building. The landlady had two sons, Kenneth and Eric, who were both a little older, so they kind of took me under their wing and showed me the ropes. It was still summer, so there were lots of kids on the sidewalks playing hide-and-seek, and shooting marbles and soda-water bottle caps. At first, I just watched from our first-floor window, but after a while I began to learn how to play the games and joined in.

I didn't actually enter elementary school until a year or two after the other kids my age, because my mother didn't enroll me at that point. She and my aunt taught me my alphabet and numbers at home. I tried to learn quickly, perhaps because I always wanted to please my mother. I studied even if they weren't around and learned my alphabet so well that I could say it backward.

When I finally did go to school, I was given some tests to decide what level I should be in, and put in first grade. Eventually, I was reunited with the other kids my age because they had me skip a level or two. I was a very good student, and spelling was one of my strong points. When the teacher asked for someone to spell a word, I'd be like, "Me! Me!" with my hand waving in the air.

My mother was working downtown at a laundry on Lexington Avenue in the sixties or seventies when I first started school. Every morning at seven o'clock, she would drop me off at P.S. 89 (at West 135th Street and Lenox Avenue), then catch the subway at the corner. School didn't start until eight-thirty, but the hour and a half passed like crazy because we were playing handball. I was always the first kid there, so I got a court before the other kids came. They'd say, "Can we play on your court?" and I'd say, "Yeah, man, come on!"

When I got out of school at three o'clock, I would go across the street to the Lincoln Theatre on West 135th Street, just east of Lenox Avenue. My mother had a friend who worked there as an usher, and this lady would let me go into the theater to watch the show for a couple of hours until my mother came to get me.[1]

This was a vaudeville theater. There was a movie following the stage show, with the whole thing repeated four times a day. Since I went every day, I saw the same program over and over and had the opportunity to watch a lot of famous performers, like Bert Williams, Bill Robinson, Paul Robeson, Eddie Rector, the Whitman Sisters, and Noble Sissle. I was actually more drawn to the comedians than the dancers, but the funny thing is that most of the comedians did a comic dance routine. Of course, sometimes I would just sit and do my homework by the light coming from the hallway and the projectionist's booth.

In fourth or fifth grade, I got transferred out of P.S. 89 to P.S. 5, which was located at West 140th Street and Edgecombe Avenue. I actually lived closer to P.S. 89, but the board of education realized that my address was not in that school district. P.S. 5 was in the opposite direction from the subway, and too far from the Lincoln Theatre for me to walk by myself, so my mother came up with another plan.

While she continued to live in our apartment, she paid for me to board just up the block with Mrs. Johnson, an elderly, heavyset widow who was a friend of the Lincoln Theatre usher. (My mother thought it would be better for me not to be living with her anyway, because she was always working and, you know, partying—not every single night, mostly on the weekends, but this was grown folks' partying.)

A little later, my mother and Aunt Marie moved down to West 121st Street into a brownstone that gave them a bit more privacy. I continued to live with Mrs. Johnson so that I could finish up at P.S. 5 and not change schools again. When she died suddenly six months later, I moved in with her friend and next-door neighbor, Mrs. Lawson, and stayed with her until I graduated from P.S. 5.

People sometimes ask me now if I felt abandoned by my mother, but I never did. Mrs. Johnson and Mrs. Lawson were like mothers to me. They treated me as if I was their child. And my mother used to come around a lot. Most days she would stop over on her way home from work to see if there was anything we needed, and I could also go visit her whenever I wanted to. So I didn't really feel neglected in any way. I guess I was just too busy with other people, with other kids.

Summertime

For several summers after we moved to New York, my mother sent me to my Aunt (my father's sister) and Uncle Gowdy's farm in Aiken, South Carolina. She wanted me to get to know my cousins, and spend time with my father and Grandmother Hadley (her mother), who had moved there when my parents separated. They were both from South Carolina originally, although I believe my father had some Cherokee blood. My mother had been born in West Palm Beach.

Each visit south lasted four to six weeks. I traveled alone by train, always in a separate coach for blacks because the railroad was segregated then. My mother would attach a tag to my clothing with my name, address, and destination so the conductor, who she asked to look after me, would know when to put me off the train. She tipped him, and gave me a dollar in case I wanted to buy something to eat.

It was fascinating to be on the farm. Just about everything we ate was grown there. We had this long table covered with all different kinds of food like fresh corn, peas, rice, hot biscuits, and cornbread. Whatever meat there was, like pig's feet or cow, came from the farm. I must have been pretty young the first time I went because I couldn't reach the table, so they got a very thick Bible for me to sit on.

During the growing season, my aunt and uncle hired workers to help in the fields. They lived on the farm, and I used to play with some of their kids. We liked going into the fields and eating watermelon and green peanuts until we got sick, and had a lot of fun playing games like hide-and-seek. My father put a swing on the limb of this gigantic oak tree in our front yard, and all the kids in the area used to come over to swing on it with me. He worked in a factory where they made barrels for beer, pickles, and other items, so sometimes I'd take a shortcut through this wooded area to bring him his lunch pail, then wait until the workday was over to walk back to the farm with him.

My earliest musical memory (this is even before I went to house rent parties) was in Aiken when my family would sit outside on the porch or in our front yard, in the evening after the week's work was finished. The farmhands would sometimes gather there to play music, maybe on a washtub bass and harmonica, and sometimes a friend of my father's would come over and play banjo with them. The musicians would stand in a circle and people would get up and dance in the middle. They'd take turns getting out there, just improvising, doing whatever they felt like doing. An older person might pull a child in, but the kids mostly just jumped up and down. I never wanted to participate, but after my grandmother would push me into the circle, you couldn't get me to stop. I'd always try to copy what I saw the grown-ups doing.

On Sundays, and occasionally other evenings, I also remember hearing all this singing and shouting coming from across the river that ran in front of our house. There was a church tent over there with revival meetings going on inside. Even though they didn't have any microphones, it wasn't that far away and it was loud, so we could hear the preacher preaching and the people clapping their hands, shaking tambourines, and singing all this fantastic gospel music.

In most Baptist churches, when the preacher's getting deep down and he's talking to the sisters and brothers, they start carrying on, and sometimes you'll see somebody jump up. But in revival meetings, the Holy Rollers do that constantly. They carry on, shout (by this, I mean a movement where they clench their fists, then throw their arms in the air), and go into all kinds of contortions as if they're possessed by the spirit and they want to let it go, baby! That's the feeling those people had, and it was very inspiring.

On the farm, the grown-ups would be rocking to the music from the tent, and to entertain ourselves, the kids would re-create what was happening inside. We'd imitate the preaching, singing, shouting, and carrying on of the Holy Rollers, just cutting up. That music and the movements we did were so exhilarating that they kind of stuck with me from then on. Even as I got older, I remembered those rhythms very clearly.

Although my grandmother lived in Aiken, she had a lot to say about my upbringing. Kids in the South were taught to respect their elders as a way of life, but things were different up North. When I first moved to New York, I would hear our landlady tell her kids, "I told you to do so and so." They'd answer, "Oh Ma, we'll do it when we're finished." When my mother said now, she meant now, not when *you* get ready. I never talked back to her. If my mother got mad at me, she chastised me, but when my grandmother got angry with me, she'd whup me.

Once, we were eating at the table and I put some butter on my plate even though I didn't want any. Instead of saying, "Grandmother, I don't want the butter," I smeared it on the wall. I guess I was thinking that she might tell me to eat it because it's good for you, and I didn't want to hear that. She whupped me for not saying I didn't want the butter, and for spreading it on the wall. Afterwards, when I was crying, she hugged me and said, "You know that I love you, but when you do something bad you're going to get punished." I didn't get angry, though. She was strict, but she was fair. And afterwards she'd bake me a sweet potato pie.

Although racism existed in the North, Aiken was the first place where I experienced it outright. My older cousin and I had driven into town on a horse and wagon to do some errands and were walking on a narrow sidewalk when we noticed three young white men coming toward us. As we approached, it didn't seem like they were going to move, and just when we got up to them, my cousin took my hand and pulled me into the street. I could hear those boys laughing as we walked by.

Afterwards, my cousin didn't say anything and I didn't think about it. It wasn't until much later that I wondered why the hell we had to step off the curb. Eventually, I understood that they had the right of way because they had more rights than we did. But that wasn't the way I saw it at the time.

Another time, also in Aiken, I helped this white fellow load his wagon in exchange for a ride back to my aunt's farm. When I went to sit on the seat next to him, he told me I had to go in the back of the wagon. This time, I knew why.

They had signs down there saying "colored" and "white" on fountains and restaurants, which was strange to me. I was very young and if that went on in New York, I didn't know much about it. However, as I grew older I saw plenty of examples of prejudice up North. For instance, I found out that there was at least one restaurant on 125th Street, right in the middle of Harlem, that blacks couldn't enter. We could go into Woolworth's and buy whatever we wanted, but we couldn't sit down and eat at the counter. And, although 125th Street was right in the middle of this black neighborhood, the stores along it didn't hire African Americans. Adam Clayton Powell Jr. said if they won't hire blacks, then we won't buy anything. In the late '30s, he picketed and organized demonstrations against the stores until they agreed to start hiring some blacks.

I can tell you about stuff that happened even in the 1970s. I was driving on Long Island, near Riverhead, when I stopped at a roadside confectionary store to get something to drink. There were two white fellows inside. Before I could even order anything, the counterman said, "Look, you better get out of here, because I don't want any trouble." I said, "I just want a bottle of soda," but he said, "You better go ahead." I didn't want to have a problem, so I turned around, walked out, and drove away. Things like that happened up North too.

Competitive Edge

As I got a little older, I began to participate more in all of the street activities going on in my neighborhood in Harlem. By about age seven, one of my favorite games was our version of follow the leader, which we played on construction sites because they weren't boarded up then like they are now. Any kid who couldn't run along the exposed beams or climb the building's frame was considered chicken.

There were two groups in the neighborhood: the Boy Scouts, in their uniforms, hats, and badges; and us poor kids, in our raggedy pants and worn-out sneakers. Since we couldn't be Boy Scouts, we said that they weren't any good. Even though those goody-goodies were supposed to be so great at sports and could afford special camps, we trained in street ways and were always trying to beat them at everything. And we did, a lot. Anyway, they were Boy Scouts and had to follow the commands of their leader as if they were in the Army, but we were just free and could do anything we wanted to . . . except when our mothers told us not to.

Sports were very important to me, and if I didn't have the winning edge, I would practice until I did, or at least until I improved. When I played stickball, which was the most popular game on the street, we would have teams, say 138th Street against 137th Street, and if you wanted to play, you had to get picked. Naturally, they picked the best ones, so of course I wanted to be the best. Now, I could hit the ball and I could run, but I wasn't much at catching. I just couldn't close my hands quickly enough. I knew it was one of my weaknesses, so I used to spend hours by myself throwing the ball against the wall and catching it, practicing and practicing until I got better.

We also had a lot of races out on the street. I was considered a pretty good runner, so one day I challenged this fellow who was on the senior high school track team to a race from one manhole to the next. Even though I was pretty swift getting off the mark, Mason shot out of there and beat me. Right away, I started making excuses about how I didn't get a good start and suggested that we race again. I ran as hard as I could, but this cat also won the second race. After he won the third time, I stopped giving excuses. Instead, I said to myself, *Okay, I did the best I could, and maybe someday I'll be able to run that fast.* In order to improve, I got lots of tips from the coaches and some of the older kids and, of course, I practiced, practiced, practiced.

It was in junior high school that I also got into boxing. We would have little matches to see who could outbox each other, but we were real street fighters. After high school, I spent a brief period of time training with an ex-prizefighter who offered to work with me because he thought I showed promise. Since I was always trying to box some cat who was older than me, I got beat up a lot, but I learned a lot too. At that period of time, it was rough out there on the streets, and when you showed that you weren't afraid guys respected you more. I liked knowing how to take care of myself.

When I was about ten or eleven, shortly after I started living with my mother again on West 121st Street, we moved around the corner to West 122nd Street between Seventh and Eighth avenues. Some kids on the block warned me about Butch, the neighborhood bully, but, being the new kid, I soon became his favorite victim.

One afternoon, after I had just bought a box of chocolate snaps at the grocery store, Butch came over and said, "Give me those chocolates." I told him I wouldn't, so he said, "If you don't, I'm going to beat your butt," and grabbed them from me. I started begging him to give them back, but he kept pushing me away, and I wouldn't fight.

At that moment, my mother came walking down the street on her way home from work. I ran to her, with tears in my eyes, hoping that this would win her sympathy and that maybe she'd get in there and grab the cookies. Instead, she said, "He took your chocolate snaps from you, right? Well, he can keep them if you don't take them back."

Right then and there, I decided I'd rather fight Butch than have my mother be mad at me. I turned slowly and walked toward him, looking back at her every few steps. Just as Butch was about to eat the first cookie, I grabbed the box from him. He was very surprised and threatened to beat my backside again, but after a stern glance from my mother, I raised my fists and threw a punch. We hit each other a few times before Butch finally said, "Keep the chocolate snaps. I don't want them anyway," and stomped off.

When I went back to my mother and said, "Look Mommy, I got them back," she replied, "See, if you don't stand up to people, they'll take advantage of you. I didn't say you could beat him; maybe he would have beat you. But from now on he's going to respect you." I learned a lesson from that incident.

Although I would fight if I had to, from an early age, I preferred to take care of tense situations without getting physical, if possible. For instance, some of my friends used to try to talk me into sneaking into the movie theater, which I didn't want to do because I didn't want my mother to find out. When I'd say no, they'd call me a sissy, but I'd just brush them off, saying, "Okay, I'm a sissy, but don't introduce me to your sister." They didn't have too much to say after that.

Stoops and Roofs

Occasionally, my fascination with physical challenges got me into hot water. All of us kids used to hop the trolleys running up and down Lenox Avenue without paying the fare. I knew it was wrong, but I did it anyway because it was so much fun. Once, when I climbed onto the rear of a moving car, this white passenger yelled at me and slapped my face. He didn't call me names, but he socked the hell out of me. Man, did my cheek burn! I wasn't sure if it was because I was black or because I was doing something I wasn't supposed to be doing. Whatever it was, I jumped right down and never did it again.

Another thing I loved doing was leaping over the storage basement doors that alternated with apartment stoops along Lenox Avenue. I'd get a running start, then vault from one stoop to another, flying over the open hatch in between. One time, I didn't quite make it. The front of my foot got caught, and as I fell I scraped my shin against the sharp edge of the iron door. The skin along my lower leg peeled back like a banana and blood started gushing out.

Harlem Hospital was a couple of blocks away, so I ran there. As soon as this nurse saw me with this flap on my leg and goopy blood all around my feet, she threw me on a gurney and rushed me into the emergency room, where they wrapped a tourniquet around my thigh to stop the bleeding. It's funny, but the whole time that they were washing it out and sewing me up, the only thing I could think of was, *Are they going to tell my mother?* Of course, I had to tell her when I got home and she saw this big bandage.

A couple of years after that incident, this group of kids and I discovered a new playground: the roof. Rooftops on tenement buildings in New York City were generally five or six stories high, and were often separated at the rear by air shafts that provided apartments with additional windows. Folks would string their laundry from window to window and gossip with their neighbors across these air shafts.[2]

My friends and I came up with a stunt that was inspired by this setup. We used to put a board up to the raised edge of one roof, run up the board, and jump across the open space to the opposite roof. One day, one of the fellows didn't quite make it. He fell five floors, but since his fall was kind of broken by the clotheslines, he only broke both of his legs. We tried to run down the stairs to get to him, but the door to that particular apartment building was locked from the inside. So we actually jumped back over to the other side, opened the door, and ran down. Apparently, we weren't so scared that we couldn't make the jump again so we could go help him.

Again, this was something I had to tell my mother. She said, "I don't want you on that roof anymore." "Yes, Mommy." As if that was going to stop me.

One Christmas season, when I was nine or ten, I went into the Woolworth's on 125th Street to buy a box of candy for my mother with money I had earned by doing chores for elderly people around the neighborhood. I had been saving to get this gift, and I had just enough money. While I was looking around, I noticed some very small toy automobiles in shiny colors and got the bright idea that I could slip one into my hand and walk right on out of the store, which is what I started to do.

When I got to the door, this security guard, a white fellow dressed in street clothes, stopped me and said gruffly, "Hey kid, open your hand. I saw you taking that toy!" I was terrified. "I'll put it back," I stammered, "I'll put it back. I didn't mean to take it," but he said, "I've got to punish you and take you to jail." "You can take me to jail," I pleaded, "but *please* don't tell my mother."

Instead, he took me downstairs to the basement, which was filled with boxes, and said, "I want you to clean up this room. Stay here until I come back for you." I told him I'd do anything as long as he didn't tell my mother, and began putting the boxes in order and sweeping up the room. The whole time, the thought of my mother trusting me so much and that I let her down was killing me inside.

It might not have been that long, but after what seemed like a couple of hours, the man came back. He looked around and said, "You cleaned the place and it looks very nice." I asked him if there was anything else he wanted me to do, but he told me to go on upstairs. As I was leaving, he asked why I had come into the store in the first place. When I told him, he went behind the counter and came back with a box of candy. "Give this to your mother," he said. "And I don't want to see you in this store anymore." I took the box and ran all the way home. The only thing I told my mother was that I cleaned this guy's basement and he gave me a box of candy. It was the first and last time I tried stealing.

If you hear me say "mother, mother, mother," all the time, it's only because after my parents separated, I stayed with her. She was always the one who was there. My father eventually moved to New York, around my tenth birthday. After that, my mother stopped sending me to South Carolina for the summers. Instead, for the next couple of years, she enrolled me in a day camp run by Abyssinian Baptist Church with activities such as arts, crafts, and sports. I especially loved the field trips to Orchard Beach in the Bronx, and the lemonade-and-cake parties that my counselor and her husband had for her campers in the backyard of their brownstone.

I saw a lot more of my father once he came up North. He worked as a manual laborer for several years, then ran a newsstand in Harlem. On his day off, we'd often go sightseeing, walk through Central Park and stop in at the zoo, or visit his brother, a music teacher who lived on West 99th Street. This period lasted from about age ten until fifteen. After that, I didn't see him as often because by then, I had developed other interests.

2 • EARLY BALLROOM FORAYS

Determined

After my mother told me I was too stiff to be a dancer, I felt pretty sad. I honestly thought that I was dancing like everybody else at the Renaissance Ballroom. That night, I was really dragging on the way back home. But by the next day, what she said kind of lit me up.

My mother wasn't trying to get me to improve; she was just telling me the truth. Maybe I looked so bad that she felt like she had to say something. I didn't see it as harsh; no, I took it as constructive criticism. If she had never told me I was stiff, I might never have become a dancer. In fact, that's when I *really* got interested in dancing.

Whenever I couldn't pick up something right away, I used to try to teach it to myself, so I started buying records to play on my own little record player in my own little room. I'd take a broom or a chair for a partner and try to dance like the grown-ups I'd seen, moving my shoulders, waist, and hips. I'd bend from side to side, doing any little thing just to keep myself from being upright and straight. Sometimes my mother would open the door and see me dancing with a broom. When she asked what I was doing, I told her that I was trying to get unstiff.

For the next year or so, I continued to practice by myself, playing the two or three dance-band recordings that I owned over and over. I also wanted to watch anybody who knew how to dance, so I kept going to parties with my mother, where I saw the latest social dances. I began to notice that there was a difference between these private get-togethers and what I had seen at the Renaissance Ballroom. When a club put on a social dance at a ballroom, everybody would be out there dressed up in what we called their "Sunday best," doing ballroom dances like the foxtrot, peabody, two-step, and waltz. You'd never think that these people who looked so grand would ever go to a real down party with folks drinking and having a lot of fun, but they did. My mother was a very good ballroom dancer but, whew, she could also get down and wiggle a mean butt. I could hardly tell it was my own mother compared to the lady I saw in the ballroom.

There was some crossover of dances done at parties, but they'd handle it a little differently at a ballroom. If someone was in the mood to do the black bottom, they'd go off and do it in a corner. They might do a Charleston, but they'd cool it down.

Usually, I just watched my mother and her friends while they were dancing, but occasionally I would participate, and it was at these parties that I first started to really learn *how* to dance.

There was one particular time I will never forget. I was sitting watching the goings-on as I usually did when one of my mother's friends said, "Come on, Frankie, dance with me." It was a slow tune. She started holding me very close . . . and then she began gyrating at the hips! Because she was a little bit hefty, we were really pressed together. It was probably just how she danced with any other man, except I wasn't a man. Except that night I found out I was.

I was kind of relieved when the music ended because I was embarrassed! It was the first time this had happened to me while I was dancing, although it definitely wasn't the last. I didn't even say thank you, and I did *not* dance any more that night.

Playing Hooky at the Alhambra

During that first year of dancing, I also worked at improving my skills by practicing in the basement with Herman Jackson, a friend who lived in my building. I'd show him the steps I learned from watching my mother and her friends. Sometimes I'd act the girl, sometimes he would. We were getting interested in going to parties with kids our own age so we could see what dances they were doing, and we were about to get our chance.

I was thirteen. On Sundays, my mother, Aunt Marie, and I went to Metropolitan Baptist Church for services, which were followed by a big midday dinner. Then, I would spend the afternoon at Baptist Young People's Union (a church-sponsored religious activities club for teens), and around seven o'clock my mother and aunt would often return to church.

Every Sunday, Herman would stop by to pick me up for BYPU, and we'd walk from 122nd Street up Seventh Avenue to our church at 128th Street. Each week, we passed by the Alhambra Theatre on the corner of 126th Street without paying it any mind. But one afternoon, when we left a little earlier than usual, we noticed some kids our own age by the Alhambra box office under the theater marquee. Herman and I got a little bit curious, so we crossed the street and asked what was going on. They told us there was going to be a dance with a big band for youngsters age twelve to fifteen in the ballroom on the top floor.

Now, we were supposed to be in BYPU from three to five. But this orchestra, Claude Hopkins,[1] as I recall, was playing at that time. Herman and I looked at each other, then asked how much it cost to go in. The kids told us five cents. Can you picture that? A live big band, and it's a nickel to go in! We said we could make that, so we plunked down our money and took the elevator upstairs.

The Alhambra was a typical ballroom, nicely decorated with a band-stand at one end of the room, an upstairs balcony, an arched ceiling, and a partition surrounding the square dance floor.[2] We stood behind the railing, just looking, taking it all in. The band was *swinging*, and all these kids our own age were out on the floor dancing like *crazy*! These cats were jumping! I'd never seen anything like it.

Occasionally, they did some of the same ballroom and party dances that my mother and her friends were doing, but the most popular was a dance that I found out was called the breakaway, which was very lively. These youngsters were much wilder; they just had more energy, which might have been partly because they had more room to dance than at house parties.

Herman said, "Oh man, we've been missing out on this!" so I punched him in the arm and said, "Why don't you ask one of the girls to dance?" He replied, "Why don't *you* ask somebody to dance?" We kept boasting to each other that we could do that step or this step, and then saying, "So why don't you get a girl and do it?" In the end, neither one of us danced that Sunday, but when we left, we agreed that we would go back there the next week. Forget about church, man.

The next Sunday, I told my mom I was going. I didn't say where, just "I'm going." Generally, Herman and I strolled to church, but this time, we cut out of the house and were running up Seventh Avenue. We were going to the dance, man!

We were so thrilled to get up to the ballroom and hear that great music and see that fabulous dancing again. For the second week in a row, Herman and I stood by the rail and, once again, even though we kept daring each other, neither of us could actually get up the nerve to ask a girl to dance. The same thing happened on our third visit.

On our fourth visit to the Alhambra, we vowed that we would both ask girls to dance that afternoon. When we got there, I saw this young lady standing by the railing, near the opening onto the dance floor. I knew she wanted to dance because her fingers were poppin', her foot was tappin', and her head was bobbin', and the music wasn't even playing. I told Herman,

"I'm going to ask that girl to dance," and he said, "Okay, man, that's great. Go ahead."

In those days, you generally asked people to dance before the music started, so I strolled over and said, "May I have this dance, miss?" I don't know why women do this, but she stepped back and looked me up and down before she said okay. I took her by the arm and we went out on the dance floor. I was very nervous as we stood there waiting for the band to strike up, because I had never danced with a young lady my age. I had danced with Herman . . . or a broom. I looked over at him and he reassured me with a thumbs-up.

Up until now, everyone had been swinging on the dance floor, so I figured I could do whatever they were doing. Finally, the band started playing—a waltz! This girl was waiting for me to take her in my arms, but I was at a complete loss. I didn't want to say, "Well, I don't know how to waltz," so I looked over at my buddy to see if he could help me. He was laughing his butt off.

Just then, a young couple passed by, so I put my arm around my partner and started following the guy all around the floor. If he went this way, I went this way. When he turned, I turned. It was a funny thing because my eyes were so riveted on this other couple that I never once looked at my partner. When the music was over, I thanked that young lady and split the scene. I cut out of there so fast, I think I left my shadow behind. Herman was still dying laughing, and told me how funny I looked out there. So that was my very first experience going out social dancing on my own.

The Charleston

ACCORDING TO FRANKIE, the Lindy hop developed out of three social dances that were being done in Harlem in the late 1920s: the Charleston, the collegiate, and the breakaway.

Like many African American vernacular dance forms, the Charleston can be traced back to Central Africa. Various resources have identified Charleston-like steps in dances of the West Indies, Ibo ethnic groups,[3] the Ashanti,[4] and Bari speakers.[5] The Charleston may have been based on a more relaxed African American step called the Jay-Bird,[6] and is reputed to have originated in Charleston, South Carolina, where it was sighted as early as 1903.[7] During the next two decades it turned up around the country in contests, on social dance floors, and in a variety of performance venues. By the dawn of the 1920s, the Charleston had made its way to Harlem via the first wave of the Great Migration. Ragtime pianist Willie the Lion Smith attributed its northward spread to Gullahs and Geechees, peoples of the South Carolina and Georgia Sea Islands.[8]

Although the Charleston was introduced to New York's general public in "various nightclubs and stage productions, on and off Broadway"[9] during the early 1920s, its real launch took place in late 1923. In *Runnin' Wild,* one of the earliest African American Broadway successes, choreographer Elida Webb featured Charleston variations in a routine performed to "Charleston," a tune written specifically for the show by James P. Johnson.[10] The uniquely spectacular staging captivated audiences, created a hit song and show, and finally "put it [the Charleston] across."[11]

By 1925, the Charleston had achieved nationwide popularity with revelers of the Jazz Age, and soon came to signify the rebellious hedonism of the Roaring Twenties. Josephine Baker introduced Europe to the Charleston during the 1925 Parisian stage show *La Revue Négre,* stirring up a frenzy of enthusiasm for African American dances among French audiences, critics, and artists.[12] In 1928, Joan Crawford paid tribute to what was by then an international craze with her performance of the Charleston in the film *Our Dancing Daughters.*[13] Just about any visual image of the era includes a bobbed flapper energetically tackling the leggy dance. In addition to the sensation it created, Marshall and Jean Stearns cite the Charleston on three counts for its significance in the history of American popular dance: "For the first time a step was taken over generally by men"[14]; "The distinction between popular dances to watch, and popular dances to dance, was wiped out"[15]; "For the first time, too, ballroom and tap dancing merged on the professional level as tap dancers worked out a tap Charleston."[16]

Some pinpoint the Charleston as a bridge between the demure foxtrot and the more vigorous Lindy hop. Musicologist Mervyn Cook even credits it with affecting the course of jazz music: "The growing popularity of dances such as the Charleston led to the development of a livelier style [of jazz] in which the original march-like mood was abandoned in favor of headier tempos and snappier rhythms."[17]

Additionally, the Charleston marked the most pervasive involvement to date of all the socioeconomic classes, from tycoons and socialites to domestics and laborers, in the same social dance behavior. Reflecting the pluralistic principles embodied in the new art forms of jazz music and dance,[18] the Charleston made history due to the extent of its saturation. The Lindy hop rode this trend toward popular culture when it swept the country in the mid-1930s. ●

The Collegiate

AT THE ALHAMBRA BALLROOM, Frankie first saw a dance that he soon discovered was called the collegiate. This minor social dance was based on an eight-count foot pattern similar to the Charleston and the breakaway, but allowed for none of their separation between partners. Rather, it placed participants in a relatively close, almost rigid embrace from the waist up and focused on fast footwork. Its distinguishing feature was the turning in of the leg as each dancer kicked up their heels behind their bodies, much like the famous Charleston knock-kneed stance. Frankie describes it as "doing the Charleston, but with your partner, and without swinging your legs so much." The collegiate reminds Frankie very much of the shag of the 1930s, an example of which is found in the 1937 Arthur Murray promotional short subject, *How to Dance the Shag*.[19]

Frankie has only hazy memories of the collegiate. Indeed, he found the dance less appealing than others of the period, and reports that its popularity was already waning by the time he was exposed to it. Nevertheless, although it was the least influential, Frankie considers the collegiate to be one of the foundational dances that blended with the Charleston and the breakaway to form the Lindy hop. ●

Renaissance Man

After my waltz fiasco, Herman and I decided to bring our own partner to the Alhambra. A young lady named Virginia who lived in our building agreed to join us, and we spent the entire evening taking turns dancing with her. We got through the next couple of months this way, until we finally got up the nerve to ask other girls to dance, that is, when it wasn't a waltz. (Later, I learned how to do that too.)

One Sunday, maybe six months after we first went to the Alhambra, I said something to Herman about going to the dance before we left my apartment without realizing that my mother could hear us. She came into the room and wanted to know, "What dance?" I had to confess. Of course she was peeved, and I got grounded for a week. But she also said that if I wanted to do something I wasn't supposed to, I should at least tell her and see if she approved.

Altogether, I spent two or three years dancing at the Alhambra, although at one point it closed down for a while, then reopened.[20] After about a year, we started going to their evening dances, which were for adults, but no one ever said you can't come. Being around the better dancers in the evening helped me improve quite a bit. So did the fantastic music at the Alhambra. There was always a live big band; they didn't play any recorded music in ballrooms at the time. I can't remember all of the bands that played there, but I know I heard Mills Blue Rhythm Band and Louis Armstrong. From all the dancing I was doing at the Alhambra, eventually I got to be pretty good. I never thought I was the best dancer there, but one of the better ones, I think.

At the Alhambra, my friends and I heard about the Sunday evening dances at the Renaissance Ballroom, which were aimed at older teenagers aged fifteen to nineteen. The Renaissance, located at the southeast corner of Seventh Avenue and West 138th Street, was open for dancing on Saturdays, Sundays, and special occasions such as community affairs, just like the Alhambra. On other nights, the Renny, as it was called, might have other kinds of events, including boxing matches and basketball games. It was home base for the Renaissance basketball team, which was known as the Renny Five.

The Renaissance was known to have a higher level of dancing than the Alhambra. My friends and I had begun to have more confidence in our dance abilities, wanted to be with people our own age, and thought we could learn something new at the Renaissance, so around 1929 or 1930, we began going there.

For a while, depending on the band, we alternated between the two venues since we couldn't afford to go to both. The house band at the Renny was Vernon Andrade's Orchestra (the band I think I was dancing to when my mother told me I would never be a dancer). They played most of the time, but we thought that the bands at the Alhambra sounded better. Of course, sometimes the Renaissance would bring other orchestras in. Fletcher Henderson appeared on rare occasions, and some of the other local bands played there also. Occasionally, we also checked out the music and dancing at other spots like the Audubon Ballroom or Dunbar Ballroom, or Saturday evening dances put on by social clubs.

The dancers at the Renaissance were much better than the youngsters we had been dancing with up till now. They were doing movements we'd never seen before, and had better footwork. There was such a difference. Once it became clear that our chances for improving were greater at the Renaissance, we overcame our mixed feelings about the music and began going every week.

I don't remember the exact moment when I first saw the Lindy hop, but I'm pretty sure it was shortly after I started going to the Renaissance Ballroom. Originally, the Lindy and the breakaway were really the same dance. However, it took a while for the new name to take hold. Remember, things didn't get around as fast as they do now. At first, I didn't actually realize that I was seeing the Lindy. I just thought these kids were doing the breakaway, but a very flashy version of it with some variations, a different style (such as releasing the girl in a long swing-out), and more energy. Of course, this was just a transitional stage. It still wasn't anything like what we saw them doing later on up at the Savoy. At the Renaissance, people actually called the dance everybody was doing the Lindy hop, not the breakaway, and I started calling it that too.[21]

Breakaway to the Lindy

I N THE DOCUMENTARY *WATCH ME MOVE,* tap dancer/choreographer Honi Coles characterizes the downtown "white" version of the Charleston as being very upright and perky, while the more authentic, uptown "Harlem" version was grounded and swinging.[22] In Harlem, the Charleston was a wildly popular dance, "very big," as Frankie puts it. "You heard it all over, on records, at parties, and in vaudeville shows. Chorus girls or showgirls or somebody was always doing it, and there were lots of Charleston contests."

Frankie recalls that originally, Charleston steps were done by individual dancers or by a separated couple, while the breakaway was always a joined partner dance. As these early social dances evolved, the Charleston also began to be done, at times, as a partner dance in standard ballroom position. Soon the breakaway began to incorporate some Charleston footwork, and the two dances eventually merged to form the foundation of the Lindy hop. This early transitional stage of the Lindy is demonstrated by Shorty Snowden with a partner and two other couples in the 1929 film *After Seben,* the earliest moving image of the Lindy.[23]

By the turn of the decade, the Charleston had to a great extent been absorbed by the Lindy hop. Throughout the 1930s, dancers at the Savoy Ballroom created many new Charleston variations, including turnover Charleston, hand-to-hand Charleston, flying Charleston, long-legged Charleston, squat Charleston, etc. As these individual figures became part of the Lindy's vocabulary, the Charleston found new life. However, Frankie and other Savoy dancers saw themselves as doing Charleston steps within the Lindy. They no longer considered themselves to be dancing the Charleston.

The Lindy hop had a considerably longer lifespan than the breakaway, and thus a more extended period of growth during which it could respond to outside influences. A major difference between the two dances was the amount of space they inhabited. As the vertical, staccato impulses of ragtime and early jazz began to elongate into the elliptical, smoother sounds of swing, uptown social dancing also began to broaden. In the breakaway, dancers' feet circumscribed a small circle, but the Lindy soon lobbed out into a larger, oblong floor pattern. In testament to this, it was while Lindy hopping at the Renaissance Ballroom that Frankie first remembers "really swinging a girl out."

Most enhancements to the Lindy hop were a direct response to Harlem's evolving dance music. In the breakaway, while maintaining a ballroom hold, partners stepped slightly apart on counts one, two, affording a separation that was brief in time and narrow spatially. Toward the end of the breakaway's lifespan, just prior to its metamorphosis into the Lindy, this separation included a brief release of hands, left for the woman, right for the man. The driving rhythms of swing music were reflected in the Lindy by a wider and longer-lasting breach between partners, featuring one-handed releases or, on occasion, the freeing of both hands. The expanded time and spatial allotment promoted improvisational dancing by increasing the opportunity for it.

The advancement soon became a defining feature of the Lindy hop, opening the floodgates for a deluge of new dance steps. Although the breakaway and the Lindy shared the same basic eight-count footwork, the latter eventually incorporated a much wider variety of steps, reflecting the more complex rhythms and dynamics of the new form of jazz to which it was done—swing. ●

For the next few years, I spent almost every Sunday evening at the Renaissance. Now I had a group of buddies to hang out with. Besides Herman, I had become good friends with two other kids named Frank, and we were known as the Three Franks—Little Frank, Middle-Sized Frank (me), and Big Frank. Virginia had moved out of the neighborhood, but I had a bunch of new dance partners, including my first real girlfriend, Julia (who was a very good dancer), Willamae Briggs, Frieda Washington, Rebecca, Florence, Eleanor, and Thelma, among others.

It was at the Renaissance that I first I met Billy Ricker and George Greenidge, who became my very good friends on and off the dance floor. The three of us liked to trade steps, give each other tips, and talk endlessly about dancing and music. We were the core of this group of kids that spent Sundays at the Renaissance and got together for parties at each other's apartments on Friday nights. If it was at my home, my mother might join in and dance with us. By this time, she knew how much I was into dancing.

I picked up this new dance, the Lindy, the same way I did other dances—by watching people do it. By now, my observational skills had become a little more honed. I had gotten better at listening to the music and copying steps. It wasn't that I wanted to dance exactly like other people, but if I saw someone doing something I would try it, then maybe improvise on it and make up a step of my own.

There were several of us right in my group who were creating steps; so were a lot of other people. After all, it was a new dance, so a lot of moves were being invented on the spot. We often showed each other our ideas, but I never heard anybody bragging, "Ooh, I just made up a new step!" We'd just say, "Hey, dig this step." Of course they weren't all good. For a new step to stick, someone had to say, "Wow, that's great!" and try it. Then somebody else had to copy them, and so on.

By the time I hit the floor at the Renaissance, I also had a much better idea of how things worked in a ballroom between girls and guys. In all the ballrooms, people were there for dancing, so we watched each other to see who could and who couldn't. Boys almost always asked girls to dance. If you'd never seen a young lady dance you usually didn't ask her just because she was a fox. If you did, and she had just walked in, she might say no thanks because she didn't want to get stuck with a guy who couldn't dance. But it didn't always happen that way. Occasionally, she'd just look you over and say okay.

Sometimes, you'd notice a girl standing on the edge of the floor watching you, possibly thinking she wants to dance with you. You'd start doing a little something extra, so when the dance was finished and you sauntered over, she'd be interested. She might act all sophisticated, but maybe she'd be dying to get out there with you. One girl told me, "I saw you from over there on the side, and I sure wished it was me you were dancing with."

Another thing too: If there was a girl who you knew was going with a fellow, you would walk over to the guy and say, "Hey look, is it okay if . . . ?" and he would say okay or no. Some guys would say no even if she wanted to dance with you. In that case, she might drift over later in the evening, and then you could ask her.

Of course, this is where some of your female friends came in handy. You'd say, "I want to dance with that girl, but I don't want to go over there and ask her." Frieda Washington and I were such good friends that she would help me out by standing next to the girl's boyfriend, acting like she wanted to dance. This cat had already seen Frieda on the floor, and knew how good she was, so he'd start dancing with her. And then—BAP!—I'd go over and ask his girlfriend to dance. We had it down to a tee.

The more interested I got in dancing, the more I wanted to pick up new steps, hear the latest music, meet new partners, and discover other places to dance. In Harlem, there were a lot of social clubs for kids as well as adults. The kids' clubs would play basketball and stickball in the streets against each other, but they were really a bit like gangs because it was all guys and sometimes things got a little rowdy. It wasn't as if we would engage in gang clashes—if there was a fight, it was generally between the leaders of the groups—but both sides would show up to make sure it was fair.

Even after I moved down to 122nd Street, I would go back to see my buddies in the 138th Street club. But I was a funny kind of kid because I didn't say I was in any particular club. I knew guys from all the different groups, and for some ungodly reason I ventured into all those territories. Other kids would say, "Man, you're going there? That's Reindeer territory!" Or "That's Tiger territory!" I'd say, "So what?"

These social clubs often gave dances and parties. They'd clear out all the furniture from one room in someone's apartment and charge five or ten cents to get in. The music came from the Victrola. We were still in school, so the parents might be home, and there was never any alcohol. Sometimes one gang would go to another gang's dance, but they usually brought their own partners because they didn't want any fights. I didn't have any sense, though. If another gang was having a party and I wanted to go dancing, I'd go alone.

One night, this young lady was standing on the side at a party given by the Buffaloes, and I asked her to dance. They were playing a slow tune, and in those days when the music was slow you held the girl close. At the Renaissance, we'd be out there Lindy hopping to most songs, but if they played a romantic ballad or a slow blues everybody would grab their girl and rush straight for the middle of the floor. Just the squares danced around the edges, while all the grinders crowded into a bunch. Guys and girls would be glued together with only our tops swaying, our feet moving just a few inches from side to side in a slow drag. At parties, we'd put the lights down low, grab a girl, and just lay her up against the wall. Of course, this wasn't what we did for every slow tune. If it was a slow foxtrot, you'd have to hold your head and body just so. But for the blues, you'd get real funky and uninhibited.

Anyway, this girl was all over my shoulder, I was hugging her, and we were just grinding away. As it turned out, she was the girlfriend of the leader of the pack. He saw me dancing with her, came over, separated us, and pushed me away from her.

Right away, I was ready to take him on, which must have surprised him. He said, "You've got some goddamn nerve. You're in my territory and you want to fight." I said, "If I'm just fighting you, yes, but if you need your whole gang, then you're no leader. If you want to duke it out, come on downstairs. We don't need to tear up the furniture." I tell you, I was crazy. So, we had a bout, just him and me, but it was fair and turned out kind of even.

A Double Life

During the whole time I was getting into dancing, I was still in school and also working different jobs to help out my family and get a little pocket money. If my mother knew what one of the guys I worked for really did, she would have made me quit. He was a pimp, and he was big-time with all these women and a fancy car, but he was a nice guy. I cleaned and waxed his floors, washed his windows and his car, all for four or five dollars, good money at the time.

I also did jobs for Harry Wills, a world-class prizefighter whose career was held back by racism.[24] He owned a townhouse on Striver's Row, which were these immaculate, tree-lined blocks, West 139th Street and West 138th Street between Seventh and Eighth avenues, where lots of famous

African Americans lived. When I cleaned his home, Wills gave me ten dollars, which was almost as much as my mother made in a week.

One summer, I took a job on a Hudson River Day Line boat that traveled back and forth between Manhattan and New Jersey. The cruise began at 125th Street in the early evening and lasted for several hours. I worked as a fourth cook in the ship's galley, peeling potatoes and onions and serving the captain his meals. Another cook and I were the only blacks on board.

After dinner, I'd put on my best suit, my only suit, and go up on deck, where I'd sit off to the side watching the passengers' festivities. They only had a small band and it was just ballroom dancing, nothing spectacular. When the musicians were supposed to be heating it up, they'd play a ragtime tune, something hot, and people would do the Charleston.

As for school, I was a good student with an almost perfect attendance record. I was practically never late, always brought in my homework, and was never a behavior problem. I rarely studied very intensely, but I used to skim my textbooks and notes before tests, and I had a pretty good memory for what the teacher had said in class.

I tried to do well at Frederick Douglass Junior High School 139 (between 139th and 140th streets, just below the Savoy Ballroom on the opposite side of Lenox Avenue) so my mother and grandmother would be proud of me, but I admit I was more enthusiastic about athletics than academics. I liked to go to school because I could play sports, and I played all of them, baseball, basketball, football, handball, and ran track. One year I got the award for best athlete of the whole school. You won by racking up points for each sport that you did. I wasn't the best in any one area, but the best overall. I felt very good about that. Every kid in school wanted that award.

I was so into sports that I once deceived my mother in order to play baseball. She had started sending me for violin lessons with my uncle, who I mentioned was a music teacher. At first we did classical music compositions, but soon we switched to more popular tunes. After a few months, he felt I was doing well enough to play in a trio with him and another nephew for weddings and other social occasions. To get to my uncle's house, I walked through Central Park past a field where these kids were having a weekly baseball game. After a while, I just couldn't resist joining in.

My uncle finally called my mother to find out why I wasn't coming anymore, and the jig was up. As I was getting ready to leave a couple of days later, she confronted me with the violin, which she'd found hidden in a closet. I was carrying my bat and glove in the case. She said, "How are you going to play the violin with that? If you didn't want to take lessons, why didn't you just say so?" I explained that I thought she really wanted me to take the lessons, and said I was sorry. My punishment was getting grounded for a few weeks.

Sometimes, my interest in sports and dancing kind of came together. Nowadays, you see athletes dancing when they make a touchdown or a basket. That's exactly what I used to do after I'd made a couple of points on the basketball court. The coach would yell, "Manning, you're not on the dance floor now!" I'd say, "Okay, Coach," and dance on down the court.

I think being an athlete helped me with dancing, particularly once we started doing air steps. It wasn't so much because of the strength I developed, but because of the timing and the ability to anticipate or react to what was coming next, like when my partner didn't do an air step exactly the same way twice.

There were no high schools in Harlem at the time, so I had to commute to Haaren High School, which was a specialized vocational school on West 47th Street between Broadway and Sixth Avenue. I had been going around New York by myself for some time (it was a much safer place for kids back then, and I loved seeing all the sights), so I didn't mind traveling downtown for school.

Most of the students at Haaren were white, but about a quarter were black. I became friends with several white kids, including this fellow named George Murphy. We helped each other out a lot in class, and hung out together after school in Harlem or at his home in the Bronx. Our families knew each other and sometimes I'd stay over at his house, or he'd stay at mine and we'd go to school together the next morning.

Our girlfriends were also very friendly with each other. Naturally, he had a white girlfriend and mine was black. A lot of times the four of us would go out together in Harlem, which was not a problem. We also used to go to the movies and Central Park together. Eventually, George's girlfriend quit him and mine quit me. Then I started going with his girl and he started going with mine, so the four of us would still be together. This was very unusual at the time. It didn't last all that long, but no one really knew because we were already hanging out.

By the middle of twelfth grade, I decided to drop out of school and work full time. I hate to say it, but one of the reasons I left was because of prejudice. All of my teachers in high school were white, and most of them tried to talk us black kids out of going to college. That had actually begun in junior high school. They said we should take up plumbing or auto mechanics or carpentry. I wasn't interested in any of those things, although I didn't know what I wanted to do. So I thought, *What the heck, I'll just go get a job and help my mother out.*

A while after I left school, I started working as a furrier. I got my first job in the garment industry through a friend who was making pretty good money ironing fur coats. When I started in the factory at Hershkowitz and Hershkowitz, on 29th Street and Sixth Avenue, I was just a porter, which included sweeping the floor and laying down the pattern boards. I always liked to advance, so I learned to do practically everything there. I was a hard worker, and eventually I was promoted to making patterns and, later, to stretching the furs out. I worked in a couple of different places and got to the point where I was making fourteen dollars a week. Big money! But the work was seasonal, although once I got some real skills there was one factory where the owner kept me on for a few hours a day in the off season because he liked me.

With the exception of my relationship with George's ex-girlfriend, all of my romances during my teens were with girls I met on the dance floor. One of my more serious relationships during this time was with Dorothy Young, who was a couple of years older than me. We met at the Alhambra Ballroom. In 1932, she got pregnant and gave birth to Charles Franklyn Young on November 8. So, at age eighteen, I became a father.

I want to be straight about my early relationship with Chazz, as he was later nicknamed. Although Dorothy and I stopped going out with each other, I did visit her and the baby, and offered whatever help and financial support I could. However, because of my intense involvement with dancing, and later, my professional career and time in the Army, I did not have extensive contact with my son during his first fourteen years. Up until then, he was mostly raised by his mother and her family.

Getting Hooked at the Lafayette

Around 1930, some of my friends encouraged me to enter a Lindy hop contest at Harlem's famous Lafayette Theatre. All the top black stars appeared there before it went out of business because of competition from the Apollo Theatre. The Lindy hop was starting to become more popular, and Lindy contests, including this weekend event, had begun sprouting up throughout Harlem. This was the first time I danced on a legitimate stage, and it was a *disaster.*

At first, I refused to enter because I didn't think I was good enough. But my friends kept egging me on, and when my girlfriend Julia chimed in, I agreed to give it a try with her. Our friends promised to cheer and applaud for us, so by the night of the competition, we were feeling pretty good about getting onstage.

The Lafayette was known for its legendary "Tree of Hope," which stood in front of the theater and was supposed to bring good luck to everyone who touched it. Just before the contest, we rubbed the trunk of the tree to help us win, but it didn't do any good. When our turn came, we went onstage and began doing our thing, just social dancing. At first, it was fun and we felt good, but after a few bars, we started to realize that the audience didn't like us. I guess we just weren't that good. When some people actually started booing and yelling, "Get them off," we began to think the contest was never going to end, and it only got worse before it finally did.

The Lafayette had this comedian who would come dancing out onstage if the audience didn't like you, and give you the hook. As humiliated as I was, I still remember that this guy was very funny. He started cavorting all around us, making comical noises, then got us round the waist with this big hook and started pulling us off the stage! I was intent on finishing my turn, so we kept dancing as he kept trying to drag us off. *Finally* he got us off that stage.

Afterwards I told my friends, "I thought you guys were going to clap for me, but I didn't hear any applause." They said, "Yeah, well you weren't doing too good. We were afraid to applaud because everybody else was booing."

Besides this being my first contest, if I'm not mistaken, I think this was the first time that I encountered some of the people who danced at the Savoy. I think some of them were in the contest, and they were very good. I had seen them dancing right before the show, and said to myself that I didn't have any business competing with these folks.

My buddies tried to get me to enter another amateur contest at the Alhambra Theatre soon after that. Julia had moved away, and my new girlfriend, Florence, was considered a very good dancer, but I refused, so she entered by herself. The whole gang rooted for her as she danced alone on the stage, and we were thrilled when she took a prize.

Success at Last

As frustrating as it was to flop at the Lafayette, I kept dancing just as much as before because I loved it. Besides, I had to keep trying and trying until I got it right. About a year later, I finally had my first success as a dancer. It was on New Year's Eve, probably in 1931, at one of Harlem's ballrooms, most likely the Renaissance. If I close my eyes, I can see the confetti, balloons, and lights around the edge of the ballroom, picture everybody all dressed up as best they could, and hear the band playing.

My mother, who was involved in organizing the affair, had arranged for my new partner, a neighbor and friend named Frieda Washington, and I to do a little dance exhibition. We weren't professionals, but sometimes onlookers told us that we could Lindy hop, and asked us to get out there and show our stuff.

When Frieda and I began dancing that night, much to our surprise, after a few bars people started throwing money out on the floor! It was just nickels, dimes, and quarters, but that adds up. I whispered to Frieda, "You go ahead and dance while I pick up the money," so she was up there shaking and doing the shimmy, mess-around, and all that kind of stuff while I was running all over the floor raking in these coins. Then I said, "Okay, now I'll do something and you pick up the rest." While I did the Charleston, snake hips, and other steps like that, I was asking her, "How much did you get, girl? Ten dollars! That's great, baby!"

The audience saw us running around and thought it was so comical that they threw even more money. It seemed like the more we raked in, the more people tossed out. I know, because after we gathered as much as we could and brought it over to the side to count, there was still a lot left over for the sweepers. We must have gotten twenty dollars in change. It was my first big payday as a dancer.

PART II
SAVOY DANCER
(Circa 1933–1936)

3 • TO THE SAVOY AT LAST

Courage

Ayear or so after I left high school, and at least a couple of years after I had first seen the Lindy hop, I was playing basketball on a pickup team with a bunch of friends. Herbert Roper had just scored two points, which put his team ahead of mine, and he started doing this little step. He was moving so gracefully, doing this smooth swing, that I just stared with my mouth open. "Hey, Herbie," I asked, "what's that you're doing?"

"The Lindy hop," was his reply.

I asked, "Man, where'd you learn that?" and he answered, "At the Savoy."

"That's great! Do that again." So he started moving as if he had a girl in his arms.

I had never seen the Lindy hop being done like *that* before. It just took my breath away. It was so rhythmic, and his body movement . . . Man! I'd seen kids at the Renaissance Ballroom do the Lindy, but they weren't as smooth as this guy. I don't know if he was a top dancer at the Savoy, but he was older, so he had *been* there.

"I've got to learn this!" I told Herbie. So he showed it to me a couple of times, and I began doing the Lindy hop just like him. When I went back to the Renaissance that Sunday, I tried doing the same thing with each girl I danced with. And I told my friends, "We gotta go to the Savoy."

If you loved music and you loved dancing, the Savoy was the place to go. At the Renaissance, going to the Savoy was our one ambition because they had the best bands and the best dancers. It had been on our minds for a year or two, but we were afraid to venture there because we put the Savoy on a pedestal. Nobody but the greatest dancers went, or at least those who thought they were.

Everything was being created at the Savoy—all these steps we had heard about—and we wanted to learn something new. We knew all the dances being done at the Renaissance so well that we had to invent new steps, but we didn't feel like we were good enough for the older crowd at the Savoy. Those cats were killers.

•

I think we were probably up to Billy Ricker's house in Harlem for our usual Friday night get-together when we finally came up with a plan: we'd go as a group to give us courage. That way, we wouldn't have to worry about whether we had anybody to dance with. We could just dance with each other. Everybody agreed, so we decided to go the next day.

I can't recall the exact date, but I was about nineteen years old, a couple of years out of high school and working as a furrier. I remember there were six of us all together: Billy Ricker, Willamae Briggs, and Frieda Washington, my best friends, and George Greenidge. There was one other girl, but I'm not too sure who it was.

The entrance to the Savoy was at street level. You went down one flight to check your coat, then you walked back up two flights to the ballroom, which was on the second floor. As I was climbing the steps that led to the ballroom, I could hear this swinging music coming down the stairwell, and it started seeping right into my body. I got to the top step, went through the double doors, and stopped for a moment with my back to the bandstand, taking it all in. When I turned around and faced the room . . . well, I just stood there with my mouth open. The whole floor was full of people—and they were *dancing*! The band was *pounding*. The guys up there were *wailing*! The music was rompin' and stompin'. Everybody was movin' and groovin'.

When you walked into the Renaissance or the Alhambra, you might see some people dancing the Lindy, but others would be doing a foxtrot or two-step. At the Savoy, it seemed as if everyone was doing the Lindy hop.

We'd been to several other ballrooms in Harlem, but we had never seen anything like this! Everybody was dressed elegantly and looked like they were having the time of their lives. The ballroom itself was so beautiful, like nothing we'd ever seen before. It was more than I had dreamed of![1]

The Savoy was laid out differently from any of the other ballrooms. The Renaissance and Alhambra were more square, but the Savoy was *long*, a whole block long, from 140th to 141st Street. And it was about 75 feet wide. Huge! The dance floor, with a railing around the edge and tables and comfortable chairs separated by wooden dividers behind the railing, took up half of the space. The other half of the room was a lounge area decorated in blue and gold. You could get soft drinks, beer, and snacks at the fountain, then sit at the nearby tables and chairs, or in the booths that were under the windows along Lenox Avenue.

We started saying, "Wow! Look at that!" "Man! You hear this music!" "Look at all these people dancin' and jumpin'!" "This is dancin' heaven!" It even looked like the floor was getting into the mood because it was bouncing up and down too. There was such a mass of people—their heads bobbing up and down—that we were wondering how the heck all these folks could dance on that floor. The Savoy could actually hold about 2,000 people without anybody even getting kicked. It was like, man, this is the place where we should have been all the time!

Right away we got busy taking in the sights. We walked across the floor to the bandstand, stepping right in time to the music, which was out of this world. The Savoy had two bandstands side by side. Every night, there were two big swing orchestras, each with about twelve or thirteen pieces. The top band that evening, Fess Williams's Royal Flush Orchestra (he blew clarinet and wore this high hat and a sequined jacket), was playing on the number one bandstand, which was on the north side.

When it came time for Fess Williams's break, the Savoy Bearcats (I'm pretty sure) came onto the number two bandstand on the south side and started picking up their instruments. As Fess Williams's orchestra slowly faded out, the Savoy Bearcats began playing, so there was always continuous music.

Once in a while, two bands at the Savoy had the same arrangement for a song, and they would actually play the end together, so you'd have both orchestras doing the same tune at the same time. For instance, Chick Webb and Teddy Hill both had charts for "King Porter Stomp."

We had heard a lot about "the Corner," and this was what we wanted to see. There was a crowd standing in a circle to the left side of the bandstand, so we decided to check it out. It wasn't to keep anybody out; it was to give some of the better dancers more room. We watched them and, man, my eyes popped! They were dancing up a storm!

The music was a bit faster than what we were used to, so the dancing was faster. I didn't know any of the couples out there that night, but I remember somebody saying, "Man, that Speedy can go!" I'd never seen anything like this guy's footwork before. We were so impressed with these new, more advanced steps that I said, "We ain't never gonna be able to dance like this."

We watched these cats for quite a while until we learned that those who weren't as good could go to the south side of the ballroom, near the number two bandstand. The dancers down at that end had their own little circle, so we went and watched them, and decided we might be able to fit in there.

After we started dancing, I said to Billy, "I'm going back to the other side to see what those guys are doing," and ran up to the north end of the ballroom. I caught a couple of steps, then came back to show my friends what I had picked up. After that, we all took turns. Billy would go, or George would go, get a step, come back, and show it to us. Okay, I'll give it to you, we were stealing, got it and gone, and we practiced everything we'd grabbed over and over.

That night, when we left the Savoy, we were very excited. We kept talking about everything we had seen, agreeing that we *had* to come back. What a night!

When we returned the next week, Chick Webb and His Orchestra were on the lead bandstand. As good as Fess Williams and the Savoy Bearcats had sounded, his band was even better. He had a bigger orchestra that swung more than the others. And of course, Chick Webb was far better than the house band at the Renaissance. When he started playing, people were out there just *swinging* and *swaying* with the rhythm. It was such a wonderful experience, such a wonderful moment in my life, going to the Savoy Ballroom and being exposed to this kind of music as a youngster.

···················· The Cat's Corner ····················

THE NORTHEAST CORNER OF THE SAVOY, located directly to stage right of the number one bandstand, was the place to be. During the '30s, it was known to Frankie as the "Corner," although swing dance revivalists now refer to it as the "Cat's Corner."[2] It was the spot where the Savoy's best congregated to dance with each other, and for the benefit of awed onlookers. From its intuitively enforced perimeter, bystanders had a bird's-eye view of the dancers within, who were thus guaranteed enough floor space to shine during their impromptu performances.

Shorty Snowden and George "Twist Mouth" Ganaway, two of the Lindy hop's earliest stars, claim to have staked out this turf for themselves in 1928 and dubbed it the "Cats' Corner."[3] But Frankie credits Lindy hop promoter Herbert "Whitey" White with convincing Savoy manager Charles Buchanan that the north wing of the hall would be an ideal place for the better dancers to really kick up their heels without disturbing other patrons. "The Lindy hop was so wild that the Savoy's management felt it was a problem for the other patrons. So Whitey suggested designating an area where the kids could really cut loose. The more sedate Lindy hoppers could dance in the rest of the ballroom."

A column from a 1936 New York newspaper confirms this:

> In 1927 [White] was the floor manager at the Savoy, and it became his painful duty to throw hopping dancers, the wild kids, off the floor, because other patrons didn't like to be kicked in the shins, ankles, and thighs. But soon he came to see the merits of the dance, and he caused the north end of the ballroom to be reserved for the wild dancers.[4]

Martha Hickson, a social dancer who frequented the Savoy in the early 1940s and whose husband, Foster Hickson, performed with Whitey's Lindy Hoppers, suggests that this particular area was anointed for two reasons: It bordered the stage where the lead

Exterior of Savoy Ballroom, circa 1950s.

A crowded dance floor at the
Savoy Ballroom, midsummer 1941.

Savoy Ballroom dance floor, 1950 (looking north from south end).

HILDA + FRANKIE
1934

OPPOSITE: Jam circle at the Savoy Ballroom, circa late 1930s. Herbert "Whitey" White encourages Ann Johnson (with leg bent) to enter circle with George Greenidge (facing Ann). Johnny Innis stands to Whitey's left.

Hilda Morris and Frankie Manning, winners of the Apollo Theater Lindy hop contest, December 1934.

Cotton Club entrance and marquee, fall 1936 through spring 1937.

FRANK DRIGGS COLLECTION.

Jimmy Valentine in a dance contest at the Savoy Ballroom with an unidentified dance partner, midsummer 1941.

PHOTOGRAPH BY CHARLES PETERSON. COURTESY OF DON PETERSON.

Whitey and the eight members of Whitey's Lindy Hoppers who appeared in *A Day at the Races* in California, early 1937. *Left to right:* Herbert "Whitey" White, Willamae Ricker, Snookie Beasley, Ella Gibson, George Greenidge, Dot Miller, Johnny Innis, Norma Miller, Leon James.

Publicity photo of Bill "Bojangles" Robinson, inscribed: "To Frankie, The Greatest Lindy Hopper of Them All."

Frankie doing ace-in-the-hole with Naomi Waller at the Cotton Club. The drawing, inscribed "WHOOPS! NAOMI AND FRANKIE, LINDY HOPPERS," was presented to Frankie by an unknown artist after a performance circa fall 1936 through spring 1937.

COURTESY OF FRANKIE MANNING.

Whyte's Hopping Maniacs performing with "Le Cotton Club de New York" at the Moulin Rouge in Paris, summer 1937. *Left to right:* Naomi Waller and Frankie Manning, Lucille Middleton and Jerome Williams, Mildred Cruse and Billy Williams.

PHOTOGRAPH CREDITED TO STUDIO C. BRACKEN. COURTESY OF FRANKIE MANNING.

band sat, and it was more spacious than the opposite end of the ballroom, which housed Charles Buchanan's office and a telephone booth.[5]

Everything Frankie saw in the Corner was more intense than at the Alhambra and Renaissance ballrooms. The footwork was more complicated and better synchronized with the music. The movements had a more swinging quality. The dancers were so much better than those at the Renaissance that he thought of them as being on the level of professional dancers.

According to Marshall Stearns, "Only the elect were allowed to sit or dance there."[6] But Frankie thinks this view of the Corner is exaggerated: "It wasn't like that section was prohibited to us when we first began going to the Savoy. Anybody could dance there if they had the nerve. Some couples had the attitude that they were good enough—kids from the Bronx or Staten Island or Jersey—so they'd get out there. Maybe they didn't look like much, but it wasn't as if anything would happen to them. Nobody told them to get out of the circle. At worst, another couple might swing out on the floor to show them how it was supposed to be done, then look back as if to say, 'That's the way you do it.' And sometimes people from other places were good. No matter what, somebody always thought they were better; there was always that kind of competitiveness.

"In *Jazz Dance*, Al Minns says that Leon James was the king of Lindy hopping, and that when Leon went in the circle nobody else could dance there unless he said they could.[7] That is not true. Nobody ever said, 'He's the king, and I can't put him down.' Nobody bullied anyone into staying out of the circle, because lots of people thought that *they* were the best. Many dancers had a particular step that they featured and were the best at. People watching would applaud when they did it and others might try to imitate them, but weren't as good.

"Even though people crowded around the dancers in the circle, when they finished we didn't clap and applaud. It was just, 'Man, that was great,' or 'That wasn't so good.' A lot of people came over to the Corner to watch, but there was still social dancing going on in the rest of the ballroom. It wasn't like the whole room stopped." ●

●●

Regulars

At first, we went back and forth between the Renaissance and the Savoy because we had a lot of friends at the Renny. We would go to the Savoy on Saturday, pick up some steps, and bring them back to our old stomping ground on Sunday. The kids there would say, "That's great. Where'd you get that stuff?" We'd say, "We were up to the Savoy." "You went to the Savoy!" That was the way they reacted. If they asked how it was, I'd say, "Watch me dance."

The Savoy was open every night from 9 p.m. to 4 a.m., so after a little while I began going three or four times a week. I was there on Saturday for sure, because that's when they had the contest.

We also found out that they had this club on Tuesday nights called the Savoy 400. The Savoy regulars told us that the ballroom wasn't as crowded on Tuesdays, so the better dancers came that night in order to have more room and not be restricted to the Corner. We couldn't believe it: "You mean to tell us that they're better than the guys we saw in the Corner on Saturday night?!"

Being in the 400 Club meant you could buy a Savoy 400 jacket and, more importantly, get benefits like reduced admission on Tuesdays. Many young Lindy hoppers today, and even some of the original members, mistakenly believe that this was an exclusive club open only to the best dancers. That is not true. Anyone who filled out the registration form could join.

Thursday was "Kitchen Mechanics' Night." This was for folks who were working all week, so you got a lot of one-nighters. Most of them were women, domestics who got Thursdays off, and they were ready to party.

Monday was kind of slow, so they called it "Ladies' Night" and let them in for half price. Sunday was always dress-up night, although of course back then, anytime you went to a dance you dressed. I didn't go too much on Wednesdays or Fridays because those were society nights. A social club might give a dance or community affair, and they played a lot of foxtrots and waltzes. Men dressed up in their tuxedos and women in their evening gowns. I didn't have a tuxedo, so if I did go, I just dressed up the best I could. The other nights at the Savoy were more swinging.

····························· *The 400 Club* ·························

T HE 400 CLUB, begun in 1927, was actually a marketing strategy devised by the Savoy's management, which boasted that the club had 400 members. A 1951 Savoy publication celebrating the twenty-fifth anniversary of the ballroom claimed, "a total of 17,234 persons having been club members at one time or another."[8]

The name was a spoof on the pinnacle-of-society gatherings of Lady Caroline Schermerhorn Astor,[9] with four hundred deemed just the right number to fill a ballroom. According to Kenneth T. Jackson, "During the 1890s the wealthy were often called the 'Four Hundred' in newspapers after society figure Ward McAllister remarked that Mrs. William Astor limited her guest list to four hundred names,"[10] the richest in the country.[11]

The term stuck, was bandied about by the rag press to the great amusement of its readership, and, several decades later, was recycled up in Harlem. ●

Within a year, I was down to visiting the Alhambra very rarely and the Renaissance only on occasional Sunday nights, usually if Jimmie Lunceford was there, because he didn't play the Savoy all that often. Some of the people who were still at the Renny would say, "Oh man! You learned all that stuff at the Savoy and now you come back here and show us up!" I'd say, "I just came back to dance, that's all."

There were quite a few of us who didn't mind dancing in the south corner of the Savoy. George, Billy, Willamae, Frieda, and I were this core group, but we had some other friends who were a little younger. Because we five were the best in our corner we were bossy, but those younger kids would challenge us. They'd say, "You ain't did nothing, man," then come out and dance.

During this period, if we saw anything interesting in the Corner, we continued to take it back to the south side and show it to each other. Of course, we didn't always copy steps exactly. Some, like hand-to-hand Charleston, didn't allow for much variation, but you could really make some changes with other types of steps, those with a lot of footwork. For instance, I added a heel-toe movement to the double scissors. We were stealing from all the cats in the Corner, but mostly from Shorty Snowden. At that point, I still didn't know the names of any of those guys except for him. Shorty won most of the Saturday night contests, and everyone knew he was king of the ballroom.

Even though we were improving, none of us thought we were good enough to dance over on the 141st Street side. I didn't have the nerve to ask those girls. Are you kidding? It's possible that one of them might have said yes, but she would have shown me up.

The Hot Spot

Sometimes, I speak of the Savoy as if it was the only ballroom in Harlem. It wasn't. Harlem was a unique place in the '20s and '30s. There was a ballroom with a big band playing for dancers on practically every corner: the Renaissance, the Alhambra, the Dunbar Ballroom, the Audubon Ballroom, the Rockland Palace [formerly the Manhattan Casino], and the Golden Gate. There were also a lot of nightclubs, each of which had a band and a dance floor, although I was too young to go to those places.

These were the depression years (which didn't make that much difference to my family since we were poor anyway) and dancing was an outlet for people because there wasn't much else they could do. We all stayed in Harlem, but you could find someplace to step out every night of the week. Going to a ballroom became our social life.

When church was over on Sunday, I'd take my girl to a vaudeville show where seats in the balcony cost 25 cents. Afterwards, we'd get ice cream sodas at the ice cream parlor, then go to the Savoy (admission was also 25 cents) and dance to two live bands from 9 p.m., when it opened, to 3 a.m. The whole day cost a dollar fifty, and we'd have a wonderful time.

Even though we were poor, we always dressed up. People in Harlem felt that they'd get more respect if they dressed well. Guys felt that the better they looked, the more likely a young lady would be to dance with them. I only owned two suits, but I always wore them with a shirt and tie and nice shoes, not two-tones, just black or brown ones. This was the fashion, and everybody dressed that way.

The Savoy Ballroom opened in 1926, and right from the get-go it was one of the major places in Harlem. Moe Gale, who was white, owned the Savoy, but Charles Buchanan, a black man, was the manager. We didn't see Gale around very often because he ran a booking agency that hired orchestras for the Savoy, placed individual bands in theaters and nightclubs, and packaged entertainers into touring shows. At the end of the '30s, he also opened up the Golden Gate Ballroom two blocks away, but it was not a success. If Gale did show up at the Savoy, it wasn't any big deal. As far as we were concerned, he was just another person who couldn't dance.

Buchanan, who was really the man behind the Savoy and also managed the Golden Gate, couldn't dance either. Actually, his relationship with Gale was more like a partnership. I heard or read somewhere that he eventually became a part owner of the ballroom.[12] It sure seemed like it, because the Savoy was his baby. He knew what was going on with everyone who worked there, from the cleaning ladies to the bouncers to the musicians on the bandstand. All employees were accountable to him. He insisted that the hostesses look attractive and dress well, and I think it was his rule that they were not permitted to make dates with the customers. If they did, they certainly couldn't leave the ballroom with them.

Buchanan did everything it took to run the Savoy. He took care of the payroll, played emcee, and sometimes hired the bands. He made sure it was a respectable place that people wanted to patronize at the end of the day or after a week of work. He didn't allow fights. If one started, the bouncers stepped right in and got you out of there. Of course, if there was someone on the dance floor who was kicking people, the Lindy hoppers would all surround him and kick him back. Buchanan was a pleasant fellow, and he could be fun, but mostly he was all business and demanded respect. I knew him well, but I can't say I was buddies with him.

Musicians from the South and all over the country came to the Big Apple, to Harlem, because there were so many places for them to work. Every band leader wanted to play the Savoy because they knew that if they got people out on that floor, their reputation was made. An orchestra had to keep the floor crowded. If nobody got up to dance, that meant they weren't any good and wouldn't be around much longer.

Big names like Duke Ellington, Cab Calloway, Count Basie, or Jimmie Lunceford only played the Savoy on special occasions because the ballroom didn't pay that much. They usually just came in for one night, although Basie was sometimes on the bill for a whole week. House bands, including Erskine Hawkins, Lucky Millinder, Teddy Hill, the Savoy Sultans, Buddy Johnson, Fess Williams, Tiny Bradshaw, and Willie Bryant took up residence at the Savoy for extended periods of time, maybe a month or longer. The Savoy became home base for these orchestras. They played there regularly, and came back to it after they had worked at another ballroom or gone on tour.

Chick Webb, who was my favorite, was there more than anyone else. His orchestra continued to play the Savoy regularly even after he died in 1939, and Ella Fitzgerald took over. Chick always sat on the number one bandstand. No one else held that honor unless he was out on a tour booked by Moe Gale. If he was, Erskine Hawkins, Lucky Millinder, or Buddy Johnson might get that spot. The Savoy Sultans was a good little jump band (only about eight pieces) that got quite a name from playing at the Savoy in later years. They were always on the number two bandstand, which I'm guessing was because Buchanan didn't want them wearing a groove in the floor on the other stage from all their stomping.

Bands such as Earl Hines, Andy Kirk, and Cootie Williams weren't house bands, but they would appear at the Savoy for longer than a guest band, maybe for a week.

I don't remember any white bands playing the Renaissance or Alhambra ballrooms, but quite a few worked at the Savoy: Tommy Dorsey, Jimmy Dorsey, Artie Shaw, Benny Goodman, and Glen Gray and His Casa Loma Orchestra. Guy Lombardo's orchestra broke all attendance records the night they played the Savoy. I couldn't believe it! If the music was good, it didn't matter to the Savoy crowd whether the band was black or white. By the same token, if the music wasn't good, they wouldn't blame it on the color of the musicians.

The Savoy was *the* ballroom because it had the best orchestras, and from that they got the best dancers. Even though a lot of people went to ballrooms just to listen to the music, back then bands played for the dancers. After all, they were called dance bands. Band leaders knew the tempos that would keep people on the floor, and played a range from slow to fast that appealed to us. Savoy patrons liked variety, not the same steady tempo from one song to another that some dancers today prefer.

Savoy Lindy hoppers liked dancing to fast tunes (like Chick Webb's "Clap Hands! Here Come Charley," flag wavers as he called them, which meant crowd pleasers), but not all the time, so orchestras didn't play fast numbers all night. Dancers today like doing jam circles[13] to "Sing, Sing, Sing," but we never jammed to music like that. We didn't even like "Sing, Sing, Sing." There was too much drum. I'd dance to a fast tune if it was swinging and I liked it. Otherwise, I'd sit it out. Same thing with a moderate-tempo song, for that matter. And we knew what to do with a slow number . . . mooch and grind with your best girl, body swaying, your feet hardly moving.

Other dances besides the Lindy were done at the Savoy. Many dancers got to the point where nothing was too speedy for them, but when the band played very fast music, rather than Lindy, they sometimes did the peabody, a ballroom dance (something like a foxtrot) that is basically a walking step. It was done in a big circle around the edge of the dance floor, with couples racing to get around as many times as they could. (That's why we used to call the Savoy "the track.") Usually "Long-Legged George" Greenidge won. Eleanor "Stumpy" Watson told me that when she did the peabody with George, her feet hardly touched the ground. My friends and I would start at the north end of the ballroom, and after two or three times around, we'd finish out the song with some Lindy hopping.

The shim sham is a tap routine that was developed by tap dancers Leonard Reed and Willie Bryant in the 1920s.[14] It's made up of four basic steps: the shim sham, pushes with a crossover, tacky Annie, and half breaks. At the Savoy, we sometimes did the shim sham as a group line dance, without taps, but it was different from what swing dancers do nowadays. Mr. Buchanan never announced it, we only did two choruses, and it wasn't associated with any particular music. We danced to whatever made us feel like doing it, which was usually something with thirty-two-bar choruses. A bunch of guys would just jump up and start doing the shim sham on the side of the ballroom, over in the corner. Although a few people might join in, most everybody else kept on dancing without paying any attention to us. It wasn't an organized thing, and it was not a big deal at the Savoy.

Although it was not a big thing either, we also did the shag, which had been around for a while. Mildred Cruse and Billy Williams, who were the best at it among us, were always shagging. There was also some Latin dances done at the Savoy, but they were much bigger after World War II.

The only way they could get us out of the ballroom was for the band to start playing waltzes and slow foxtrots at around 3:30 in the morning. We all knew what that meant. "Time to go home now," we'd say to each other, and start heading out.

Whites had been coming up to Harlem since the 1920s to see black entertainers perform in nightclubs such as the Cotton Club, the Plantation Club, and Connie's Inn, among others. Even though Roseland had opened earlier, once the Savoy opened, many people started going uptown to dance there and hear the music.[15] The Savoy wasn't just *the* ballroom in Harlem, it was *the* ballroom of the entire city because of the fabulous bands and the outstanding dancing.

Although there were spots right in Harlem that blacks couldn't enter, the Savoy was integrated. In fact, as far as I know, it was the only integrated ballroom in the country at the time, and by that I mean that blacks and whites could dance with each other.[16] It was an extraordinary place. At the Savoy, it didn't matter what color you were, black, white, green, yellow, or whatever. I don't even remember noticing people's skin color. The only thing they asked when you walked in was, "Can you dance?" They never looked at your face, only at your feet.

Celebrities came because they knew they were going to be entertained, not bothered. People wanted to watch the dancers, not stare at stars or ask for their autographs. We frequently saw Joe Louis and Sugar Ray Robinson, and sometimes movie stars came in, like Carol Landis, Tyrone Power, Claudette Colbert, Mickey Rooney, Orson Welles, and Lana Turner, who's said to have dubbed the Savoy "the Home of Happy Feet." I also remember seeing Marlene Dietrich with an entourage of about ten or fifteen people. She was wearing a top hat, just like in one of her movies.

Lots of musicians stopped into the Savoy when they weren't playing elsewhere, including Count Basie, Duke Ellington, Cab Calloway, Ethel Waters, Benny Goodman, Lionel Hampton, Tommy Dorsey, Harry James, Gene Krupa . . . I can't even name them all! Norma Miller even remembers seeing Leopold Stokowski.

The Savoy was the great equalizer. We didn't pay that much attention to famous people if they couldn't dance.[17] If somebody said, "Hey, there's Clark Gable," the only thing we wanted to know was, can he dance? Bill Robinson might be a great tap dancer, but could he Lindy hop? Actually, he could, a little. Ella Fitzgerald used to come down off the bandstand to dance quite a lot and, once we got to know each other, she often Lindy hopped with me.

Battle of the Bands

One of the reasons the Savoy became so well known was that, for a certain period of time, they broadcast live music programs every night that were heard across the country. Of course, there were other ballrooms in Harlem, but mostly only local people knew about them because the music coming out of these places wasn't being put on the radio.

The Savoy was also famous for its battles of the bands, which produced some of the greatest nights there that I can remember. The management would pit a big-name band against the house band in order to attract more people. There was never an official winner—the enthusiasm of the dancers decided who won—or any prizes, but I say that everybody won, the bands *and* the dancers.

Usually, Chick Webb's orchestra competed against the guest band, but if he was on the road, the guest band would battle whoever the house band was at the time. Once, in 1939, I remember Jimmy Dorsey's orchestra went up against Benny Carter's band. Both were alto sax men. Dorsey, who was supposed to be king of that instrument, came out and did the first set, followed by Benny Carter. After that, Dorsey didn't pick up his saxophone for the rest of the evening. For the last two sets, he would only play his clarinet because Benny Carter, who was one of the best alto sax players ever, blew him out of the joint.

If I could go back to any one night at the Savoy, I think it would have to be the time Chick Webb battled Benny Goodman. It happened on May 11, 1937. Benny Goodman was touted as the king of swing to the world, but Chick Webb was the king of swing to dancers at the Savoy, and when those two came together, it created a tremendous amount of excitement. Plus, Gene Krupa, Goodman's drummer, and Chick Webb were both huge, so it was almost like there was going to be a battle between them as well.

To me, it seemed like all of Harlem turned up for this electrical night, and a lot more people than normal came from downtown. The Savoy was packed, and I'm told there were thousands waiting outside to gain entry. It seemed like there were as many folks on the street as inside the Savoy, and I remember police on horseback patrolling the crowd, which wrapped around the block.

I got so caught up in the excitement that some of my buddies and I cooked up a little scheme to make a few extra bucks. We snuck people into the ballroom through the 141st Street delivery entrance for half price, which was a dollar that night, a little higher than usual. We only did it for an hour or so, just long enough to make fifteen dollars apiece, because I wanted to get up there myself.

I had been looking forward to hearing some great music, and this was one night when the bands were awesome! I danced to every single song, and sweated so much that I had to change suits three times! I'd tell Big George, the Savoy's doorman, "I'll be right back," and run home as fast as I could.

We used to buy Benny Goodman's records, and a lot of people may not realize that both bands had many of the same arrangements, which made it easier to compare them. Fletcher Henderson, who was Goodman's main arranger, had many arrangements out on sheet music, which a lot of bands used. And Edgar Sampson, who was Chick Webb's arranger, had also done some arrangements for Benny Goodman. The next day, everyone was shooting their mouth off, talking about who won the contest. Someone would say, "Man, I'm sorry for Chick 'cause he was lost when Benny Goodman was playing 'Sing, Sing, Sing'." Somebody else would jump in: "Are you kidding? Did you hear Chick play 'Clap Hands! Here Comes Charley'? Benny Goodman couldn't touch him." I loved putting in my two cents as much as everybody else did.

In my opinion—and I'm not saying this because he's black, or because he represented the Savoy, or because I performed with him—Chick Webb outswung Benny Goodman. In fact, when Chick was playing, I saw Gene Krupa standing onstage just shaking his head.

Another big night was the time Count Basie, with Billie Holiday, battled against Chick Webb and Ella Fitzgerald. It took place on the same date as that famous Benny Goodman concert at Carnegie Hall.[18] I didn't go to the concert, but we all knew it was happening. Phil Schaap, the jazz historian, told me that Basie and a couple of his men (Lester Young and Buck Clayton) were actually at Carnegie Hall that night. Apparently, because they had been invited to jam on a few numbers, Duke Ellington sat in for Basie at the Savoy for part of the evening. I must have gotten to the ballroom late, because I don't remember seeing him. Basie was playing by the time I got there.

Basie's records had just started coming out the previous year, so he was still a little new to us and his popularity was still growing. I was in Whitey's Lindy Hoppers by this time, and I remember Snookie Beasley, another member, coming into the Savoy with a new record by Basie saying, "Frankie, you have *got* to hear this."

Chick Webb was still our man, but we thought Basie was really swinging. His sound was very unique. Some of the Lindy hoppers still preferred Chick, but others, including me, were leaning toward Basie. The two factions used to like to argue in fun for their man: "Hey, you Chick Webb guys, Basie's cats are going to blow you away." "Nah, Chick's going to kick Basie's butt." "Okay, you dance to Chick, we'll dance to Basie." It went back and forth like this right up until the battle.

This is really Norma Miller's story[19]—I don't remember it happening—but apparently just before the battle, Chick Webb got a little pissed off because he found out that some of the Lindy hoppers were talking against his band. He said, "Who cares about those damned Lindy hoppers? We don't need 'em." Whitey happened to be within earshot, and when Chick turned around and saw him, he added, "Yeah, I said it and I mean it. What do you want to do about it?"

Whitey didn't say anything at the time, but the word went around that the Lindy hoppers were not to dance when Chick Webb was playing. Everyone had been looking forward to it, but if Whitey said not to do something, we all went along with it.

That night, none of Whitey's dancers got up for the house band, but as soon as Basie began playing, they all started swinging out. Eventually, Buchanan helped Chick and Whitey straighten things out, and the Lindy hoppers started dancing to both bands, but Whitey was able to show his muscle and get his point across. It was as if he said to Chick Webb, "Without the dancers, it doesn't mean anything."

As I said, I got this story from Norma, but I do remember that both Basie's and Webb's bands were swinging, and I danced harder than I ever had that night. And yeah, as far as I was concerned, Basie won. It's the only time anyone ever blew Chick Webb off the bandstand.

We used to say that the Alhambra was like elementary school; the Renaissance was like high school; and the Savoy, well, now you're up in the big time. Going there was like going to college. The Savoy was like home for me and my friends. I'd wake up in the morning and want to be there. It was such a warm place, it seemed like it just embraced you. To me, the Savoy was paradise. When I die, if I go to heaven, I want it to be just like the Savoy.

4 • WHITEY, SHORTY, AND STRETCH

Invitation to the Dance

By the time I started going to the Savoy, Herbert "Whitey" White was already well established as the person who had brought a special group of Lindy hoppers together. He thought these youngsters were very talented and wanted to expose them to better dancing, so he gave them a section to dance and enjoy themselves in. I never asked, but I think he wanted to help keep some kids off the street. They were under his auspices, but this wasn't an organized kind of thing or a performance group yet. It was just the cats in the Corner who loved to dance.

There were about nine or ten couples, but they weren't called Whitey's Lindy Hoppers yet, just the Savoy Lindy hoppers or "those Savoy dancers." During the day, they would meet up at the ballroom to shoot the bull and practice steps. They entertained, but just as social dancers. The only performances, if you could call them that, that I saw them do at the Savoy were in the Saturday night contests.

Whitey was a tough guy. He started as a bouncer at the Savoy and, like most of the other bouncers there, he had been a prizefighter at one time. He'd also been a dancing waiter at a nightclub in Harlem.[1] He was called Whitey because of a white streak in his hair, and whenever there was a special occasion he'd make it even whiter with shoe polish. We'd say, "Something special is happening tonight, 'cause Whitey done whitened his streak." He seemed about thirty or forty years old, around 5'10" (my height), a little on the stocky side, maybe about 200 pounds, with a cherubic face. He always had this charming smile and a beautiful laugh—he loved to have a good time—and he was a sharp dresser.

Whitey was always at the ballroom. You'd see him walking up and down the floor, back and forth, looking for dancers who were very good. If they had potential, he'd ask them to join his group. Every time Whitey came by, we'd put on a little extra stuff, trying to get his attention; each of us had our own special thing. Our group was stealing a lot of stuff from his group, and creating little variations. I think that's why he began to notice us.

•

At first, he'd just come over, watch us for a little while, and move on. One night—I'd say this was the early part of 1934—Whitey walked up to me, told me I was a pretty good dancer, and asked if I wanted to dance with the Savoy Lindy hoppers. I told Whitey I would *love* to join the group. You kidding? We all knew they were the best. He said, "Well, come on over and I'll introduce you to some of the guys."

I started to follow him, but when I got halfway across the floor I realized that my friends hadn't come along. "What about them?" I asked. "Can they join too?" Whitey told me that he didn't want them right now, just me, so I said, "If they can't come, then I don't want to either." He said okay, turned around, and left me standing there.

As soon as I went back to the group, everyone wanted to know what Whitey and I had been talking about. They started carrying on and congratulating me, saying that I was going to be one of the Savoy elite and learn all the steps now. When I told them that I had turned him down and why, they were amazed, shocked. I'll never forget what Billy Ricker said: "You *stupid* jerk! If that had been me, boy, I would have forgotten all about you dudes. I'd a' went and danced over there!"

For the next couple of weeks, Whitey kept coming by to size up the rest of the group. One night he said, "All right, I'll take you *and* your friends." I went to tell the gang the good news; then Whitey took us over, told the Corner cats that he had some new dancers, and introduced us around. I don't know about the rest of them, but I was nervous as hell. This was our chance to meet the supreme dancers.

Right away they wanted to see what we could do. I was nervous about getting out there, but the music started playing, so we started dancing. George went first; he just figured, what the hell. None of us did anything near as good as the regulars, but Whitey said we had some possibilities, so we stayed.

The Savoy Lindy Hoppers

Once I was part of the Savoy Lindy hoppers, I had the privilege of being with the best dancers all the time. That's when I learned the names of everybody I had been watching in the Corner: There was George "Shorty" Snowden, who was just a little over five feet. His partner, Big Bea, was a foot taller. We called Leroy Jones "Stretch" because he was just about six feet tall. He danced with Little Bea, who was tiny. I never could understand why she and Shorty Snowden, who was the same size, didn't dance together, but it wouldn't have been funny.

Maggie McMillan and Edith Matthews were two of the top female dancers. Madeline and Freddie Lewis, who were brother and sister, also danced together. There was Speedy, the guy I had noticed the first night I went to the Savoy. Rabbit could also do a lot of very fast footwork.

There are a couple of stories about how Shoebrush got his name. One is because his hair was flat, but he also had a shoeshine box on one of the street corners in the neighborhood. "Twist Mouth" George Ganaway's mouth was twisted so that he had to talk out of the side of his face. Blackjack was a heck of a dancer and a muscle man for Whitey. If anything went wrong, he'd take over. We called Clyde Brown "Brownie." He stayed on and eventually became Whitey's right-hand man instead of Blackjack.

William Downes came in right before I did. So did Leon James, who was a year older than me. Although Norma Miller is five years younger than I am, I think she was already in the group when I joined.[2] She says she knew me from the Renaissance Ballroom.

The Savoy Lindy hoppers got started because Whitey had been president of a social group called the Jolly Fellows in the late 1920s and early 1930s. Shorty Snowden and Speedy and most of those guys belonged too. (My mother was a member of the Jolly Flapperettes, counterpart to the Jolly Fellows, and knew Whitey, although she hadn't ever mentioned him.)

At the time, they had a million social clubs in Harlem, from pinochle and whist clubs to all kinds of buddy clubs.[3] Quite a few social clubs had a dance group in them. Sometimes two of the clubs would give a dance together—anybody could go—and they might have something like a competition, although there weren't actually any prizes. Each group would just do a little show, usually with ballroom dancing, which they were very good at. Once the Lindy hop started coming into the fold, occasionally they'd have a Lindy contest. By the early '30s, some of these clubs had gotten kind of rough, and were more like gangs. Clubs like the Jolly Fellows started dying out, and that's when Whitey began to get the Lindy hoppers together.

Being in the Savoy Lindy hoppers meant I could get in without paying—even my girlfriend Dorothy Jackson, who I began seeing around this time, could come in for free—and I could go in the afternoons to practice. Some of the kids were up there all day long, but I was working as a furrier. During the very busy season, which was the summer because we were making coats for the winter, I might work a twelve-hour day. As soon as I got off, I'd run home, clean up, eat, then go to the ballroom. In the wintertime, when I'd get laid off for a few months or work shorter hours, I would go there to practice during the day, also. It was tough financially but, like most of the kids, I was living with my family, so we didn't have to worry about going hungry.

Sometimes I would stay at the Savoy until it closed at four in the morning. Since I had to be at work at eight, I'd be dragging in and could hardly make it through the day. But when night came, I was ready to go. This is when I really stopped going to the Renaissance.

One benefit of being part of the group was that we got to watch the experienced Lindy hoppers a lot more and could ask them to show us steps. This was much better than stealing from them. But you know what? I found out that we really weren't stealing, because if we had asked any of those guys what they were doing, they would have shown us. They gave us moves like the back Charleston (now called the tandem Charleston), face-to-face Charleston, and heels, which were much more advanced than what we had been doing before. That seemed like kindergarten stuff to us now.

Us newer dancers started to make up more sophisticated steps and show them to the older guys, who would approve or disapprove. Instead of taking so much from them, we began to be more creative. Eventually, even though we were younger, they accepted us into their group.

During the day, we would dance, dance, dance, trading steps off and on to records on the Victrola or to the bands when they were rehearsing a new arrangement. Occasionally, they'd rehearse after the ballroom closed, and only the Savoy dancers would be allowed to stay and listen. Sometimes the leader would ask us if we liked the tune or if the tempo was good for dancing. We'd say, "No, pick it up a little bit," or "Oh, yeah, that's just right!" They listened to us because if we liked what they were playing, we'd dance to it when they got up on the stand.

At night, our energy came up because we could dance to a sixteen-piece orchestra. Some of the Lindy hoppers practiced with special partners, but when we were social dancing we'd all dance with each other. My group was getting out in the middle of the circle by now, doing the steps that we had practiced during the day, but it wasn't like we were putting on a performance or dancing for applause. One couple would start dancing, and a crowd would form around them. Then another guy standing on the side would say, "I can cut that," swing his chick out, and do his little bit. Then someone else would come out, and you had a jam. It was always impromptu. Maybe we looked good or maybe we didn't, but we danced the way we felt like dancing, just for enjoyment.

Over time, I became very good friends with the other Savoy dancers. One day, I got into an argument in front of the ballroom with this street kid named Apples who often went dancing there, and was considered dangerous. I don't remember what sparked it, but he pulled out a knife and threatened me. Maybe I was just too stupid, but for some ungodly reason, I wasn't scared.

Instead, I just stood there with my hand in my pocket and warned Apples that if he cut me he better not ever show his face again at the Savoy or it would be the last thing he ever did. Of course, I didn't have a thing in there, but he didn't know that, and because I confronted him he got confused.

Right then, Big George (the front door ticket taker) separated us, told me to get on into the ballroom, and pushed Apples away. The next time he turned up at the Savoy, Blackjack, Speedy, Rabbit, and those guys cornered him and told him not to ever pull a knife on "that kid" again or else . . . Yeah, those cats were all for me. Later on, I heard that Whitey told Apples that if he had been upstairs dancing, he wouldn't be downstairs using his knife.

When I began to pal around with the older dancers, I also got to hear their stories. I got this one from Shorty himself. He was a wonderful, humorous person, and I'm telling it just the way he told it to us: Shorty was dancing in a marathon contest at the Manhattan Casino in Harlem, up on 155th Street off Eighth Avenue. Whoever danced the longest won the prize. During the day, when hardly anyone was in the ballroom, the dancers would just be dragging along, and it was a chance to sleep. You would tell your partner to take a little nap while you held her up, then you'd wake her and take a nap while she held you, back and forth.

At night the place would get crowded because a lot of people came to watch, and if a couple was lively the audience might throw them a little change. Shorty used to cut all kinds of tricky steps that he did up at the Savoy Ballroom so he could outshine everybody else and make a little money.

One night, this reporter came over to him and asked, "Hey Shorty, what's that dance you're doing?" Shorty told us that after Charles Lindbergh had flown the Atlantic, the headlines in the paper read, "Lindy Hops the Atlantic," so he said, "I'm doing the Lindy hop."

As I've mentioned before, at that point, they were still doing the breakaway. You only separated a little from your partner, but it was this release that gave dancers the opportunity to improvise on the footwork. That's what Shorty was playing around with when the reporter asked what he was doing. Shorty gave the breakaway a new name and—*voilà!*—the Lindy hop was born. We called Shorty Snowden the father of Lindy hop because he actually named the dance.[4]

At one point, some of the papers had all this stuff about Whitey creating the Lindy hop, but it was all hype.[5] He never said that. There were too many guys around who could set the story straight. He would never have gotten away with it. Of course, Whitey didn't deny it either. At the time, I don't think most people had the slightest idea *who* invented the Lindy. They only knew that it came out of Harlem.

It was after I began dancing with the Lindy hoppers that I really started idolizing Shorty Snowden and Leroy "Stretch" Jones. When either of these guys got out on the floor, they put fire to it. Nobody could top them. Everybody just stood back and said, "Go out there and dance? Who, me? Behind Shorty? No way."

To me, Shorty Snowden was an exciting dancer who could really swing. He had very, very fast feet and even though he was small, he was durable. Shorty was creative and he started a lot of steps. He had so many moves I can't even name them all. He could improvise while he was dancing and look really good. He was very funny too. A lot of times he won contests doing comical stuff. But what I mostly got from Shorty was the foot movements—that's what I wanted to do.

Leroy was like Fred Astaire—sophisticated, classy, full of rhythm, with an overall elegant style. You know how Fred Astaire used his hands and legs with such grace? Leroy would do the same thing. He had the personality of what we called a strutter because he was short-waisted with very long legs, which he would use to advantage. He looked fantastic doing the cakewalk,[6] which had a strut in it that he incorporated into the Lindy.

If you watch the better dancers, hear great music, and dance often, if you're any good you'll start improving. I got so that I could look like almost any of the Savoy Lindy hoppers—Freddie, Speedy, Rabbit, Shoebrush, Blackjack. I wanted to dance like Shorty and Leroy, but didn't feel that I was good enough to imitate them in their presence, so I only did it when they weren't in the ballroom. It took a while, but it got to a point where I could copy their style down to a tee. People told me I looked just like them. Since they were the top dancers, I thought I must be getting pretty good. Except nobody ever said, "You dance like Frankie."

Going Horizontal

Shorty and Leroy came out of the old school, a little before my time—so they danced real upright. About six months after I joined Whitey's group, after I started getting more comfortable, that didn't feel exciting enough to me anymore, so I started changing things around. What I did was I took a little bit of Shorty and a little bit of Leroy and created my own style. I did the same steps they were doing, but I started bending my body at the waist and stretching out their movements to make it look more exciting. I found that I could still use my feet like Shorty, but move more rhythmically and use my body to express what I was hearing in the music, which was changing over from a more up-and-down rhythm of the '20s to this real smooth type of swing. I was trying to imitate the new sound. We didn't have any mirrors, so I didn't actually know what I looked like, but it felt so-o-o good.[7]

I think that another part of what inspired me to dance this way had to do with my mother telling me I was too stiff. Her words came to the front of my mind and made me want to relax. That, coupled with memories of seeing all the sisters and brothers in those Holy Roller churches getting down and shouting. When they dance, they move every part of their body all over the place.

Soon, I was dancing almost horizontal to the ground—way down in here—and I had the idea to extend my leg in the back for better balance. When I'd swing out, my leg would just kick back—JOOMP, BAH!—and my arms would reach forward—OOOH! I cut a lo-o-n-ng figure there. I guess people began to notice because dancing like that was such a drastic change from being upright. Folks started to say, "Man, you look like you're flying!" And I said to myself, *Yeah, that's exactly the way I want to look, like I'm flying!* And that's just how I felt. It was wonderful![8]

Pretty soon, the guys who joined the hoppers when I did, Billy Ricker and George Greenidge, and those who came in a little while after me, like Jerome Williams, Billy Williams, and Snookie Beasley, picked up on it. Even William Downes and Leon James adopted that style. This was the point at which a lot of the younger dancers started dancing like we do today. So we moved from Shorty Snowden "up here," to Frankie Manning "down here." But most of the older dancers—like Speedy, Shoebrush, and Blackjack (those three never went professional) and Shorty, Leroy, and Freddie—were so used to dancing straight up that they never changed.

Because we were dancing at a new angle—I got the guys bending over and touching the floor with their hands while they stretched their leg way out in back—it felt like we could do more movements. Lindy hopping was still developing from the Charleston, and we began creating new variations, like the hand-to-hand Charleston, front-to-back Charleston, and side-to-side Charleston. Long-Legged George (Greenidge), who was our master creative genius in Charleston, was instrumental in making up a lot of new ways of doing that step. And it seems to me that swinging out like that might have helped my partner feel the motions of my body better, and give her more time to respond and express herself.

5 • WIN WIN

Saturday Night

As I've mentioned, there was a contest every Saturday night at the Savoy. When I started going there, Shorty would win four weeks in a row, then one week Leroy would take the prize. Then Shorty would get it for the next five weeks, then Leroy for one. Speedy, Rabbit, or Blackjack would enter, hoping to catch Shorty on one of his off nights, but that would be the night that Leroy was on.

Mr. Buchanan was the emcee. Just before the contest, he would ask Whitey for a list of everybody who was entering. Any number of people could go in. The orchestra leader picked the music, which was almost always "Christopher Columbus," because it was so swinging. Each couple danced alone, and there was no time limit; they just stopped when they felt like it. Some couples went out there and just did a few steps. Others tore up the floor for two or three choruses.

In a way, the contests were like performances, except we'd just get up on the floor and social dance. After each team had danced separately, Buchanan would line them up and hold his hand over each couple's head in turn. If you didn't get much applause, you were out immediately. Then he'd go down the line again for third and second place. The team that got the most applause won. This crowd was very knowledgeable about Lindy hopping, and they were fair. If you were good, you got it; if you weren't, you didn't.

It didn't cost anything to compete, and anybody could go in, but most of the dancers were put up by Whitey, who would take a couple of bucks off the ten-dollar prize if one of his teams won. Generally, if you weren't connected with him you wouldn't enter, because you wouldn't feel like you were good enough.

Occasionally, a couple from the boroughs or Jersey would jump in there. Each area had its own style of dancing. A lot of times, we could tell that a couple was from Staten Island or Queens or the Bronx because we'd recognize their style. It might be different from ours, but we never said it wasn't Lindy hopping. Sometimes they weren't that good, just like some of the dancers at the Savoy, but if they were, they'd get respect.

Once in a while, a couple from another ballroom would luck out and win. They might have come with a bunch of friends who applauded for them, but usually there were so many regulars from the Savoy that outsiders were wiped out. It wasn't a popularity contest, though. I had a lot of friends, but if I wasn't dancing well, they'd let me know. I'd say, "Man, I thought you were my friend! You should applaud for me," and they'd tell me I wasn't looking too good that night.

I didn't begin entering the Saturday night contests until after I joined Whitey's, but then I went in almost every week. Sometimes I might not have any intention of competing—I just wanted to watch—but when I got up there I'd say, "Hey, Frieda," or "Hey, Maggie, you want to go in the contest tonight?" and we would just do it. At one point, when things were kind of slow in the fur business, Buchanan had given me a job bringing sodas up from the cellar, working behind the counter, and sweeping up when the dances were over. Once I started competing, he told me I had to choose between working and dancing, so I chose to dance.

Whoever won the contest felt like they were just the greatest dancer there was, because they'd gone up against quite a few good ones. There were four girls who usually won: Norma Miller, Helen Bundy, Willamae Ricker (she and Billy had gotten married soon after we all joined the Savoy dancers), and Frieda Washington. I generally danced with one of them. We all switched partners around. Billy Ricker, George Greenidge, Snookie Beasley, Billy Williams, Jerome Williams, Brownie, Leon, and me were tops among the younger guys. At first, any one of us would win, but after a while it boiled down to George, Billy Ricker, Snookie, or me. Every once in a while some other guy would win. When that happened, these cats would always announce, "I'm the best; I'm the greatest." Of course, Shorty Snowden wasn't dancing in the contests anymore. He used to win so often that he told us they barred him from entering.

I think that because the Saturday night contests were so competitive, they had an important role in the development of the Lindy hop. People wanted to have something special for these contests, so they would add to the steps they were getting in the ballrooms or come up with something new. When I was social dancing there were certain steps, little crazy stuff, that I did by myself while the girl was swinging out, and that's what I would do in the contest.

Showtime at the Apollo

Around this time, there were a lot of contests in Harlem. On Wednesday nights, the Apollo Theatre had an amateur competition,[1] and on Thursday nights they had a Lindy hop contest. Every performer who was anybody played the Apollo, or wanted to, because that audience really knew about entertaining. If you were good, they would let you know. And if you were bad, they would let you know, for sure!

After I started dancing with Whitey, he paired me up with a very good dancer who was new to the scene named Hilda Morris. In late 1934, we entered the Apollo Lindy contest and won. The prize was to appear for a week in the revue that opened there the next day. You worked with whatever band was on the bill, so my very first stage show was doing a whole week with Duke Ellington! Can you imagine?

The next morning at rehearsal, all the acts in the show were giving him their music, but we were such amateurs that we didn't have any. After everybody had handed theirs in, he walked over to me and said, "What's your name, kid?" I was shivering in my shoes with the great Duke Ellington standing before me, but I told him and introduced Hilda. Then he asked if we had any music. We said no, we were just going to dance, so he asked what tune we wanted to use. In all innocence I said, "How about 'Let's Get Together'," which is by Chick Webb. "We don't play that," he said. "Well, how about 'Nagasaki'?" "We don't play that either." I figured all bands did these songs because they were so popular. As I later learned, Ellington rarely played other people's music, unlike, say, Lucky Millinder. I was about to suggest something else when Ellington said, "Is there any music of *ours* that you'd like to dance to?"

Now, we used to go see Duke all the time at the Apollo and the Harlem Opera House, and we loved his music, but there wasn't anything I'd heard that was all that danceable. It was fantastic music, and it was exotic—we used to call it jungle music—but his band just didn't work for the Lindy hoppers. This was 1934, so it was before he came out with all those swing tunes like "Jack the Bear," "Cotton Tail," "In a Mellotone," and "Take the 'A' Train." I'd been listening to "Black and Tan Fantasy," "Mood Indigo," "Sophisticated Lady," and all this other beautiful music, but nothing that was swinging.

Finally, Ellington said, "We have a tune called 'Stompy Jones.' Would you like to hear it?" I said, "I've never heard of it, but just play it and we'll dance." So Hilda and I performed the whole week to "Stompy Jones," which worked just fine.

We did four shows a day, with the first show beginning at eleven o'clock in the morning and the last show finishing at about midnight. When there was a big draw like Duke Ellington, the Apollo management ran five shows on Saturday by cutting out the short subjects and just showing the feature film before each stage show. All Hilda and I did was get up on the stage and dance. I would talk to her while we were out there: "Hey, let's do this step." She'd say, "Yeah, okay! Now how about this step?" And I'd say, "Sure. Then let's do this." It was just as if we were social dancing at the Savoy Ballroom, except that we were in a theater with Duke Ellington's band and all these other acts. And, we were each getting fifty dollars to do something we loved!

Touring

Right after our appearance at the Apollo, Hilda and I went out on the road for the first time. In fact, I believe this was the first time Whitey sent anybody on tour. Some producer in the audience at the Apollo came backstage and told me he would like us to be part of a show he was putting together for a theater in West Virginia. He was also planning to bring a tap duo and a singer from the Apollo, but had the band and a comedian already lined up down there. I didn't know anything about show business, so I called Whitey, who came down and talked to him about how much money we'd get for the week-long gig.

Before Hilda and I left, Whitey sat me down. "Listen," he said, "you're going out on the road, and I want you to take care of everything. When you get down there, I want you and Hilda to get a room together because it's cheaper, but I do not want you to bother her." I knew what that meant. Whitey trusted me with that kind of responsibility. He used to hear me tell the Lindy hoppers—a lot of them were street kids—that we shouldn't be cursing around the girls. At first, the guys just laughed at me, but I said it so often that eventually they began to calm down. Later on, some of the younger girls started using worse language than the fellows, and I would ask them how they expected boys to respect them if they didn't respect themselves.

Hilda and I slept in the same bed every night, and I did not try anything with her. As a matter of fact, I was her protector. One night, one of the tap dancers wanted to seduce her, so he gave her a couple of drinks. She got high because she had never had liquor before. He was older, but I told him he'd have to deal with me if he messed with her.

Later on, when we came back off the road, the restrictions were lifted. It was an open field, but it wasn't a long affair. Hilda and I just went out a couple of times. That was the only time Whitey ever asked me not to fool around with my partner.

At the end of our week on the road, the producer disappeared with all the money and left the whole show stranded. That happened a lot in show biz. Still, we were all pissed. I sent Whitey a telegram, and he wired us money to pay the hotel bill and get back home. After that experience, I *never* wanted to go out on the road unless I had enough money in my pocket to get back.

Sometime in here, I'd say by late 1934 or early 1935, Mr. Buchanan started getting calls asking if he could send some Lindy hoppers down to perform at private parties, or at an affair or benefit at one of the big hotels. I don't think he and Whitey were hiring out dancers before that. I think we were the first ones. We still weren't professionals, but people were beginning to notice, and they called the Savoy because they knew we had some exciting dancers. Buchanan would ask Whitey to pick out one or two couples and pay us when we got back, or we'd get paid on the job; not much, maybe five dollars.

I remember one benefit at an elegant hotel, either the Waldorf-Astoria or the Pennsylvania. It was a really big-time show with Eddie Cantor and his protégée, Dinah Shore, who was still a youngster, not a famous singer yet. Whitey sent three or four couples. To start, each team did their own thing, and as soon as we swung out, people loved it. Then, to finish, everybody jammed, meaning we all danced at the same time, although we weren't doing routines yet. At that point, Eddie Cantor decided to make a comedy out of it by grabbing the girls and then the guys while we were trying to dance! Then he acted like he was trying to get the hell out of our way. It was hilarious. Over the years, a lot of comedians have pulled this gag with us.

Around this time—I know it was before the first Harvest Moon Ball in 1935—Whitey had the idea to build an act out of Leon and me, like Stump and Stumpy, Buck and Bubbles, Cook and Brown, and all those comedy/dance teams. This was before the Lindy had developed into a major attraction, and I think he wanted to get a top-notch act together. We rehearsed in the basement of the Apollo Theatre a few times, but Whitey really didn't know what to tell us to do. He just wasn't a coach in that sense. Leon had showmanship and I had dance abilities, but I was still an amateur and we weren't good enough singers. It just didn't work out.

Once, when we were the only two who happened to be around, Mr. Buchanan sent Leon and me out on a gig at a hotel. He usually left all that to Whitey, but he must have been out of the ballroom at the time. When we got to the job, Leon and I just clowned around doing jazz steps, Charlestons, and a little comedy, traded steps, and sang, "Back in Nagasaki where the fellers chew tabaccy and the women wicky wacky woo," just stuff to entertain the people. We also incorporated some Lindy hopping into the act, with me dancing the girl's part.

After we finished, the hosts of the show paid Leon, who had the idea to split the money with me and not tell Buchanan. I was stupid enough to go along with it. Back at the Savoy, Buchanan paid us again, then called the hotel to collect the fee. When he found out what was going on, he got mad at both of us, but he said we could keep all of the cash as long as we didn't do it again.

Ladies' Twist

When I first started going to the Savoy, I heard a lot about Twist Mouth George Ganaway. I haven't said much about him, but Shorty, Leroy, and Twist Mouth were considered the three best dancers at the Savoy. Actually, Twist Mouth always said that he could outdance Shorty any day, but to me he didn't have that same kind of rhythm in his body. I never saw him compete in the Saturday night contests, but I heard that he did, and won occasionally. I didn't see Twist Mouth all that much because he had gone out as a professional single act before I started going to the Savoy. He mixed singing, eccentric dancing, and jazz steps with Charlestons, boogies, legomania,[2] and stuff like that. He was tall, so he used his legs a lot, and he was very flamboyant. You'd see him walking down Lenox Avenue in his white suit and white hat with his white dog on a white leash.

Even though he worked at Smalls' Paradise, Twist Mouth George was never a real star, just one of the acts there. I wouldn't put him in the same category as Snake Hips Tucker, who was a big name, but he and his partner were instrumental in changing the Lindy hop.

Up until then, the girls always did the back step, a rock step, on the swing-out, just the same as the fellows. One day, Whitey and I were sitting in a box at the Savoy alongside the dance floor when Twist Mouth came over with Edith Matthews and said, "Hey Mac, watch this." (That's what we called Whitey sometimes; it was a word for "boss.") He swung Edith out about three or four times, and she twisted each time [pivoted left, then right, then left on counts 8, 1, 2 while emphasizing her hip movement] instead of doing the rock. It was the first time I'd ever seen that in the Lindy hop. You might see something a little similar in shake dancing, what we call exotic dancing nowadays, so it didn't come totally out of nowhere, but those girls were shaking more than twisting.

Whitey started nudging me under the table, whispering, "Get that. Get that." He knew I was very good at copying people, and he was starting to take me more into his confidence. By now, Leon and I were his top dancers. I said, "Hey, that's great. Do that again," and watched intently. When they left, Whitey asked if I could do the step; then he swung me out and I did what I had seen Edith do. Even back then, I always tried to do the girl's part because I wanted to be able to dance both ways. It was fun to get out there and imitate the girls as a comic routine, but I had also gotten into a teaching role. A lot of the guys in my group looked upon me as someone who knew how to help them with a step.

After Whitey and I tried doing the twist, I brought over Helen Bundy (who had joined the Lindy Hoppers after me) and told her to twist with the music. Then we started showing it to the other girls. They were kind of getting it, but when Edith came around another time, I got her to demonstrate it for everybody, and she did a much better job of explaining it than I did. Once the rest of the girls learned to twist, they started to add their own little touches and began advancing it.

So that's the night the twist was introduced at the Savoy Ballroom. It must have happened just before the 1935 Harvest Moon Ball, because you don't see twisting on the newsreels.[3] It hadn't gotten to be a big thing yet. I didn't know it was going to be history or I would have asked whether it was Twist Mouth George's or Edith Matthews's idea. At the time, you never heard anybody going around saying, "I made up that step." We never thought about who created this or who created that.

Harvest Moon Ball

The first Harvest Moon Ball was held in August 1935. It was sponsored by the *Daily News* as a way to promote the newspaper. Major ballrooms in the boroughs of New York City held preliminary contests in each category: foxtrot, waltz, tango, rumba, and Lindy hop.

Most of the people who entered the preliminaries at the Savoy Ballroom were Lindy hoppers from the Saturday night contests. We could all ballroom dance, and Shoebrush was very good, but only two couples went into that category. The preliminaries were the only contest at the Savoy where we had to register, had a specific amount of time to dance, and were not judged by the audience. The judges picked one or two out of each group, and then had one last heat with all the winners. Eventually, they picked about ten or fifteen couples to send to the Harvest Moon Ball, and there was a lot of speculation about who was going to win. Leon and his partner, Edith Matthews, and me and Maggie McMillan, who was very elegant and upright with a big personality and smile, were favored to win.

I had noticed that when we did the elimination rounds at the Savoy, we would start off with a whole gang of energy, but by the end of the two minutes, which is how long we were going to dance at the competition, we were very tired. If you know anything about Lindy hopping, you know that's a lo-o-n-n-ng time. So right away I started working to get an edge on the other contestants. First, Maggie and I began practicing to a recording that was two and a half minutes long in order to build ourselves up. Then, since this was the very first Harvest Moon Ball and the judges hadn't seen much Lindy hopping, I concentrated on steps that I thought would catch their eye. Figuring that they would look at the flashy stuff, I put in as much of that as I possibly could. I had a pretty good idea about what steps aroused the crowd from having been in the Savoy contests, so I added those to our dancing. I know we did the sailor step,[4] which I still teach, and a Charleston step that I've since dropped. And naturally I tried to project more. It took a lot out of me to practice like this, but I think it helped, and everybody else got into it too.

Finally, I decided to check out the Roseland Ballroom dancers because I didn't know what they were like, so a bunch of us went down there one night when Fletcher Henderson's band, a *black* band, was playing. When we got there the doorman told us we couldn't go in. We asked why not, but he just kept repeating himself. We got very indignant, but it was one of *those things*, so we said, "We don't have to come in here, anyway. We can go back on up to the Savoy." We just wanted to go where we could dance without anybody saying anything about whether it was with a white person, a black person, a green person, or what! The Savoy was ours, *ours,* and we felt that our place was better anyway.

Originally, they were going to have the Harvest Moon Ball competition in Central Park on August 15, but when the day came it was so jam-packed the dancers couldn't even find the platform where they were supposed to compete. The event was canceled and rescheduled for August 28 at Madison Square Garden, which was more controllable. Ed Sullivan, who was a columnist for the *Daily News* at the time, was the emcee, and they put different stage and screen stars on the bill as an added attraction. The Garden was packed for this one-night affair with about 20,000 people.

Right before the contest began, Whitey gave us a pep talk. He told us to go out there and do our best, and said that he wanted his dancers to take first, second, and third prize in the Lindy hop contest. He didn't want any other ballrooms, like Roseland or the Arcadia, to walk away with that.

The dancers for the other competitions—the foxtrot, waltz, rumba, and tango—came out before us during the grand march. They looked beautiful and walked on very properly to thunderous applause, but when they announced the Lindy hoppers, a wild commotion erupted in the crowd. Naturally, we danced through the house—not swinging out, but holding our partner's hand and laughing, skipping, jumping, cutting little steps, and

WIN WIN WIN

89

carrying on. We didn't walk out like kings and queens; we were the jesters. It wasn't any straight parade, and the people reacted to that. The energy from the Lindy hoppers spread through the whole auditorium, and by the time the first dancers hit the stage, the audience was ready for us.

Five teams danced at a time. Sometimes it was all Savoy Lindy hoppers; sometimes we were mixed in with competitors from other ballrooms, all of which sent white dancers. Four couples were each given a designated corner of the stage to dance in. The fifth was told to stay in the center. The judges sat in a row at the front of the stage.

In the heat of competition, dancers often forget where they are supposed to be. Because of this, and because they wanted to be seen, everybody in my group ended up congregating in front of the judges. Leon, especially, was very audience-minded, and no one could get him out of that front spot. He and Edith stayed right there, showing off and carrying on—his arms flying and his legs wiggling—so the rest of us just had to do the best we could to get noticed. Even though we were competing for the Savoy, we were also trying to outdance the other guy. Occasionally, we tried to dance around Leon to the judges so we could show off our stuff too, but he hogged the spotlight.

We had been told that we were going to be judged by the same rules used for ballroom dancing, like we couldn't separate from our partner or jump up off the floor. Even though we had protested—"What are you talking about? We're Lindy hoppers!"—that was the way it was supposedly going to be. But Leon and Edith, who went out there and did their own thing, won. I had tried to adhere to the rules, but it just didn't work. Maggie and I came in second. Norma Miller and Stompin' Billy came in third.

It's a funny thing, but I didn't feel sorry for myself. The Harvest Moon Ball was just a contest that we needed to win for the Savoy, and we got the three top spots. It didn't faze me that someone else won first place. You see, to me, the Savoy Ballroom . . . that was the world. I was considered pretty good there, so it didn't matter what anybody else thought. As long as the Savoy thought I was good, nothing else counted.

It was a really fantastic experience, but that first contest in '35 was very hard for us. Even though Fletcher Henderson's band played for the Lindy hop contest, my recollection is that the music wasn't very good. Maybe he was having an off night, but I remember that a lot of us complained.[5] And it was really tough to be thinking about those ballroom rules while we were out there trying to shine.

Still, I think the first Harvest Moon Ball was a great showcase for Lindy hopping. It was the first time we had been exposed to so many people at once, and the contest was filmed for newsreels that were shown in the theaters. (Of course, we didn't know this at the time.) This was the beginning of the spread of Lindy hopping—some people had never seen it, only heard of it—and the audience was very enthusiastic about the way we danced, especially those of us from the Savoy. The Harvest Moon Ball also inspired dancers to generate new steps.

Nobody won any money, just prestige and a medal, but the top winners in each division got a paid, week-long engagement with Ed Sullivan at the Loew's Theatre. After that, the Moe Gale Agency, which was a partner in the Savoy, also booked the first- and second-prize winners of the Lindy contest for a tour of Europe.

This was the first time any Lindy hoppers had the opportunity to perform outside the country. Whitey asked Leon, Edith, and Maggie if they wanted to go, and they were all for it. When he asked me, I said, "No." "What do you mean?" he protested. "I've got a contract for you and Maggie. You're going to Paris, to London, to Ireland. You're going for free, and they'll pay you. You'll get prestige, a name. When you come back, it could get you work in a nightclub. You'll see all these things that you probably won't ever get a chance to see again. Go to Europe, man."

I listened to Whitey talk, but I just kept shaking my head no. You see, I was working as a furrier, making beautiful furs for beautiful ladies. I liked the business and thought that was going to be my career. I probably would have lost my job if I went. Don't get me wrong, I *loved* dancing; I went to the Savoy as often as I could—like all the time. If somebody asked my mother, "Where's Frankie?" she'd say, "Over at the Savoy, I guess." But I didn't think that I was good enough to be a professional. Even though I had taken second place in the contest and everybody around the Savoy said I was a great dancer, I genuinely didn't feel that way. Dancing was just something I did in a ballroom for enjoyment.

Whitey must have spent a couple of hours trying to convince me to go. I didn't even get to dance that night. I can't remember everything he said, but his words just didn't overwhelm me. Somebody else would have jumped at the chance, but that wasn't me. After a while I told him that I didn't want to talk about it anymore and I was going to see my girlfriend, Dorothy.

When I got down to her place on 134th Street, who was sitting on the stoop waiting for me but Whitey! Now, this cat was a stone con man. He could talk the shell off a turtle, but I have a little bit of a stubborn streak in me. Whitey asked if I would give him just a few minutes, so we sat down . . . until five o'clock in the morning, and the sun had started coming up! That's when he threw in this business about how I was his best dancer and he depended on me to take care of the rest of the Lindy hoppers. He said he saw something special in me. I never did get up to see my girlfriend, which made me mad. I definitely wasn't going anywhere after that.

Since I refused to go overseas, Norma Miller and Stompin' Billy went with Leon and Edith. Maggie's boyfriend, Speedy, was glad she didn't go to Europe, but she was very angry with me.

After the Harvest Moon Ball, things started to get busier for the Savoy dancers. As champions, Maggie and I got a gig doing the Lindy hop at a nightclub in Jersey for four weeks. We were billed as something like, "Frankie and Maggie: Harvest Moon Ball Lindy Hop Champions." I would finish work, go home, wash up, and take a train to the club, where we danced in two shows until around two in the morning. Since I had to be at work by eight o'clock, I wasn't getting a lot of sleep. At first it wasn't so bad, but it got to the point where I had to buy this Big Ben alarm clock that made a lot of noise and put it right by my pillow.

Maggie and I danced together a few more times, but eventually she left Whitey to work as an extra for Shorty Snowden's group. My refusing to go to Europe turned out for the best, though, because I think the man upstairs had something else in mind for me.

6 • UP IN THE AIR SHE GOES

Pros Versus Upstarts

When I first joined Whitey's group, Shorty and Leroy were at the Savoy every night and were still entering the Saturday contest, but that didn't last much longer. It's possible that Shorty was thinking about leaving or had already formed his own performing group, and Whitey was getting some replacements when I came in, but the idea of a professional group didn't occur to Whitey until Shorty went big-time. At this point, there still wasn't much demand for Lindy hoppers. Sometimes Buchanan would ask Whitey to have us dance in front of the boxes—the tables and chairs at the edge of the dance floor—for celebrities or for tourists who came up to the Savoy on buses. We would swing out so they got to see what Lindy hopping was all about, and it promoted the Savoy. Of course, we didn't call it a performance then; we were just dancing in a different place. We didn't get paid, but the people watching might throw some money on the floor near the dancers, and we would divide it up.

I also have a memory from around this time of a whole bunch of us making a movie, a short, out in Astoria, Queens. It was the first movie Whitey's dancers did. I don't know the name of it or what company made it, and I've never seen it. The setting was a house with columns on a plantation. I think we were the children of slaves playing around in the yard, dancing and carrying on. A lady—this belle in a big dress with hoops and a white sash—came out and said, "You kids are going to town!" I was the one with a speaking part: "No, Miss Julie, we're not going to town. We're going to dance right here." Then we did the Lindy, just some improvisation. If we got paid at all, it wasn't much, but it was a very exciting experience. It was like, "Damn, I'm making a movie!"

Shorty Snowden was the first to take a Lindy hop group out of the Savoy and dance with them professionally in a club. I don't know what else they had done, but after I became part of the Savoy dancers, they began working at the Paradise Restaurant in Times Square with Paul Whiteman, who was called the "King of Jazz," and it was big-time.[1]

The act was called something like Shorty Snowden and His Lindy Hoppers. There were three teams: Madeline and Freddie Lewis, Little Bea

•

and Leroy "Stretch" Jones, and Big Bea and Shorty Snowden. I never actually caught them at the Paradise Restaurant, but I was told about it and saw them later on at Smalls' Paradise in Harlem, and after that at a club in Atlantic City in 1936. From what I heard, they kept repeating the same thing in all three places. It was all single work, meaning that they danced as if they were in a contest or a challenge dance, like in the movie *After Seben*.[2] One couple would finish and go off, then the next, and the next. There was never any ensemble work because that hadn't been created yet.

Their act featured three distinctive styles: flash, smooth, and comic. Madeline and Freddie were the first to dance. They did flash, which meant they were doing very energetic movements. His style was a little bit like Leroy's, but I don't put him in the same class as Leroy or Shorty. Freddie was wild. Saying somebody was wild wasn't always a complete compliment. You could look wild and be a good dancer or not, but Freddie was good.

Leroy had a very upright ballroom style, as I've mentioned, and he was very smooth, but this cat's feet would be moving! He was very handsome with a big smile, and he had personality plus. Little Bea, who was very graceful, complemented that. If she was twisting (which many of the girls were doing by now), his hands would outline her shape in a way that said, "Look at her," really showing the girl off. When he did something himself, he would move in such a way that said, "Dig this step I'm doing."

It was quite a contrast to the others when Big Bea and Shorty Snowden came out. He could do any style of dancing, and if he was with another girl he did a lot of footwork, but these two used their partnership to do a comic style of Lindy hop. They were hilarious! They didn't do particular steps to be funny (like we do peckin' now), but there'd be this little cat down there turning this big chick while he jumped over her head,[3] and you'd just start laughing. He'd rock back on his heels and shake his toes. When they'd do a jig walk,[4] you'd see her long leg kicking up between his legs, almost over his head. At the end, when Big Bea picked him up, it was the funniest sight you'd ever want to see. All of a sudden, they would get back to back, lock arms, she'd lift him up, and you'd see this very large woman walking off with this little guy on her back, kicking his legs. They always went last because that got the big laugh.

Sometime after the 1935 Harvest Moon Ball, we heard from Whitey that Shorty was going to be leaving the Paradise Restaurant. The management of the Paradise was mounting a new show, so Whitey took us down for an audition. We had three couples, just like Shorty, and the manager wanted us to do the same kind of thing they did. Now, we were strictly amateurs, and I mean amateur amateurs. Each couple was supposed to dance two choruses, but I didn't know what the heck they were talking about! Even before he began working with Paul Whiteman, I think Shorty knew more about choruses than any other Lindy hoppers. If you watch *After Seben*, the other two couples are still going when the music stops, but he dances for two choruses right on the money.

At that time I didn't know anything about counting. We were used to working with bands that played the Savoy, like Chick Webb. When they started playing, we started dancing, and we knew that they would stop when we finished. We were always with the beat and always danced with the music, and if someone said do this step so many times it would always come out with the phrasing, but we didn't have any time limits or sense the natural end of a chorus. We might start in the middle of a chorus and finish up before the song ended.

I went over to Leroy (Shorty's whole group was there), and said, "What's the hell's a chorus, man? How do I know when it starts and when it ends?" He tried to give me a quick rundown: "You hear the music, then it's going to sound different in the middle from what they were playing, and that's when you'll know that you only have a short period of time until the end of the chorus. Then it's going to start all over again."[5]

Each of us went out and did our little bit. When Maggie and I got up there, I was busy worrying whether I was dancing to one chorus or two choruses, or what! We danced wildly all over the stage, backs to the audience; I messed up the whole thing. We did not act like professionals because we weren't, and we did not get the job.

After Shorty and all of them started dancing in the Paradise Restaurant, they would go out on stage doing their improvisational steps and get applause for a certain movement. Naturally, they'd want to do what the audience liked again, so they'd start doing that step every night. Then they'd get a heavy hand for another step, and put that in. Pretty soon Shorty and his dancers were repeating many of the same steps every night, and to me, they got kind of stuck. When Shorty and Leroy would drift back to the Savoy—they didn't come as often anymore—they couldn't social dance like they used to. Their minds were so set on those steps that that's what they did even at the ballroom.

In the meantime, we youngsters were coming up in the Savoy and getting a name for ourselves. When this got back to Shorty Snowden and his dancers, who still considered themselves the champion Lindy hoppers, they started coming around to the Savoy again. Everybody was telling Shorty how great these young upstarts were, and people were forgetting what he had done. So Shorty had a friendly conversation with Whitey: "I hear that your Lindy hoppers are supposed to be so great. I know they're good, but the audience still thinks we're king of the hill, so we want to have a contest."

Whitey admitted that Shorty could outdance us—we all agreed with that—and told him that he didn't need to prove it, but Shorty insisted. "Never mind all that stuff. We'll have a contest right here in the Savoy Ballroom two weeks from tonight and let the public decide who's the best." It was going to be when Shorty got back from a trip out of town. "You pick out your three best teams to go against us."[6]

When Whitey came over and told a group of his dancers about the challenge, some of us began to walk away because we didn't want to be picked to go up against Shorty and Leroy. Whitey called us back and said, "Aw, come on. It's just a contest. Just dance and have some fun." Everybody was hoping it wouldn't be them when he picked the three teams: Lucille Middleton and Jerome Williams, Mildred Cruse and Billy Williams, and Frieda Washington and some guy named Frankie Manning.

Now, an idea had been floating around in my head for a while from watching Big Bea and Shorty do their pet step every time they performed, and this challenge must have brought it to the surface. I got together with my partner, Frieda, and said, "I have an idea for a step. You know how Big Bea carries Shorty off on her back?" "Yeah," Frieda said, "but I ain't taking you off on *my* back. You can forget that."

"No, no, no. That's not what I mean. What I want to do is put you on my back, but instead of you just laying there, I'll roll you over like in a somersault so you land in front of me in time with the music. Then we start dancing again." I wanted it to be a step, not just a lift. Now, here's something Frieda had never seen, and I sure didn't know how to do. She took two seconds and said, "Okay, let's try it." She was a brave girl.

Instead of practicing at the Savoy, I decided to work at home because I wanted it to be a surprise. Frieda and I lived next door to each other on the top floors of two walk-up apartment buildings. I was at 230 West 140th Street (we had moved again); she was at 228. I would holler out my window for her to come on over to practice, and she'd run across the roof and down the stairs to my place.

On the first day, I took the mattress off my bed and put it on the floor. Frieda looked at it, then looked at me and asked what that was for. I told her it was in case she fell. That's when she got a little reluctant. "*Fall!*" she said. "Whaddya mean, 'fall'?" That had never occurred to her. I didn't have the slightest inkling of how to do what I had in mind—neither of us had paid any attention to how Big Bea and Shorty did their step—so I just bent over and told her to get up on my back. Unfortunately, I didn't realize that she was standing five feet away and, as I stood there waiting, she ran and jumped on me. It was the only way she could think of doing it. Naturally, we both hit the floor . . . BLAM! I said, "Not like that, girl!" and she answered, "Yeah, I know . . . *now*!" We tried it again, with her standing closer to me, but I didn't know how to tell her what to do, so I said, "Just get up on my back." "Okay, but how do I do that?" "I don't know. Just get up there." While I was bending over, I grabbed her by the ankles, trying to lift her, and she fell . . . on the floor, unfortunately. Another time I managed to get her on my back, but we both went over and landed on the mattress right as my mother walked in. She looked at us lying there and said, "What is this?" I tried to tell her that we were practicing a step, but there was no explaining. "What kind of step do you need to do on a mattress?" she asked. But my mama was cool and just told us not to hurt ourselves.

It got to a point where we could lock arms and I could draw Frieda up on my back. There she was with her feet sticking up in the air, so I said, "Now roll over." "Roll over where?" "Roll over in the front and bring your feet down on the floor." "Well, how do I do that?" "I don't know . . . just do it! Don't be kicking me, just bring 'em down. You're getting heavy up there!" There should have been a video, because the two of us trying to get this step was pure comedy. We had so many laughs. One day, I told her to pull her knees in, kick her feet, and roll over, which she did and landed in front of me. "*That's* the way to do it! But next time don't land on your knees. Bring your feet underneath you, girl." She wanted to know why I didn't tell her that in the first place.

To make a short story long, that flip was much harder to work out than I thought it would be. For a while, I wasn't sure we could do it. We must have practiced for about two to three hours every day for the two weeks, and didn't even enter the Saturday night contest. Finally, with a lot of work, we got to the point where I could flip Frieda every time. Then I moved the mattress out of the way and put a record on the Victrola so we could learn the maneuver to the music. Finally, we tried different ways to get into the step without breaking our rhythm. We picked out the best way and practiced until we could do the whole sequence each time.

Big Night

Now, for two weeks there had been this murmur all through the neighborhood about the big contest at the Savoy Ballroom, and come that Saturday night it was packed. People were sitting all around the edge of the floor waiting for the contest, not even dancing. They wanted to get a good seat because they thought they were going to see the six greatest Lindy hop teams in the world. Of course, we were just about the *only* Lindy hoppers in the world. Everybody was very excited, but I was scared as hell.

Shorty Snowden came over and laid down the rules: "One of my couples will dance first." He wanted to wipe us out right away. "Then one of yours. After that, we'll alternate." Whitey said okay, and chose Billy and Mildred to start for us.

The first team to go out was Freddie and Madeline. They danced, and when they finished, the audience applauded and stomped their feet. Then Billy and Millie got out there. We called them Fred Astaire and Ginger Rogers because they moved so smoothly. And that girl could twist! I mean, it was a shame. When they finished dancing, everybody just tore up. Next came Leroy, the second-greatest Lindy hopper around, and his partner, Little Bea. Leroy did all his fancy stuff, and when they came off the floor the whole place caved in.

Jerome and Lucille were the best comedy dancers we had. Jerome was so funny that if he just walked in front of you, didn't do nothin', you'd start laughing. He started doing all this comedy stuff with Lucille, and the audience was cracking up—I mean, rolling on the floor. When they finished, the people jumped to their feet, clapping and yelling.

Then came the masters: Shorty Snowden and Big Bea. They got out there and danced like I had never seen before in my life. Shorty was swinging Big Bea all over the joint, and doing all this footwork. Man, they dug a hole in the floor! When they finished, the house just parted and came down.

Now, I want to tell you that I was ner-r-r-*vous*. All those cats were *on* and that floor was *hot*, and I hadn't even danced yet! And you know who didn't want to? I didn't feel like I could do any better, so I said, "Whitey, just give it to them. Ain't no sense in me going out there." But he told me to go ahead, it was all in fun. I said, "What am I gonna do behind *that*?"

Frieda tried to convince me too. "Don't think about it. Let's just dance."

"Are you crazy, girl?" It was fun to them, but not to me. They really had to urge me to get out on the floor.

Just as I was getting ready to swing out, reluctantly, Chick Webb leaned over and said, "Frankie, what tune do you want me to play?" I was quite surprised because he hadn't asked anybody else.

Now, Chick Webb always played for the dancers. There was this wonderful communication between his band and the Lindy hoppers. If it wasn't crowded and we were able to dance in front of the bandstand, he would often focus on somebody doing a certain step, and he'd catch it. We'd try to do things to trick him, and he'd play back at us: "You ain't going to trick me, man.

No, I got you." Same with his wonderful trumpet player, Taft Jordon. He'd play a solo to the way we were dancing, and we'd respond by doing little rhythmic steps with the music.

As I've said before, the tune we always used in contests was "Christopher Columbus." But earlier in the evening, Chick had played "Down South Camp Meeting," which is this real swingy tune. If you heard it, you'd dance to it. I had found that I could catch all these little breaks in the music, so I said, "How about 'Down South Camp Meeting'?" "You got it," he said. "What tempo do you want?" "Something about right here," I said, snapping my fingers. That little humpbacked man up there on the drums hit off the tempo, and those cats started swinging!

Now, I danced to Chick Webb almost every single night, and we always had a lot of fun with the guys in the band, but this night it felt like they were all saying to me, "Frankie, we're going to play this for you!" Every one of them was really blowing. It was like they were telling the audience: "This is our man. We're gonna swing for this cat." When they started stomping this music out, it got me going and I forgot about the contest. I hadn't even swung out yet—I was just jockeying—but I was feeling that music because the band was driving.[7]

I said, "Okay, Frieda, I'm ready," and we swung out. I flung that girl so far across the floor that we almost took up the whole ballroom! This was one time when we *really* danced to the music, and it seemed like the band was catching everything that we were doing. Every time I kicked my leg out, Chick would say, "DJBOOM!" If I did a little swing-out, Taft Jordan would play, "BEOOOOWWW!" Frieda had one of the greatest twists of any of the girls, and she could really show it off. When she was twisting around me, Chick Webb was playing "CHEEE-CHI-CHI, CHEEE-CHI-CHI" on the cymbals, keeping time with her. They'd play a riff behind me, and I'd think: *Yeah, keep up with me, guys!* I was feeling everything that they were doing, and the band was hitting every step that we did. Frieda and I were just talking—"Let's do a crossover Charleston." "Yeah, okay." "How about a boogie?" "Sure enough."—and having such a good time that I wasn't even thinking about the contest. Everything was going so right that even the crowd was rocking with us.

It was coming down to the end of our turn, so I said, "You ready to do the step?" "Yeah, let's go for it." That's exactly what she said. I remember it as if I was there right now. I swung her out and did a jump turn over her head while Chick said, "SHUUMMP!" Then I jumped so we were back to back and flipped her. While she was going over, he played "CHI-CHI-CHI-CHI-CHI-CHI-CHOOO." And when she hit the floor right on the beat . . . "BOOMP!"

The crowd had been clapping in time with the music and yelling, "Go, Musclehead!" (my nickname), but when Frieda landed, for one second, it seemed like everyone in the audience caught their breath. Their mouths opened, but no sound came out. It was as if people weren't sure they had really seen what they'd seen, like they were trying to figure out what we had just done. They were awestruck. Then all of a sudden, the house *erupted*! Everyone jumped up and started stomping, clapping, hollering, and grabbing each other saying, "Did you see that?" "What the heck did he just do?" "He threw that girl over his head!" Folks were just carrying on. It was turmoil!

After Frieda landed, she fell onto me and we fall-off jig walked right on off the floor.[8] People started crowding around, slapping me on the back and exclaiming about what we had done. Buchanan was up on the bandstand saying, "I guess the youngsters won," but nobody was really paying attention. Normally, he would have put his hand over each couple so the audience could choose the winner, but he didn't get a chance because everybody was all over the floor. I remember thinking, *Gee, maybe I did something.*

Just then, Whitey pushed his way through the crowd and said, "Hey, you got a new step you didn't tell me about."

"Well, I didn't know if I was going to do it," I said.

Even Shorty Snowden came over. "Hey, man! That's a great step. Where'd you get it from?"

"I got it from you."

"Oh no you didn't. I don't do anything like that." So I told him about the step he did with Big Bea, and he said, "Oh. Yeah, that can be done."

"I know," I said. "I just did it."

Aftermath

A lot of the Lindy hoppers wanted me to show them the step, so I told them to be at the Savoy on Monday. I knew they would be doing my move in the next Saturday night contest whether I taught it to them or not. That was always a problem when you went into contests, even with floor steps. If they thought they could do it, they didn't care where it came from.

I just want to say something here about stealing steps. In Marshall Stearns's book, Al Minns said that Lindy hoppers never stole from each other, that it wasn't allowed. I don't know why he said that, because everybody was always showing their moves to other people, and we were all copying off each other. If you didn't get steps this way, then you'd always have to make them up. There was a friendly competitiveness when we got out on the floor, but I never heard anybody say, "You shouldn't do that step because it's mine." Nobody ever thought of copyrighting their moves, making people pay them for a step, or saying, "I'm the only person who's going to do this."

If you stop and think about it, how far would the dance have gone if people didn't steal from each other? Back in the early '30s, there weren't any dance schools that would even teach the Lindy because they didn't accept it as a dance. It wasn't until the latter part of the decade that Arthur Murray and other dance teachers decided that this thing was so big, they might as well put it in their schools. So the only way we could learn was by exchanging steps.

If another person learned your step, they might improve on it, which happened all the time. Then when someone else did it, it could spread, and the dance could advance. Otherwise, you'd be the only one who knew that move. If we couldn't steal, I don't think Lindy hopping would have lasted as long as it has. It would have stagnated right there in one spot, but that's not what happened. I stole things from all kinds of dancers. In fact, I was the biggest crook in the Savoy. Yup. Still stealin'.

Come Monday, all the Lindy hoppers were at the Savoy, and I taught them over-the-back, which is what I called my step because that was the trajectory the girl took. We didn't use exotic names. We'd ask, *Which way is she going? I'm throwing her over my back. Then that's the step.* If I pick her up on my shoulder to carry her off, and she drops down my back, that's drop-down-the-back.

Dancers today don't always know the original names of the steps, so they sometimes make up their own. Like they call around-the-back the "Lindy frog." Or the Rhythm Hot Shots call down-the-back the "dive." Down-the-back is where the girl dives down the fellow's back while he's bending over.[9] Snookie Beasley used to put so much personality into that step. After the girl had gone over and was holding his thighs with her head between his legs, he'd jump up and down while moving back and forth to make it look more exciting.

Dancers come up to me and say, "Frankie, do you know how to do such and such?" I say, "No, I've never heard of it." But when they show me the step, I say, "Oh, you mean *that*. Yeah, I know how to do that."

People say "aerial" nowadays, but I called my invention an air step. I wanted to distinguish it from ballroom dancing, where the male lifts his partner gracefully, twirls her above his head, and gently lowers her to the floor. You saw folks doing that at the Savoy when the band played a waltz. In the Lindy hop, you *throw* the girl in time with the music, and she's got to land right on the beat and start dancing again.

Air steps were mostly done in contests at the Savoy. Once in a while, someone might do them in the Corner, where there was more room, especially if they had something new to show off. And we occasionally did them in front of celebrities in the boxes, but rarely while social dancing. When you see air steps on film clips or in photographs taken at the Savoy, they were done for the cameras.

I had to find another air step after the contest, so from then on I was always looking for something new. The second one that I did was over-the-shoulder. I had seen this acrobat raise his partner up in front and lower him down in the back, so I made it into a step where you throw the girl backward over your right shoulder[10] and used it a week or two later.

The next air step was the side-flip,[11] which George Greenidge made up. After that, I don't know who made up what because everybody started creating air steps. My name got kind of lost in the shuffle, and I never mentioned what I had done to anybody. Leon James and Al Minns probably didn't even know who started doing air steps, because Leon was in Europe at that time and Al hadn't joined the Lindy hoppers yet. When *Jazz Dance* came out, I read that Al said he and some other dancers had come up with air steps. That's when I first had the thought, *Hey, wait a minute, I did that.* I confronted Al about it later, and he admitted he didn't know who had done the first one. That's because I hadn't run around saying it was me.

George and I would go to circuses, movies, and vaudeville shows to see balancing acts, comedians who might do something acrobatic, and the Five Crackerjacks, a comedy/dance team. We were looking for anything we could put into a rhythmic pattern. Back at the Savoy, we tried out a lot of ideas, but we had to discard some because we just couldn't do them.

Some of the air steps were created by accident. For example, I introduced ace-in-the-hole[12] at the Cotton Club in 1936 with my partner Naomi Waller. One time, her feet went too far over her head and she started to fall behind me, head first. To save her, I bent forward and let her slide down my back, which slowed her, until her feet hit the floor, and she ended up hanging onto my thighs, looking at the ceiling. I reached through my legs and grabbed her so I could hold her up, and right then the idea came that we could make a step out of it. Later, I finished by pulling her forward through my legs until she bounced up in front of me, and called it ace-in-the-hole-down-the-back.

I don't know who created the original handspring-front-flip,[13] but it turned into handspring-down-the-back[14] because of a similar accident. I used to be pretty strong, and I would throw Ann Johnson, my partner in the early 1940s, way up there. One time, she got scared and started falling over, so I caught her behind me. We started doing it on purpose, and had ourselves a new air step.

So that's how the first air step was created. At the time, it was just another step. I didn't realize that it was going to change the face of Lindy hopping—no one did—but it was actually revolutionary. It meant that the Lindy hop was a little more exciting than it was before. Pretty soon, we started getting dates in theaters and nightclubs all over the world. But before that happened, I also created ensemble dancing.

All the Cats Join In

Soon after I introduced the first air step, I was at the Savoy dancing to Jimmie Lunceford's "Posin'," either while he was rehearsing in the afternoon or during one of those battle of the bands. As I've said, I used to like to catch breaks in the music, and "Posin'," which he had just come out with, had a nice stop rhythm to it. Each time Willie Smith sang "Evvv-ry-bod-y *pose!*" and the music stopped, I would freeze my body, then begin dancing again when the band started up after holding for eight counts. Nobody else was doing that, but I did it with my partner because I was so in tune with the music.

When the song was over, I got to thinking that you could only pose to that particular tune. We didn't hear it all that often because other bands weren't playing "Posin'," although some of them picked it up after Lunceford recorded it in 1937. I began wondering why we couldn't stop during *any* song. That's when I realized that I could gauge other music as it was playing in order to catch those emphatic moments and stop right on the beat.

One afternoon, when I was rehearsing at the Savoy, I put a different song on the Victrola just to see if I could stop and start on the breaks, which I could. I called George Greenidge over to show him what I was doing, and he tried it. Since we were both dancing without partners, I called Frieda over. I didn't know how to tell her when to pose, so I said, "Just do what I do. I want you to stop dancing when I stop." We got that going, stopping then dancing, and I was just making it up as we went along.

Then I said, "We're going to do two Charlestons, and on the third one we're going to hold it. After the break, we'll start back in and go on from there." We did it, so then I asked George and his partner, Ella Gibson, to join in. This time I told everybody that we were going to do two swing-outs, then a reverse, then come side by side and do two Charlestons. On the third Charleston, when I said stop, I told them to bend their right leg up in front and hold it. They did exactly what I said and, man, it was great. We did it again, and when we got those steps down it looked so good that I added a third team, Billy Ricker and Helen Bundy. We got so fired up that I started adding steps and stops as we went along—skip-up, slide-back, then stop, fall-off-the-log, then stop. It was a lot of fun, and I was excited that the others were doing this right along with me.

Just then, Whitey came by and asked what we were doing. I explained about being able to do stops (that's what I called it) to any music, and he said we looked fantastic dancing in unison and encouraged us to keep it up. (He often praised me like that, but it wasn't like he would ever say that any of my ideas were going to help the Lindy hop along.) So I made up an entire routine, the first one I ever did. I don't say I completed the whole thing that day, but I did quite a bit and continued to add to it.

I wanted to get to a point where I didn't have to call out the directions, so we kept practicing for the next couple of months until the Lindy hoppers could know when to pose without me telling them. I wasn't thinking that the Lindy was a group dance now or that it would be great to do routines onstage or in a nightclub. Whitey had better foresight about that sort of thing. I was just having fun doing something different. Shorty Snowden and his group were the professionals, but they didn't do anything like this.

At the time, I didn't know what an impact my ideas were going to have. Even though I was trying to work out stops, I ended up inventing synchronized ensemble Lindy hopping. This was also the first Lindy choreography. Of course, I didn't think of it as choreography; I was just putting together a routine, even though, up to that point, we did not do routines. And, although I wasn't thinking about this, it turned out that some of the flaws in a particular dancer could be covered up by performing in a group.

Breaks

"BREAKS COME AT THE END OF AN EIGHT-MEASURE PHRASE," says Frankie, "usually the last two measures. You can hear the music coming down, like it's going into something else." "The music might get louder," adds swing dance instructor Steven Mitchell, "or there will be a crescendo, or a shouting feel, but there's always some kind of buildup. If the band is jamming hard and the tension is right, those cats, and the dancers, will want to break."[15]

Of breaks, Wynton Marsalis writes, "At certain times in the performance of a piece of jazz the entire band will stop, and one musician will have a short solo spot before the band comes back in."[16] "Customarily," observes Albert Murray, "there may be a sharp shotlike accent and the normal or established flow of the rhythm and the melody stop."[17] John F. Szwed notes, "The effect it creates is one of tension release, but when the rhythm returns it can suggest that the whole piece seems to accelerate."[18]

"During a break, the sound doesn't necessarily stop unless it's written like that, as in 'Posin'," points out Frankie. "You can freeze when you break to signify that you've finished a particular step . . . or you can keep moving. Tap dancers usually use breaks to complete a step, but Bunny Briggs talks about riding out the break, not responding traditionally like Bojangles, but with more subtlety.[19] Bunny liked to dance through the breaks and go into the next step." Mitchell concurs: "Musicians can play and sing over a break, and so can dancers."

Szwed suggests that, "Many of the most innovative features of early jazz—such as breaks and stop-time—were developed to accommodate dancers' moves."[20] *The New Grove Dictionary of Jazz* cites breaks as providing "a source of textural contrast," and offering "moments of unrestrained melodic spontaneity."[21] Similar opportunities exist for Lindy hoppers.

For Frankie, "A Lindy break is often a place for improvisation. You break the flow of the movement and do something different—like a tuck turn, a kick-ball-change, shuffles, or some little tricky step. A Lindy hopper might separate from his partner as if opening like a book, and perhaps do something like a back step or a Charleston. There can also be breaks where a couple separates completely."

In Mitchell's experience, "Once I hit the break, something always changes dynamically in my dancing; something gets bigger, smaller, or works against or complements what's come before. It's important for dancers to connect with the music leading up to a break in order to attain a true and honest response. That's what allows the improvisation to happen naturally, which gives their break character and subtlety."

"Of course, in the old days, Lindy hoppers never called it a break," recalls Frankie. "That started in the 1980s or '90s. We didn't call it anything. We just danced." ●

Slow Motion

There were some tremendous white dancers at the Savoy and, over the years, we had several in Whitey's Lindy Hoppers. Jimmy Valentine, one of the greatest, was also a one-legged dancer. I wish I had the kind of rhythm that cat did. He was so good, he could outdance a lot of two-legged guys. He would use a crutch to swing out, then throw it to the side and hop around on one leg.

One of Whitey's Lindy Hoppers' best couples was Harry Rosenberg and Ruthie Rheingold. They were a hell of a team. We didn't go out on the road with a mixed group, but we did do performances in New York that might include a white couple and never ran across any problems.

When Harry first started coming to the Savoy Ballroom sometime in 1936, he almost took over! He was one of the best dancers there, and I'm not saying one of the best white dancers, I mean one of the best dancers, period. We'd say, "That cat can dance," not "That white boy can dance."

Harry and I used to hook up in some fierce competition on the social dance floor. The Apollo Theatre once held a Lindy hop contest between black dancers and white dancers. First, they sponsored preliminaries at different ballrooms around the city. After that, my partner and I won the semifinals at the Savoy, and Harry and his partner were the winners at the Roseland semifinals for the whites, so we had to dance against each other in the finals at the Apollo. (This was before he started dancing with Ruthie Rheingold. Unfortunately, I can't remember who his partner was, or mine.)

Now, Harry and I were very, very good friends. We used to hang out together and visit each other at home. He even had a black girlfriend, Dottiemae Johnson. Harry was very interested in dancing, so he hung out with the Savoy Lindy hoppers and we taught him our routines. We used to practice together, and I showed him a lot of steps. He copied almost everything I did, including a lot of my style, and he was good at it. To tell you the truth, he could do anything I could do. If you had a curtain dropped down to our knees so you could just see our feet moving, you wouldn't be able to tell us apart.

On the night of the finals, I danced first and thought I did pretty well. Then Harry came out and did the same steps I did! As I said, I had taught him almost everything I knew. The audience was the judge. When we stood on the stage and Ralph Cooper, the emcee, put his hand over my head, I got tremendous applause, but so did Harry, so it was a tie and we had to dance it off. This was the Apollo Theatre, so you know that they were not prejudiced. They were going to give it to whoever was the best dancer. These folks were very sophisticated. They *knew* if you were good or not, and they *always* let you know.

The second time, they had me follow Harry, and I did some different steps. When the emcee put his hand out for me, the people were stomping and clapping, so I thought, *I'm gonna beat this dude*, but Harry got the same response! It was another tie, and we had to dance again. For the third round, I went first and did some other steps—I think I did stops, just improvised, not in a routine—but I had already taught that to Harry, so he did it too. When we came back, we got the same amount of applause, and had to have *another* face-off!

Harry was pointing his finger at me saying, "I'm gonna get you!" before he went out there for the fourth time. I watched him, thinking, *What the hell can I do to beat this cat?* Recently, I had started doing something at the Savoy with my partner that I called the slow motion, but I hadn't shown it to anyone else yet. The idea came from seeing a comedy team at the Apollo under flickering strobe lights, which made them look like they were moving very slowly. The next time I was at the Savoy, I told my partner that after I swung her out a couple of times, we were going to start moving in slow motion. When we got to the end of the phrase, I reached for her—she was ready to follow—and that's when we started dancing fast again. People who were watching said, "Wow!"

When my turn came for the final round at the Apollo, I started swinging my partner out very furiously. Boy, was I stretching and kicking my legs out. I jumped over her head in a spin (a jump turn) and we went into slow motion with the music still wailing. My partner knew what I wanted to do—remember, I used to talk to her while we were dancing—and after about sixteen bars of doing slow motion we started swinging out again. Well, I'll tell you, the house just fell out! This time, when we all came back onstage, I won the contest hands down. Harry said, "You dirty dog, you never showed me that." I told him it was a good thing that I had kept something to myself.

Some of the Lindy hoppers began adding slow motion into their solos, but it wasn't done by a whole group until we began doing the big apple at the Savoy in late 1937. Generally, I fit slow motion in after a couple of swing-outs and a jump turn, usually between fast sections, like Charlestons, for contrast. Slow motion usually lasts for half a chorus, and it should be continuous—slow, but not so slow that you can't see the movement. Back then, it was totally improvised. Some little drama was always acted out where the couple related to each other: I might grab my partner as she turned around and feigned slapping my hand (like in a high five), or maybe the girl would kick the guy, or he would put her through an air step like down-the-back. Mostly, I tried to go after the humor, and I always made facial expressions that helped the movement along.

There were a few special things that we did with slow motion. Whenever we played the Apollo, which was often, my partner and I would dance close to the front of the stage so that I could tumble into the audience, as if by accident. As I started climbing back onto the stage real slowly, she would grab me by the hand and help pull me up in slow motion. I couldn't do this in most theaters, but I could there because the stage was low, there weren't any footlights at the edge, and there wasn't an orchestra pit. Jerome, who was our comedy dancer, and his partner, Lucille, did this very funny truckin' bit, all in slow motion. We also had one couple who imitated Apache dancers. They held each other real close and did staccato steps, but in slow motion.

PART III
WHITEY'S
LINDY
HOPPERS
$\left(1936-1943\right)$

7 • GOING PRO

Debut

The original Cotton Club closed in early 1936 because the owners were planning to move down from 142nd Street and Lenox Avenue to the Times Square area. During the interim,[1] some of the performers who were in the final uptown Cotton Club show went into the Alhambra Theatre, billed as the Cotton Club Revue. Since the Cotton Club hired only the best in the business, from the musicians to the dancers and chorus girls, getting the revue was a prize for the Alhambra, which, like other Harlem theaters, often booked entire shows.

The Cotton Club only allowed whites in the audience, even though all of the performers were African American, so having this revue at the Alhambra was an opportunity for blacks to see a Cotton Club show. There was all kinds of dancing—tap, exotic, eccentric, comedy, shake, and chorus lines. A lot of dances that later became famous and hit the mainstream, like Suzie-Q and Snake Hips (named for Earl "Snake Hips" Tucker, who emphasized his hips and moved with the smoothness of a snake), came out of there. Because the Lindy was getting to be a big, big thing, the management of the Alhambra Theatre wanted to book us—we were billed as the Savoy Dancers or the Savoy Lindy Hoppers in these early days—so they got in touch with Whitey. It was around this time that I think he stopped being employed as a bouncer by the Savoy, and became the manager and booking agent for the Lindy hoppers. The Cotton Club had its own agreement with the Alhambra, and since we were not part of its revue, we were given a separate contract as an added attraction.

The revue at the Alhambra was a typical Cotton Club show, but without the big-name stars. I can only remember two of the acts because this was our first time working in a theater and we didn't hang around with the other performers. Henri Wessels and his partner were exotic ballroom dancers. Meeres and Meeres was a very popular ballroom team around Harlem.

There were four shows daily, starting at about 11 a.m., followed by shows at 2, 5, and 9 p.m. Even though we just had one rehearsal with the Cotton Club band on Friday morning right before we opened, when we hit that stage for the first show, boy, we tore the joint apart!

•

Our routine started out like a contest, the way Shorty's act did. First, each couple did a solo in their own style. It was Whitey's idea to pick Lindy hoppers who did three different styles. He didn't put just anyone in this show; he picked the better dancers. Mildred Cruse and Billy Williams were smooth. Lucille Middleton and Jerome Williams were comic. Maggie McMillan and I did flash. We might have done one or two air steps, but I think we were the only couple who did, at this point. It would probably have been ace-in-the-hole (which was one of my favorites because she would get up there and kick her legs wildly) and maybe over-the-back. We definitely hadn't put air steps into the ensemble section yet.

After each couple finished their solo, they lined up across the back of the stage and started jockeying. This was how we got ready to go into the stops routine, the same one that I had started choreographing to "Posin'" up at the Savoy. As soon as Maggie and I joined the line and we were all in sync, I yelled, "Go!" and everybody swung out together. We had worked really hard to bring this to perfection, and it was sensational!

This was the first time that an audience had ever seen synchronized ensemble Lindy hopping, and we got a tremendous response. People stood up in their seats, stompin' and carryin' on. Man, we stopped a Cotton Club show! We had to do about four encores even though we didn't know *anything* about encoring. We didn't have anything planned, and since we only had the one routine, I didn't know what the heck to do. So I told everybody, "Just swing out until I say to get off the stage." It made us feel so good that we did well!

Since we had a couple of hours until the next show, we changed, went out the stage door entrance, and walked around to 125th Street, which was a shopping area. The six of us were looking in all the store windows talking about what we were going to buy when we got paid. We were each supposed to get something like $50 for the week. There was a place called Wohlmuth Clothing Company where you could pick out your own material and get a suit tailor-made for $27.50, and I was going to get me one at the end of the week.

Walking back to the theater, we laughed and kidded with each other, in heaven because we had stopped the show and couldn't wait to do it again. On the way upstairs to our dressing room (which was on the top floor, 'cause we were nobodies), the stage manager called us over . . . to tell us that we were out of the show! We couldn't believe it. "Did you say we won't be in the next show?" I asked. "Why? Weren't we good?" "I'm sorry," he answered. "I'm just passing it on to you. The management says you're out."

Brownie, Whitey's right-hand man, was representing him at this gig (he also performed with the Savoy Lindy Hoppers sometimes, although not in this show), so he called Whitey, who came down to the theater lickety-split. He went in to talk to the stage manager, who told him to speak to the theater manager. We were sitting on the steps with our heads in our hands when Whitey came out and said, "Look, kids. I'm sorry. You're not going to do the other performances." He told us not to worry, though, because he had gotten a promise from the Alhambra that they would bring us back at a later date.

Eventually we found out why we had gotten kicked out. When we went into the downtown Cotton Club six months later, they had the same choreographer as the Cotton Club Revue. Clarence Robinson and I became very good friends, and one day he took me aside and said he had to tell me what happened. It turned out that the other acts were jealous of us. He made us feel a little better by saying that that was show business.

So that was our debut in a professional show. Even though they didn't keep us in the revue, which was a setback, the Alhambra was really a jumping-off spot for me. It was the first time we performed as a group (before that, it was just one or two teams doing their own thing), the first time we were in a theater, and the first performance of a choreographed, synchronized ensemble routine. It was also the first time we had a signed contract, so this was the first professional job for Whitey's Lindy hoppers. Despite the letdown of getting canceled, it was quite a highlight and we were very excited, but I still didn't feel like a professional. I just felt like I was out there having a good time.

A month or two later, we did go back into the Alhambra, but with a different show featuring Lucky Millinder and his band. Most of the time, the band would package all of the acts, but since the theater manager had promised us a place, he probably negotiated with Lucky Millinder's agent to get us on the bill. I think the agent was Moe Gale from the Savoy Ballroom, so it was all in the family.

The Lucky Millinder revue was a complete stage show, with singers, dancers, and comedians, and this time we were part of it, not an added attraction, so they couldn't put us out unless they paid us. One young star of the show was Bunny Briggs, the tap dancer, who I've since worked with many times. Even though we had a different group of Lindy hoppers who weren't quite as good, we still went over great. That band really pushed us and we were good with them. Besides me and Brownie, we had a guy named Red Elan. I don't remember who the girls were except that this was when I first started dancing with Naomi Waller.

As I mentioned earlier, Maggie had split to work with Shorty Snowden, and Frieda wasn't coming around as much, so she was just a sometimes partner. It was Whitey's idea for me to dance with Naomi. One of the things he did was to decide which guy should dance with which girl. In the beginning, he always put his top people together, so he'd pair me with girls who were very good. Naomi was terrific, one of the best partners I've ever had. She was lively, had personality, and could improvise and still be with the music—an all-round good dancer.

In later years, Whitey sometimes matched a strong dancer with a weaker one, in order to support them. He had an instinct about these things, and always tried to pair two Lindy hoppers who complemented each other. If it didn't work, he would acknowledge it and change people around. Whitey said that I could dance with any partner and make her look better, which made me feel good. Since all the girls were pretty good, I was happy with whoever he put me with. If I wasn't, I would have told him.

Truckin' Along

After we did the performances at the Alhambra Theatre, we started getting an awful lot of work. In March 1936, we had a two- or three-week run at the Roxy Theatre, the first time there for a group of Whitey's dancers. The teams were Lucille Middleton and Jerome Williams, Mildred Cruse and Billy Williams, Helen Bundy and George Greenidge, Gertie and Chick (I don't remember their last names), and Naomi and me.

Around this time, truckin' was the new vogue, and everybody was doing it. A song titled "Truckin'" had recently come out that went something like, "They had to have something new, a dance to do, up here in Harlem—so, someone started truckin'." To truck, your feet shuffle right, left, right, left with the right side of your body leading as you move diagonally forward, and your right hand shakes while your index finger points up in the air. People said truckin' was a dance, but it was really just one step, like the black bottom or the Suzie-Q. Whitey was always trying to add the latest dances into the Lindy to make it more exciting and more marketable. In order to make a routine for the stage out of any of these movements, you had to put them with other jazz steps or the Lindy hop. We went into the Roxy as truckers, according to the program, but we just mixed it into our Lindy solos, so the audience would say, "Yeah, they truckin'."

I'm not sure if Pigmeat Markham, a comedian who often played the Apollo Theatre, introduced truckin', but he helped popularize it because of his comical way of doing it. He would truck with the top part of his body practically parallel to the floor, his hands in fists, and do a ducking movement when he turned that made his neck seem like rubber. After him, quite a few comedians and dancers came out with truckin'. An eccentric dancer named Rubberneck Holmes, who could move his upper body around as if it were made of rubber, did the same type of thing as Pigmeat, but with a sharper turn.

Each of us had a different style. Jerome copied Pigmeat's version of truckin', but added some little things of his own that made it very funny. The way he trucked reminded us of an African, so we called him "Congo."[2] Jerome and Lucille developed a very comical routine. While they were truckin', with her in front, she'd lean over with her behind extended way out. As soon as they stopped, she did a grind while Jerome did a 360-degree turn. For a funny ending, I had Lucille boot him in the face with her butt, which caused him to jump back or fall down into a rollover. He'd come back peckin' at her while she trucked off the stage.

Once, when we were playing the Apollo Theatre and Pigmeat was on stage doing his routine, Jerome came out from the wings truckin' right behind him, imitating him exactly. People were cracking up, but Pigmeat didn't realize what was going on until he stopped and switched his head around. You should have seen the surprised look on his face! But being a professional, he just went along with the gag.

At the end of June, we got work at the Apollo for the first time, as an act, that is. This time it was me and Naomi, Jerome and Lucille, Billy and Millie, and one other couple. We danced to Chick Webb's orchestra featuring Ella Fitzgerald. (During the next five years, we would perform at the Apollo with many popular Harlem orchestras, including Count Basie, Cab Calloway, Tiny Bradshaw, Buddy Johnson, Erskine Hawkins, and Lucky Millinder, but we worked there with Chick Webb more than with any other band.)

Ella Fitzgerald was supposed to come on after us, but during our very first performance the applause was so loud that she couldn't even get on the stage! The stage manager called us back to take another bow, but we kept saying, "What do you mean? Ella's out there!" She had to move back to the wings while we did an encore before the audience would let us go.

The management felt that we had kind of stolen Ella's thunder, so after that they changed the order around and made us close the show *behind* her. But she wasn't mad; she wasn't that kind of person. Ella and I were already good friends from the Savoy—in fact, we used to call each other "bro'" and "sis'"—and she was happy for us.

Years later, the Congaroo Dancers (my group after the war) was working with Illinois Jacquet, Dusty Fletcher, and Ella. We were supposed to go on before her, but she told Illinois, "These kids are too great. Why don't you let them close?"

I remember that we were excited to be appearing at the Apollo because we'd had my girlfriend, Dorothy Jackson, design and make new satin costumes in a different color for each couple. We had all had too many experiences with our shirt coming out of our pants (or skirts for the girls) while we were dancing, so I had her make long shirts for all of us that buttoned underneath.

One night, when Naomi and I lined up with everybody else before the ensemble section, a hook on my pants got caught on her skirt. I kept trying to unhook myself while we were jockeying, but I just couldn't get it undone. The other dancers were looking over at us waiting for my signal while the band kept playing and playing—they must have played a whole 'nother chorus!—so I finally said the hell with it and yanked the part that was caught. I got unstuck, all right, but in the process I ripped Naomi's skirt, which fell down to the floor! Can you believe it? She was such a trooper, though. She just kicked it away from around her ankles—she had trunks on underneath—and kept dancing. Afterwards, she was mad, not about her skirt falling off, but because I tore her costume.

Norma, Leon, Edith, and Billy came back from Europe while we were playing the Apollo, and Whitey brought them to the show the night they arrived. Right away, they could see that there had been a tremendous change in Lindy hopping while they'd been away.[3] Later, Norma told us that working in Europe was entirely different from dancing at the Savoy. They weren't performing to big orchestras, just small bands that were not used to playing swing. Naturally, the dancing suffered. I don't think Leon ever recovered. He was a great dancer but, in my opinion, he was never as good as before he went abroad. And he was still doing the old style. His partner, Edith, stopped dancing entirely. But Norma was younger, so she got into what we were doing.

Hearing about their trip made me grateful that I hadn't gone to Europe. If I had, I might never have come up with the Lindy air step and ensemble dancing. By staying and hearing the music and seeing people dance at the Savoy, I was able to be more creative.

Doubling

Atlantic City was the resort area for the whole East Coast during the summer. All day long, people went to the beach and the boardwalk, which was about three miles long. At night, they filled the clubs and everybody had money. It wasn't an open gambling town then, but playing cards, shooting craps, rolling dice, and betting on horses was happening in the back rooms of all these obscure places. I'm not a gambling man, but a lot of people came for that purpose only. After Labor Day, the clubs closed down, and Atlantic City was like a ghost town.

The two major black clubs in Atlantic City with big stage shows were the Paradise Club and Club Harlem. They were top-notch. I don't say they were like the Cotton Club, but they would feature at least one big-name act as well as some other very talented performers.

We got booked into the Paradise Club, which was located several blocks from the boardwalk, on Illinois and Baltic avenues, for July and August 1936. Atlantic City was very divided in those days. Blacks could go anywhere we wanted on the boardwalk, but there was only one section of the beach where we were allowed. I don't remember seeing any signs, but all the blacks who lived there told us about it, and I never saw any of them go to any other part of the beach. Of course, in the '30s, whites went wherever there was black entertainment. Even though these two clubs were in the black neighborhood, the audience was predominantly white.

Shorty Snowden and His Lindy Hoppers were at Club Harlem that same summer, so one night we went round to see them between our shows. They looked so sharp in their matching white suits and dresses, compared to us raggedy Lindy hoppers in our mixed-up costumes.

We had already seen Shorty's act back in New York at Smalls' Paradise. Whitey had wanted us "kids" to see the pros—this was after Norma got back from Europe—so he took us. I don't know if it was in Whitey's mind for us to steal Shorty's stuff—he never said anything like that, and I know I wasn't there for that reason—but Big Bea decided that that was why we had come, and she got mad about it. In fact, Norma says Big Bea threatened Whitey. I don't remember that, but I wouldn't doubt it. At any rate, Shorty and his dancers were still doing the same thing down in Atlantic City that they'd been doing since they went professional.

We had just started doing two shows a night, seven nights a week, at Club Paradise, when Ethel Waters's people contacted Whitey because she wanted some Lindy hoppers for a week-long engagement at the Lincoln Theatre in Philadelphia. Ethel Waters was one of our biggest black stars, along with Bill "Bojangles" Robinson, Cab Calloway, and Duke Ellington. Being asked to join her show was very prestigious, and it meant that a lot more people were going to see Lindy hopping than if we were appearing with a local band. Whitey arranged for the Atlantic City group to do both jobs because we were closer to the action than his Harlem dancers, and he wanted his best people to appear with Ethel Waters.

On the Friday that the Ethel Waters show opened, we arrived in Philadelphia in the morning, as we'd been asked to do, but didn't have an opportunity to rehearse because of the tight schedule. Just before we went on, the stage manager instructed us to line up in the wings with the other acts at the end of each show, come out for our bow, then back up to the same place on stage each time. The other acts included The Chocolateers, the comedy/dance team—what we called a novelty act—who had introduced peckin'.[4] The Three Peters Sisters sang and did comedy dancing. We used to call them "one thousand pounds of joy" because they were tremendously overweight. Bill Bailey was a tap dancer. Apus and Estrellita were a comedy act.

We were scheduled to appear just before Ethel Waters. Most big stars want an act that's going to wake the audience up before they come on, and we were that type of act. We were also considered a good opening or closing act because we were so exciting. The routine that we did in Atlantic City and Philadelphia was the same one we'd been doing since the Cotton Club Revue, except we were definitely doing air steps in the solos by the summer. I think Billy and Mildred did the side-flip, and Naomi and I did ace-in-the-hole and probably over-the-back.

Everything went beautifully with our performance until we got to the finale. While all of the entertainers were coming out to take their bows, Eddie Mallory's Orchestra (he was Ethel Waters's husband) was quietly swinging in the background. Being the way we were, we started rocking with the music, finger-popping, and doing Charlestons and other actions. Everybody was busy watching us, so nobody applauded when they announced Ethel Waters as she walked onto the stage. When she saw everyone looking our way, she looked over too, just as the audience finally noticed her and started clapping.

When the curtain came down, this woman was pissed! "I am the star of this show! When I walk out, I want everyone on the stage to be quiet! And those Lindy hoppers, I want to see them in my dressing room!"

We had heard a lot of stories about Miss Ethel Waters, about how strict she was with her cast and crew and how she didn't take any nonsense from anybody. It was her show, and she was the kind of lady who wanted you to know that she was the star. Everyone thought she was difficult and tried to stay out of her way. They said, "She's gonna fire you guys," and "Y'all dead." Figuring that I would take the abuse, I told the kids I'd go talk to her, but that they should start packing in case we got fired.

After I knocked on her door, she told me to come in, and started sounding off: "Young man, do you know . . . Where's the rest of your gang?"

"Well, I'm representing them," I told her.

She went back to berating me. "How long have you been in show business? Don't you know anything about starting low? You got no business being in show business if you don't know the etiquette!" She screamed and hollered for about five minutes while I stood there and listened.

Now, I just want to tell you that we were as excited as anybody could be about working with such a big star, and I respected her, but I wasn't in awe of Ethel Waters. Whitey had always worked hard to instill pride in the Lindy hoppers and taught us not to let people talk down to us no matter how famous they were, because we were just as important as they were. I took that to heart.

When she finished talking, I said, "You through?" She was a little taken aback, but I continued: "Miss Waters, if we offended you in any way, I'm very sorry, but we were not able to get here in time for the rehearsal. We were told to stand in a particular spot, and we did, but the music sounded good, so we did our little movements with it. We did not know that it would disrupt your entrance, and we didn't mean to disrespect you in any way. But if you want to fire us, just say so and we'll pack our bags."

She ranted a little more, then she kind of calmed down and said, "I'm not going to fire you, but when I hit that stage, I don't want you moving around or attracting so much attention."

I said, "If that's the way you want it, that's exactly what we'll do," and went to tell the kids that they could unpack.

At the end of the next show, we just stood there as stiff as mummies, looking at each other with snickers. When the curtain closed, she walked over to us, put her hand on her hip, and said, "Look, I don't mean like *that*. You can move, just not so much that it distracts the audience."

After that, she started visiting the Savoy Ballroom whenever she was in town, which wasn't all that often, but she might show up three or four nights. Even though she came with people like Archie Savage, Duke Ellington, or Count Basie, I was the only person she wanted to dance with. Whitey would come over and say, "Miss Ethel Waters wants to dance with you," so I'd ask her, and swing her out a couple of times. We'd have a general conversation and she would compliment me on my dancing. She was pretty good herself.

One time when she appeared at the Apollo Theatre for a week, she was planning to dance a whole chorus with Pigmeat Markham for the finale. Singers of that era were entertainers; they could sing, dance, do comedy. That's what was required if they wanted to be a big-time star. Instead of doing the whole thing with Pigmeat, she asked Whitey if she could use me just to do sixteen bars. So for fifty dollars, I social danced with her for half a chorus, four shows a day. From then on she always wanted Whitey's dancers to appear with her. In the end, we became one of her favorite acts, and

I kind of think that I drew her attention to us by standing up to her. Maybe she respected me for facing her person to person.

Sometimes she had a group of us, but she always wanted to do the finale with me, if possible. Once I was working someplace else, so Whitey asked if she would like to use Snookie Beasley instead. She said no, so I had to finish my job downtown, then run up to the Apollo every night for just sixteen bars. Snookie was insulted.

Ethel Waters and I ended up becoming very good friends. She used to invite me down to her brownstone on 115th Street for parties or to visit, and tell me stories about what she had gone through to make it. She had to be tough to get there—that lady was salt—and she was a pioneer of women's rights. We got to be pretty close. As a matter of fact, she wanted to buy me a car, but I said no. I don't know if she had a romantic interest (even though she was twenty years older) or a dance interest, or just thought I was a nice kid and wanted to give me something, but I didn't want to be in her debt. We kept in touch for years. If we happened to be working in the same town, I'd go see her. But after she was on Broadway in *Member of the Wedding* in the early '50s, we kind of lost touch.

In addition to four shows a day at the Lincoln Theatre, starting at 11 a.m. and ending at about 11 p.m., we had to do two shows every night at the Paradise Club. During the week that we doubled,[5] we'd jump in our car as soon as the finale in Philadelphia was over, still in our costumes, and speed back to Atlantic City. Usually, the trip took an hour and 15 minutes, but it only took us about 40 minutes because our driver really put the pedal to the metal. There weren't any speed limits back then, so he could go as fast as he wanted.

The first show at the Paradise started at 11 p.m. and lasted about an hour and a half. Even though we were the closing act, a lot of times we didn't quite make it. Doris Rheubottom, the singer who went on in front of us, would have to keep singing until we walked through the door and hit the stage. It was rough. We'd finish the second show by around 3 a.m., get something to eat, then go home and sleep for a couple of hours before we got up to drive back to Philadelphia. Sometimes we'd grab a nap on a cot or a chair between shows at the Lincoln Theatre. There wasn't any sense in rehearsing that week, and we didn't party much. We were young, but we didn't have *that* much stamina.

Paradise

After that week of doubling was over, it was playtime. When we were done with the last show at three or four in the morning, we would go roller-skating up and down Baltic Avenue. Sometimes the singer Velma Middleton, a heavyset woman, like two hundred and some pounds—you've seen her work with Louis Armstrong—would go with us.

You couldn't roller-skate on the boardwalk from 9 a.m. to 11 a.m., but you could ride a bicycle. Afterwards, we'd load up on clams from this little shack that sold them just-caught, then lay out on the beach for the rest of the day or, although I didn't fish, go out on a fishing boat that some of the acts used to hire. At about 4 or 5 in the afternoon, we'd go home and rest until it was time for us to go on at midnight.

Most days, we also rehearsed for a couple of hours when the club was dark. That was something I kept up during my entire professional career whenever we had a long nightclub engagement. I had this theory that if you just performed every night and didn't social dance, you would lose your edge, so I often had the kids get out on the floor to just swing out with each other. We also worked on whatever else I thought they needed. In order to keep them from getting stale in the routine and just going through the motions, I would change things around. For instance, if someone was doing an air step at the beginning of their solo, I might have them do it at the end. Occasionally the dancers themselves wanted to put in a different step.

I also changed some things so they would be more effective for the audience, or more visible to them. I was still new to show biz, and learning a lot. If there was something I thought we were lacking and I picked it up from the older performers, I would transfer it to the Lindy hoppers. For example, we didn't know anything about bowing. After our routine, we'd all bow on our own time—never together—then scamper off the stage. I got it to where everybody bowed together and knew exactly what they were supposed to do. In case they did make a mistake, I told the kids they should throw it off as a joke so the audience would say, "Oh, he's having a good time."

I remember exactly who was in the Lindy hoppers that summer of 1936—Billy Williams and Mildred Cruse, Jerome Williams and Lucille Middleton, and Naomi Waller and me—because Billy and Mildred were involved and had a spat. Mildred fell in love with this tap dancer she'd met, and Billy was so mad that he hit her. I stopped it by grabbing a cane from a chorus girl and putting it around his neck. I was angry with him for two reasons: first, for hitting a girl, and also for hitting one of our dancers. After a while, Mildred and Billy started going with each other again and the six of us worked together for the next year, but eventually she married the tap dancer.

Routine!

Things were a little bit different when we entered the Harvest Moon Ball again at the end of the summer. This time I think we went in with a different mental attitude, partly because we had already done quite a few gigs, which gave us confidence, and also because we were doing air steps and ensemble dancing. We had a bit more sense of the audience and had adapted ways of showing off particular steps.

As luck would have it, my particular group was all Whitey's Lindy hoppers, family, so right before our heat I suggested we do the stops routine. Everyone agreed. Whitey had talked to the Harvest Moon Ball officials about changing some of those damn rules, but to no avail, so we resolved among ourselves to just forget about them.

We started out with each team doing their own individual thing. A few of us put in an air step, and Jerome did his truckin' routine with Lucille, which cracked the audience up. At just the right moment, I hollered, "Rou-u-u-ti-i-i-ne!" Everybody lined up, jockeyed until we were all on the beat, then, as soon as I yelled, "Swing out!" took off together. There was just enough time in the music for us to do all of stops right there in front of the judges. It felt great because we were really dancing, and the house was clapping and screaming.

Even though we upset the judges, they couldn't afford to take points away from us because we were so entertaining. Billy and Mildred came in first; Jerome and Lucille took second; Naomi and I were third. And Whitey was happy because he got his wish. Once again, his dancers won the top three spots.

8 • BIG TIME AT THE COTTON CLUB

Whitey's Lindy Hoppers Is Born

When Whitey came to us after the Harvest Moon Ball and told us we were going to be working at the new downtown Cotton Club, my eyes just opened up! The Cotton Club?!! Everything about it was first-rate. Each show was a mix of stars who were all headliners when they worked at any other nightclub or theater.

Although I had been getting paid since I won the amateur contest and worked with Duke Ellington, I still didn't consider myself a professional. Of course, I loved dancing and, yes, I wanted to be the best I could be. I knew that I could dance because everyone told me so, but never thought I was good enough to be a pro. I still thought I was going to earn my living as a furrier. Besides, most of the bands I worked with played the Savoy, so performing with them just seemed like dancing at the ballroom.

The Cotton Club was the turning point, the first time I felt capable of entertaining people as a dancer. Since it was the epitome of show business and anyone who performed there could say, "Okay, I'm tops," when we got that contract I thought, *If they're going to book me in* here, *maybe I can dance a little bit. Maybe this* is *leading somewhere.*

When I had performed in theaters or nightclubs before, I'd taken time off from working as a furrier, but I assumed I would go back at some point. Once I knew I was going into the Cotton Club, I gave it up forever. That's when I said, "Okay, I'm a professional now. I'm a dancer."

Whitey chose his number one team, his best Lindy hoppers, to go into the Cotton Club. At the time, that included Naomi and me, Millie Cruse and Billy Williams, and Lucille Middleton and Jerome Williams, almost the same dancers he had picked to go up against Shorty in the contest (except for Frieda).

Around this time, Ethel Waters wanted a group of Lindy hoppers to go on the road with her, so Whitey put together his number two group, which consisted of Norma Miller and Leon James, Willamae Ricker and Snookie Beasley, and Ella Gibson and George Greenidge. Norma, Willamae, Snookie, and George soon rose to be among the top dancers, as did Tiny Bunch and Billy Ricker from the number three group. Norma was a strong-minded young lady and a very intense dancer, quick to catch on to any step that was thrown at her. I feel that she was one of the few Lindy hoppers who really planned to be in show business from the get-go. Most of us were dancing just for the fun of it. She always had the notion that she could make it, and the drive to go after what she wanted. Willamae was one of the greatest Lindy hoppers ever. She made every partner look good. Snookie was a wonderful dancer, always listening to recordings of the greatest swing dance tunes. As I've said, Long-Legged George was very creative, especially with Charlestons.

Whitey had also gotten a contract for the Harlem Uproar House, a nightclub just off Broadway in the low fifties, so he formed a third group featuring Tiny Bunch and his partner. Tiny, who was very jolly and full of fun, was 6'4" and weighed about 400 pounds—okay, I'm exaggerating, but he was very heavy; looked like a big bear walking down the street, but he could move his feet. He was featured dancing with Dot Moses, who weighed only 90 pounds. We called her Dot 'cause that's all she was. Tiny would swing her around like he was King Kong and she was a rag doll, which always got a big laugh.[1]

Billy Ricker danced with Helen Bundy; Red Elan with someone whose name I can't remember; and Wilda Crawford, who was a petite, very energetic dancer, worked with Champ, who was pretty good too. Champ's real name was Ernest Harrison. We gave him that nickname because even though he knew he wasn't the greatest, he liked bragging that he could do anything we could, but better. It wasn't done in an egotistical way; he was just kidding around. We'd say, "Yeah, man, you the champ. You the champ of everything!"

By this time, there was getting to be more demand for Lindy hoppers. Whitey now had three major groups, as well as other dancers at the Savoy who were not as well trained. I've come to think of him as being like the director of a dance company. As time went on and we got more work, he was always shuffling dancers and groups around depending on who his best people were, who made good partners, how many dancers he needed, where he needed them, who was available (there were always dancers dropping out and new ones coming up), and who could manage a group. Sometimes he might have just a couple of groups working. At other times he might have quite a few out there. Some were very large, so he might have dozens of dancers on his payroll. He tried to distribute the work fairly, but if there was an important gig, naturally he wanted to send his best dancers.

Right after Whitey told us about the Cotton Club, we were all standing around the Savoy trying to figure out what to call ourselves instead of just the Savoy Lindy Hoppers. Up until now, we were so amateur that we didn't care how we were billed. Now that we had three professional groups, each one needed a different name to distinguish them so people wouldn't get confused.

Whitey came up with Tiny Bunch and the Original Lindy Hoppers for that team, and suggested that we name the Cotton Club group after me. I said no because I thought it deserved Whitey's name, so I suggested that we call one of the groups Whitey's Lindy Hoppers. Even though we were working under him, we had never used his name for the act.

Some people say Whitey wanted to be a big shot, but if that were true I think he would have put his name out there from the very beginning. Whitey preferred being in the background. I was the one who wanted him in front. At first he said no, but the other dancers all liked the idea of honoring him, so we gave that name to the Ethel Waters team. Of course, after his name started being used a lot, he loved it.

When my group actually went into the Cotton Club, I suggested Whitey's Hopping Maniacs because we were crazy. Now we had three different troupes with three different names. Whitey's Lindy Hoppers was born. Over the years, different theater and nightclub managers spelled the names of the groups in different ways on programs and in advertisements, and so did newspapers and magazines. For instance, the Cotton Club billed us as Whyte's Maniacs in their program and Whyte Maniacs on the marquee. You'll see a lot of other names for the groups, including White's Lindy Maniacs and Whitey's Jitterbugs, but we didn't think anything of it at the time. I've always just said Whitey's Lindy Hoppers to mean all of the groups.

Cotton Club shows were always headed by a big-time band—Cab Calloway, in this case. Bill "Bojangles" Robinson was the other star. The rest of the acts, including the Berry Brothers (a flash dance act), Dynamite Hooker (a tap dancer), the Tramp Band, Avis Andrews (a singer), Henri Wessells (an interpretative jazz dancer), and Tondelayo (an exotic dancer), were all fabulous.

Whyte's Hopping Maniacs was hired to do two routines. The first, a big production number with the chorus girls, was choreographed by Clarence Robinson, who did most of the Cotton Club shows and *Stormy Weather.* He had remembered us from the revue at the Alhambra Theatre and decided that he was going to use us in his next show. Of course, back then we never said "choreographer." He was called the dance director, or as the program said, "Dances Staged by Clarence Robinson." (Even though I had been choreographing Lindy hop routines for a while, I still just called myself a dancer.)

After the chorus line performed by themselves, we came out and joined them in a floor routine, a jazz routine. Then they moved back while we did variations on jazz steps by ourselves. For the finish, they joined us and the entire ensemble danced together again. Robinson demonstrated what he wanted us to do, and I also suggested steps to him. Then I worked with the Lindy hoppers until I had made up a routine that fit our section of the music and led into what he had choreographed for the finale. I complained about the music, which was corny and didn't swing, to the producers, who kept promising they would give us something different, but they never did. I should have realized they wouldn't since it was part of a production number.

Our second number was a Lindy routine in the second half of the show. For that, we were the featured act, the only ones onstage. Everything in this show was timed, which was new for us. When rehearsals began (which lasted about four weeks, seven days a week), I didn't know how much music we actually needed, so we did our routine over and over until the band figured out how long each solo was and marked it in their books. Before this, although the Lindy hoppers started and ended on the phrase (which we sensed, even though we didn't know the term), one couple might dance for a half a chorus, while another would go longer than a chorus. When a team felt like they had done enough, they would back off and the next couple would swing out. Walter "Foots" Thomas, Cab's reed player, used to rehearse the band, and he explained that if we added or took away a little bit of dancing, we would end on the chorus. Of course, we had to repeat what we did every night, but after hearing the same music over and over, it wasn't too hard.

Each couple danced for one chorus, which they built around the movements they had been doing for the last six months. We all saved our best step, the one we had each discovered would always get a hand, for the climax. And it was for this gig that we finally added air steps into the ensemble section at the end, which lasted two choruses.

After the show had been running for a couple of weeks, I invited my mother and some of her friends to come see it. When it was over, I asked how she liked it. "Oh, it was wonderful! You were great!" she said. "Am I still too stiff to be a dancer?" I asked. My mother looked at me and said, "What are you talking about?" I reminded her, but she didn't remember at all. "I never said that!" "Oh yes you did."

R-e-s-p-e-c-t

Generally, the Lindy hoppers were not the stars of the shows we were in. That only happened a few times. However, even though everybody else got higher billing, because we were very well received at the Cotton Club, we thought we had gained some kind of respect. But the fact was, dancers were considered bottom of the barrel by the entertainment industry, and Lindy hoppers were lowest on the totem pole. We were beneath tap dancers, who were known as dime-a-dozen street dancers, as well as exotic dancers, show-girls, and chorus girls. At one point, I heard that Bill Robinson had called us "scruffy" and "those raggedy Lindy hoppers." Of course, it was those raggedy Lindy hoppers who always broke up the show.

People often ask if I ever trained in a dance school. I tell them yes, but not a school like they're talking about. We practiced at the Savoy every single day, so we might have worked even harder than entertainers who went to dance school. Still, we were referred to as amateurs by other professional performers.

Gradually, I began to resent the whole situation. We worked as hard and were as entertaining as anyone else in the business; more so in some cases. It became my ambition to erase the negative image of Lindy hoppers and to elevate the dance.

The code of the era was to be well groomed all the time, even if you were just going visiting or to a movie. I don't want to brag, but I was a pretty sharp dresser—I mean shirt, tie, jacket, and, most likely, a hat. Professional entertain-ers always dressed impeccably on stage—they set the trend—and I thought Lindy hoppers should be like that too. I once had to leave a dance at the Savoy early because my cheap shoes hurt so much. It was so bad that I actually threw them in a garbage can and walked home barefoot. At the Cotton Club, I had noticed that Cab wore this beautiful pair of leather shoes that fit like a glove. One day I saw them in a store on Broadway and 48th Street, but they cost fifty dollars, three times what I could afford. Every day on my way to the club, I walked past those shoes, and finally one day I went in and put money down. It took three installments to pay off the bill, but they were worth every penny.

I wasn't the only one who wanted people to say that Lindy hoppers dressed and acted professionally. When we were starting out, Whitey made sure our costumes were clean and our shoes were polished. Once, he put rubbing alcohol in our armpits so we wouldn't smell. He didn't want anyone to call us those stinky Lindy hoppers. After I was put in charge, I had a little more opportunity to shape the group because I was always around. We often performed with class acts that were very polished and projected a con-fidence that really reached the audience. I studied the way they presented themselves down to their entrance, bow, exit, and costumes, and applied what I saw to the Lindy hoppers. I showed what I wanted by doing it myself, and everybody went along.

At the Cotton Club, we had two sets of costumes, which we supplied, but none of them matched and they were in different colors. After a while, I had two more sets made, so we each had four changes. I had another set made in Paris when the Cotton Club went overseas, this time in the same design and color for everybody. It took a while, but by the time I had the Congaroos, we went from being "raggedy Lindy hoppers" to being one of the best dressed acts with more costumes than anyone else in the business.

Off and on the Court

When we were on the bill at the Cotton Club, we were an integral part of the show—not like at the Alhambra Theatre, where we were an added attraction—so we started hanging out with the other performers. I'm a pretty friendly person, so I got to know everybody. I was tight with the Berry Brothers, especially James, who was my age, but it was very rare for the big-name stars to socialize with the regular acts. We'd see them during the show, but we didn't go into their dressing rooms and have a conversation. We definitely didn't hang out with Bill Robinson, who was very standoffish. In fact, he and I had a little altercation.

It started one night when I was talking to this chorus girl while waiting in the wings to go on. As Dynamite Hooker was leaving the stage, he bumped into her and a few other girls, then acted all annoyed. He was always doing stuff like that. As he walked past us, he pushed me and knocked me down. Now that was a mistake. I got up and punched him so hard that I sent him sprawling. While he was still down, I told him never to touch me again.

The next afternoon, when I got to the club, the stage manager told me that "Uncle Bill" (that's what he had all the performers call him) wanted to see me in his dressing room. As one of the headliners, he was the unofficial head of the show.

Once again, I knocked on the door with the star, entered, introduced myself, and said, "You wanted to see me, Mr. Robinson?" He was angry because he'd heard that I had been fighting, but I told him that it wasn't much of a fight: "Dynamite pushed me and I knocked him down." "That's unacceptable here," he said. "I don't want my people carrying on like that in this club because it sets a bad example." He continued on about how fighting made colored people look bad and downgraded black neighborhoods. I stood there and listened respectfully, but then I had to tell one of the biggest black entertainers in the country that *nobody* could knock me down like that and get away with it.

Whitey's Lindy Hoppers dancing on the set of *Everybody Sing.* Judy Garland is in front seat of bus. *Left to right:* Mildred Pollard, Eddie "Shorty" Davis, Tiny Bunch, Dorothy "Dot" Moses, Eleanor "Stumpy" Watson, George Greenidge, Herbert "Whitey" White (in checked jacket). (Lucille Middleton and Frankie Manning appear in other photographs of this scene.)

Whitey's Lindy Hoppers ending their routine in *Radio City Revels*.
Left to right: Dorothy "Dot" Moses, Tiny Bunch, Mildred Pollard,
George Greenidge, Eleanor "Stumpy" Watson, Frankie Manning,
Lucille Middleton, Eddie "Shorty" Davis. Herbert "Whitey" White
(in checked shirt) stands behind them.

OPPOSITE: Big Apple Dancers on tour with *Hollywood Hotel Revue*
in New Zealand, summer 1938. *Left to right:* Willamae Ricker,
Snookie Beasley, Eunice Callen, Billy Ricker, Esther Washington,
Jerome Williams, Lucille Middleton, Frankie Manning.

Savoy Ballroom poster advertising the big apple, circa late 1937.

Lucille Middleton and Frankie Manning doing drop-down-the-back while on tour
with *Hollywood Hotel Revue* in New Zealand, summer 1938.

Big Apple Dancers arriving in Sydney Harbor while on tour with *Hollywood Hotel Revue,* fall 1938. *Left to right:* Lucille Middleton, Esther Washington, Jerome Williams, Billy Ricker *(squatting),* Frankie Manning.

Frankie Manning arriving in Sydney Harbor while on tour with *Hollywood Hotel Revue,* fall 1938. Jerome Williams and Willamae Ricker in background.

Whitey's Jitterbugs in finale of *Hot Mikado* at the 1939 World's Fair,
Flushing Meadows Park, Queens.
First couple: Leon James and Belle Hill
Second couple: Al Minns and Mildred Pollard
Third couple: Walter "The Count" Johnson and Mae Miller
Fourth couple: Russell Williams and Connie Hill
Fifth couple: Lee Lyons and Geneva Davis
Sixth couple: Eddie Davis and Gladys Crowder

OPPOSITE: Harlem Congeroo Dancers on set
of *Hellzapoppin'*. *Left to right:* Billy Ricker,
Ann Johnson and Frankie Manning
performing the snatch, Mickey Jones,
Willamae Ricker, Al Minns, William Downes.

Harvest Moon Ball Lindy hop champions Wilda Crawford and Thomas "Tops" Lee performing at Loew's State Theatre, late summer 1940.

Ann Johnson and Frankie Manning performing a routine based on Frevo Pernambucano while on tour with Whitey Congeroo Dancers in Brazil, 1942.

When I offered to pack up and get out if he was planning to fire the group, he told me he wasn't going to, but that I shouldn't let it happen again. Just as I got to the door, he said, "You know, Frankie, what you did to Dynamite is something I've been wanting to do myself for a long time." He laughed, and so did I.

Cab Calloway, on the other hand, was very friendly. During our run at the Cotton Club, he formed a basketball team with some members of his band and the cast. We used to play the teams of other bands like Count Basie, Tiny Bradshaw, and Willie Bryant at benefits for charitable causes. I remember doing one at the YMCA and another at the Rockland Palace.

The very first game was against Jimmie Lunceford's orchestra, which was famous for dressing up. If his band played four shows at the Apollo, they would change clothes four times. When they came out onto the court, they were in these beautiful uniforms and looked like professional basketball players. We came out in our mismatched pickup clothes, but we ran those guys ragged, whipped the hell out of 'em.

A Day at the Races

While my group was performing at the Cotton Club, some Hollywood producer saw the show that Norma and the others were doing with Ethel Waters at a theater in Los Angeles, and decided he had to have them in *A Day at the Races*,[2] which was already in production. He called Whitey, who added a fourth team to the group: Dot Miller, Norma's sister, and Johnny Innis. Johnny was the driver for the group as well as a Lindy hopper.

Whitey also went out there and added himself into the dance scene as an extra. You can see him walking around clapping his hands. He wasn't a great dancer himself, but he knew all the moves and sometimes he had ideas for steps, which he would show or describe to someone. At one point, there was a lot of publicity in the papers saying that he was going to create a new dance called the Joe Louis shuffle, but that never did come about.[3]

Whitey was best at knowing whether a movement or a routine was good or not, and how to make it look better. In that sense, he was an artistic director. He was pretty critical—he had to be, in his position. Sometimes he might be specific, like he might suggest changing the sequence of some steps or tell a dancer his movement would look smoother if he did it another way. In my case, he would usually just suggest that I try something else, and leave it for me to figure out. He made more suggestions for, say, group number four (later on, when he had more groups) than he did for his top three groups. He often just told them to watch us.

When Whitey went out to California for *Day at the Races*, his wife, Goona, who was not part of the dance scene, ran the business end of things in New York. By this time, he had such faith and trust in me that I was left in charge of both New York groups. I would report to Goona and give her the money I had collected, after I paid the dancers. Billy Ricker, who was captain of Tiny's Harlem Uproar team, would keep me posted on how things were going there. If there was a problem within either group—between two people, with a routine, with the club's management, or over money—I'd take care of it.[4]

From here on, I oversaw most rehearsals and coached just about every group that Whitey sent out on the road. Once the Lindy hoppers started touring a lot and I was out of town, Whitey might have done some choreography, or asked one of the other top Lindy hoppers—Billy Ricker, Willamae Ricker, George Greenidge, Norma Miller, Esther Washington, Snookie Beasley, and Frances "Mickey" Jones—to help make up a routine, but I was responsible for the majority of the ensemble sections. All of the dancers could come up with their own solos, although Whitey might suggest changes or ask me to give them another one. If you asked any of the Lindy hoppers who choreographed the routines, they would say, "Huh?" because we never used that term. But most of the kids knew I had made up most of them.

Dancers used to ask me for a number, and I'd say, "What steps you got?" They'd show me their ideas and I'd figure out a way to help them put something together. I'd often make up a routine for my group, and Whitey would ask me to give it to another team that was going out on the road. (Occasionally, two groups going to different cities would get the same routine.) I'd have to create a new one, but I didn't mind. To me, it was a compliment. It meant that Whitey had confidence that I could whip up something else that was just as good, and it always propelled me to try something new. Anyway, we were all so in tune with each other that I would just show the dancers a step and they'd get it right away.

Some people think that I choreographed *Day at the Races*, but I don't say that. Before the Ethel Waters group left New York, each couple did their own solo, and I coached them and gave them suggestions about where to put steps. This is where their individuality came out.

Then I gave them the ensemble section, which included the horses that are done at the end of the scene. I'm talking about where the first fellow bends over, the next guy hops on his back and lays down (my part in *Hot Chocolate*), and the girl jumps over both of them and lands on top as if she were sitting in a saddle. Remember I said that George Greenidge and I used to look everywhere for ideas? We had seen the Five Crackerjacks, as well as some clowns in a circus, do something similar. As soon as we got back to the Savoy, we worked it out with Billy Ricker. In *Day at the Races*, Snookie Beasley was the bottom man, George was the jump-over man, and Willamae was in the saddle.

Billy Williams and I created the second horse at another rehearsal because we had three more dancers who needed an exit step. That's the one where the girl rides piggyback on the guy while scooping up another girl on her legs. Leon was the anchorman, Norma rode piggyback (she was the scoop) and Ella Gibson got scooped up.

The routine was shortened in the movie, so I can't say they did exactly what I choreographed, but it's fair to say that I was partly responsible. And just because some people have asked: No, I wasn't jealous that that group got to be in the movies. That's how big a deal it was to be performing at the Cotton Club.

Hi-de-ho-ing with Cab Calloway

All Cotton Club shows ran for six months. We opened on September 24, 1936, and closed in March 1937. A week later we went out on the road with Cab Calloway and a few of the other acts for a three-week tour that included Boston, Baltimore, and Washington.

Cab was always the main draw whenever he performed, but he actually had one of the best bands in the business. People don't realize this because his musicians always had to highlight him on recordings. However, during live performances, when Cab wasn't singing, those cats really got to blow. During the six months at the Cotton Club, I got to hear Ben Webster every night! He was the master of ballads, so soulful. He said that every musician should know the words to each song he was playing.

At Cab's first rehearsal for the tour, which took place just before we closed at the Cotton Club, he asked if I had sheet music, which I didn't. Since I was supposed to know what I was doing by then, and every act was supposed to have its own music, I told him I would bring it the next day. That evening, I ran out and bought the music for Benny Goodman's "Jam Session," then stayed up all night listening to the record while I followed along. I couldn't read the notes, but I counted everything out, visualizing the steps I wanted the Lindy hoppers to do. Sometimes I got up and actually did the movements. The next day, I told Cab I wanted so many choruses of thirty-two bars each of this section, so many of that section (I wanted to make the music longer), then jump back to this spot, and finish it out. Cab was laughing because, as I know now, "Jam Session" is in sixteen-bar choruses.

Because I had to work within the structure of the music, I needed to take a little more control of the choreography than I had in the past. When the kids got to rehearsal, I explained that I had choreographed a routine for each couple based on what they were already doing, which I wanted them to repeat every single performance. Since I mapped everything out so tightly, even the solos, this was the first time that a Lindy hop routine was completely choreographed.

We were only asked to do our Lindy specialty for this show (although we ended up having to do some floor work for an encore). In order to lengthen the act, I had each team dance for one chorus, then go around again. It turned out to be very exciting to have each couple swing out two times, kind of like a challenge dance. As usual, we finished with the ensemble section, which I made two choruses long.

This turned out to be the only time I used "Jam Session," and I didn't use written music again until after the war. Except for Cab Calloway, we almost always worked with Savoy bands, who knew what to play for dancers. Before the Cotton Club, we never asked any of the bands to play a particular tune. The only thing we told them was what tempo we wanted, which I would stomp off, and they'd remember for the rest of the engagement. It was generally the same with Whitey's Lindy Hoppers. Chick Webb would usually play "Let's Get Together" for us. I'd ask Count Basie, "What are you playing for us tonight?" He'd tell me, and I'd say fine. He knew what worked—"Jumpin' at the Woodside" for a Lindy routine or "Every Tub" for a jazz number—because he knew our act. Occasionally I'd request a specific song. I used to ask Erskine Hawkins to play "Swingin' on Lenox Avenue" (or later on with the Congaroos, "Tippin In," if I wanted something a little faster), but not "Tuxedo Junction," because that was his featured number. With Lucky Millinder, I might request "Nagasaki." Sometimes, if the band was already planning to use the song I wanted for their own musical program, the leader might suggest another number at rehearsal, and it always worked fine.

Billie and Basie

Later that spring, I worked with Count Basie for the first time. I had been listening to Chick Webb since I first began going to the Savoy, but by early 1937 some of us were turning into Basie-ites. To me, Basie swung more than any band out there. He had a lot of great soloists—I can't think of any other outfit that had *two* great tenor sax players, Lester Young and Herschel Evans—and he had the best rhythm section in the music world. Most of the other swing bands said the same thing. Nowadays, whenever I hear Basie, it always makes me want to dance. Some of my favorite songs for dancing are "Shiny Stockings" and "Moten Swing." If I want to show off, I use "Jumpin' at the Woodside" or "Every Tub."

For this first time, we were appearing up in Boston at a big hotel with him and Billie Holiday. I had met Billie earlier in the year when she did a week at the Savoy with Basie. After we finished our routine the first night, Billie came out to sing as we were leaving the stage. We hurried to change our clothes, then all eight of us went and sat down at one of the tables in the ballroom to listen.

Right away, a waiter came over to tell us that we couldn't sit there. When we asked why, he said, "Because you're not allowed to." It was kind of surprising because we were staying in the hotel, which some places didn't allow us to do, and we hadn't had any other problems with the management. For instance, they didn't make us come in the back entrance. We didn't raise any fuss about it; we just went on back to our dressing room.

While we were sitting there talking and kidding around, there was a knock on the door. It was Billie. She didn't realize what had happened, so she started joking: "What's the matter, you guys don't like my singing? I saw you sitting out there, then all of a sudden I didn't see you anymore."

"No, Billie," we said, "it's not like that," and explained what had happened.

She said, "*What?*" as if she couldn't believe what we were telling her. "We'll see about that. I'm going to talk to Count." Basie must have told her to handle it however she wanted, because apparently she went to the manager and said that if her friends couldn't watch her sing, she wasn't going to perform there anymore.

I don't know exactly what transpired, but Billie told us that everything would be okay, and by the next show the hotel had set up a table for us. Okay, it was in a back corner, but it was there. After that, even though normally we might not have watched her every night, each time Billie was on stage, we were at that table.

It always irks me when you hear so much about Billie Holiday being a drug addict. That's all that most people know about her. Yes, she had this sickness, but it was something that she couldn't help. She was fantastic to work with, which I know because I did several more gigs with her after Boston. People don't realize that this young lady was a wonderful person, with a very tender and warmhearted side.

During the latter part of the 1930s, Basie rarely played a theater date without booking us if we were available. I worked with him four or five times as a member of Whitey's Lindy Hoppers, and we had a lot of good times together.

In show business, Saturday and Sunday are tough because you do so many extra performances. By Monday, everybody is exhausted, so it's always a down day. One Monday morning when walked into the Roxy, where we were on the bill with Basie, Jo Jones, his drummer, asked, "How you kids feeling today?" "Tired," we said. "Don't worry," he told us, with a grin on his face. "I'll pep you up." We soon found out what that meant. Just as we were starting our act, Jo Jones gave us a tempo that was designed to kick our butts. It was *really* swinging! We laughed and let him know, "We awake, man! We awake now!"

At another gig, Basie had us scheduled to go on as soon as he finished playing the opening number. As directed, we hit the stage on the downbeat of their second song and performed our routine. At the next show, we got into position as soon as we heard Basie play his first tune. On the first note of the next number we hit the stage again—but they were playing a different song! I was out there swinging, thinking, "Oh, man, this is not our music!" and Basie was looking at us as if to say, "What the hell is happening?" After a few bars, I signaled to everybody to follow me as I swung across the stage. We flew from one side to the other, and danced right off into the wings.

We were still standing there, looking at Basie in shock, when the stage manager came running up to us and said, "I thought I told you guys that you were supposed to go last from now on." I said, "No, man, you didn't tell us nothing!" Basie had changed the schedule, but the stage manager had forgotten to tell us! I assume the change was because we were such a hit, but we never did find out why.

In late spring 1937 we did a few gigs around New York on our own and a short tour with Bill Robinson in the D.C. area. We also played the Paradise Club again, and on May 15, 16, and 17 we appeared at the Hollywood Theatre, which was also in Atlantic City.[5] (I know the exact dates because I clipped an advertisement for it.) We were considered the stars for this engagement, but it was still a helluva comedown after the Cotton Club.

Command Performance

While on the road, we were notified that the Cotton Club show was going to travel to Europe. I had refused to go a year earlier, but this time I was very excited. It wasn't something I had ever expected to happen. For financial reasons, the producers replaced Cab Calloway's band with Teddy Hill and his Cotton Club Orchestra, substituted Bill Bailey for Bill Robinson, and cut several acts. They also replaced a lot of the chorus girls and added a few acts, including Norton and Margo (ballroom dancers) and Freddie and Ginger (soubrettes; they lead the chorus). In the end, the Tramp Band, the Berry Brothers, and Whyte's Hopping Maniacs (as we were billed for this tour) were the only performers from the first show.

On May 25, 1937, we sailed for Le Havre on the French Line's M.S. *Lafayette* with the entire cast of *Le Cotton Club de New-York*. Unlike Norma and Leon, we traveled with a whole show and didn't have to worry about anything: the band, the music, whether there would be enough floor space, whether the audience would like the show.

During that period of time, management paid travel expenses, but performers were responsible for their own room and board. When we arrived, the producers had booked rooms for the whole cast at an expensive hotel, but we left after a couple of nights because we couldn't afford it. We found a cheaper place across the street from the Moulin Rouge, and by sharing rooms the whole time we were in Paris, we actually managed to save some money.

For the entire time that I toured with the Lindy hoppers, we always tried to stay together in the same place. In fact, we did everything together: eat, sleep, play cards, have fun. We were a very close group. We fought sometimes—if you're together that much, something's got to happen—but it was rarely serious. Even if some of the dancers didn't like others that much, when it came time to do anything, we were together.

We played the Moulin Rouge (a nightclub) for about a month, followed by the Palais des Sports (a theater) for a week or two, and were well received at both venues. We were contracted to do the same two routines we had done at the Cotton Club, so I gave everybody back a little more freedom for their solos. I don't remember what Teddy Hill played for either routine, but I always loved dancing to that band. They knew how to improvise on the spot. They did this thing where the rest of the band would create a background while the soloist improvised, and it was really romping, just jumping.

A lot of nights after we finished up, I'd go out with Dicky Wells, one of the trombone players, and Bill Beason, the drummer. One night, we stopped into this jazz club where Django Reinhardt, the famous guitarist, was playing. They invited him to come see our show, which he did, and for the remainder of the run he came every night and watched from the wings. Afterwards, he and some of the guys in the band would go to this little jazz spot to jam until about ten o'clock in the morning. I used to tag along (while Billy and Jerome were fooling around with the girls) because I was the only Lindy hopper who was really into going out to hear jazz.

Except for the fact that I couldn't speak French, I loved Paris—the openness of it and that it was such a jazz town. A lot of African American musicians had left the United States for France because they were better appreciated abroad than at home. They didn't run into all that racial stuff overseas. Color didn't matter there, just talent. In fact, the only unpleasant memory I have from the whole time I was in Paris is something that happened between me and my girlfriend, Lucille.

There were a lot of relationships in the entertainment world, especially between musicians and chorus girls. You kidding? You wouldn't believe what went on. I mean, they all had the same kind of hours, so they ended up spending a lot of time together going to parties or bars after working so late and so hard.

Lucille and I had been performing in the same group since early 1936. Although we were very close and had a lot of fun, we didn't really become romantically involved until before we went to Europe. Right from the get-go, she and I had a very stormy relationship. Lucille was very argumentative and would do things just to make me angry because she liked to fight, which I didn't go for. A lot of times when she'd try to start something, I'd just walk away. But sometimes she'd grab me, pull me back, and we'd get into a heated argument. My previous girlfriend, Dorothy Jackson, was the opposite of Lucille. We never argued, which I thought was remarkable.

Things began unraveling between Lucille and me soon after we set sail for France. We broke up, and both of us started flirting with other people. She became involved with Bill Beason, and I began spending time with one of the chorus girls. Even though we were no longer seeing each other, Lucille got terribly jealous.

One night after we had arrived in Paris, my new girlfriend, who was staying in the same hotel we were along with a lot of other cast members, stopped by to visit while I was hanging out with Billy in the room he and I were sharing. The three of us were talking when Lucille happened to come by. As soon as she saw this other girl, she started arguing with her, and it developed into a shouting match and then a fight. I was trying to separate the two of them and hold Lucille back when she bent down, took off her shoe without my noticing, and used the heel to hit me just above the eye. Man, my eye jumped out like that! I got very angry . . . so angry that I hit her back. Then, as I tried to prevent her from continuing to hit me with her shoe, I wrestled her to the floor. Billy pulled me off just as Mildred and Jerome came rushing into the room saying, "Frankie, stop it! Stop it!"

At that moment, I guess I kind of came back to my senses and said, "What the hell am I doing?!" It was really shocking to me. I left the hotel and walked around Paris for the rest of the night until the sun came up, trying to get myself back together.

The next day, we had a show to do. So there we were on stage, both of us with eyes swollen out to here. As soon as the band saw these two one-eyed dancers, they started laughing and kidding around. But it wasn't funny to us.

I had never done anything like that before, and it scared the shit out of me. I couldn't understand how I could lose my temper to that point. Right then, I vowed to never let it happen again, and it hasn't. Actually, it hasn't been that hard because it takes a hell of a lot to get me that angry.

In late summer, we traveled to London to play the Palladium, which was the big-time theater where all the best entertainers performed.[6] One night, we had the honor of giving a royal command performance for His Majesty, King George VI and Queen Elizabeth. After the finale was over and we had changed into formal dress (gowns or tie and tails), they came on stage to meet the cast. I was a nervous wreck because we had been instructed about what we should and shouldn't do, like you couldn't speak to them or shake their hand unless they extended theirs first.

The queen followed the king down the line, congratulating the performers, but they did not shake hands with anyone . . . until they got to me. He didn't, but the queen stopped and extended her hand. Well, I was so flustigated (I know that's not a word, but that's how I felt) that, as I took it, I curtsied instead of bowing! Boy, did I hear about it from the other entertainers. They'd say, "Frankie, I'm the queen. You gonna curtsey to me now?" They laughed for days.

The next day I bought one white glove and started wearing it. When people asked what it was for, I said, "That's the hand that shook the hand of the Queen of England, baby!" Naturally, it was the highlight of the trip.

The show went on to Manchester and Dublin, but those theaters couldn't afford the entire cast, so the director cut out the chorus girls and just sent the major acts. Everywhere we went, it was a very successful tour.

Right after we got back to New York, my partner Naomi and I stopped dancing together because she quit to become a chorus girl. Whitey didn't approve of a girlfriend and boyfriend dancing with each other, since he thought it might affect their performance if they had a fight. Nevertheless, he put Lucille and me together because he felt that we looked good as dance partners.

Except for that brief thing with Hilda, that was the only time I was involved romantically with my dance partner. Lucille and I danced together until we returned from another tour, to Australia in 1939, and we continued to be involved until sometime during that trip, but the relationship was never the same.

9 • A BIG APPLE FOR WHITEY

Getting Down to Business

In the early days, Whitey was always scrambling to get the Lindy hoppers work. He'd go to the agencies on Broadway, to theater managers, or directly to the stars like Bill Robinson or Ethel Waters and try to convince them to put us in their show. After we came back from Europe, things really started to take off for Whitey's Lindy Hoppers. During the next half-dozen years, we did a lot of theater, nightclub, and movie work. Some big things happened during this time. By the late '30s, we had become so well known that Whitey could just mention us to producers or wait for the booking agents to come to him. He had several groups, including mine, that worked almost constantly right up through 1941.

Swing bands loved working with the Lindy hoppers. The bigger orchestras, like Count Basie, Cab Calloway, or Jimmie Lunceford, which generally assembled their own revues, would book us through Whitey. In a typical vaudeville show, which we were in once in a while, you'd get 10 to 12 variety acts and a movie, all for 50 cents. But with most famous big bands or singers, there might only be 3 or 4 supporting acts. Each theater usually had its own line of chorus girls, and the band would bring along a singer, an exotic or tap dancer, a comedian, and occasionally an eccentric dancer or a Lindy hop group. Sometimes we'd get a gig when a theater or nightclub directly hired acts they wanted in their show. We also got work through the Moe Gale Agency, which often booked popular Harlem bands featured at the Savoy as headliners for a whole bill. They would usually add Lindy hoppers to a package that was designed to tour theaters or go into a nightclub.

We often did do a month-long tour starting with the Apollo in New York, then hit the Royal Theatre in Baltimore, the Howard Theatre in Washington, D.C., and the Lincoln Theatre in Philadelphia, for a week each. Usually the entire show followed the circuit,[1] although sometimes the Lindy hoppers just played one of the theaters. We were a favorite of the management at the Apollo. We played there more than at any other theater, at least four times a year, so much that we called it home. The Roxy Theatre also became very fond of the Lindy hoppers. We were one of their favorite acts and played there about twice a year.

We frequently traveled with the other acts by bus or train and got to know a lot of entertainers this way, including Tip, Tap, and Toe, Dusty Fletcher, Moms Mabley, Eddie Rector, Coles and Atkins, Pops and Louie, the Whitman Sisters, the Three Rhythm Kings, Butterbeans and Suzie, Teddy Hale, Stump and Stumpy, Moke and Poke, Son and Sonny, Jesse and James, Miller Brothers and Lois, Chuck and Chuckles, Derby Wilson, Cook and Brown, Buck and Bubbles, and Pete, Peaches, and Duke.

At the same time, there were smaller nightclubs and hotels that wanted Lindy hoppers, so Whitey might just send two teams for a night or two. Some places were so small that they couldn't have more than one couple performing on the roped-off dance floor. There were also a lot of gigs at resorts in the Catskills and Poconos. You could work almost all year round once you got on that circuit.

Occasionally, the William Morris Agency or Universal Attractions, two of the biggest agencies around, would use Moe Gale to book Lindy hoppers for a show or movie. William Morris handled quite a few black stars, including Nat King Cole, Bill Robinson, Ethel Waters, Stump and Stumpy, Buck and Bubbles, and Count Basie, through John Hammond. Gale didn't have the connections to book us directly into films, but William Morris knew that his agency specialized in small to mid-level jazz acts. I believe William Morris handled the booking for several of the movies that Whitey's Lindy Hoppers did.

How much we got paid depended on how big the date was. For example, when we first did the Apollo (which was a very low-budget theater) with Chick Webb and Ella Fitzgerald, I think the whole act was contracted for $400 for the week. That was for 8 people doing 4 shows each weekday, 5 on Saturday and Sunday. If I'm not mistaken, I think Whitey took $80 for his commission and split the rest among the dancers. If Moe Gale or William Morris was involved, they would arrange for their own commission with the theater or film producers. I don't know what Whitey got paid by the Cotton Club, but we each got $75 a week for 2 shows a night, which was good money at the time. We'd say, "Damn, I'm having such a wonderful time doing what I love, and getting paid for it too."

When the Lindy hoppers went to Europe with the Cotton Club Revue in the summer of 1937, the contract was for $600 a week. I was the paymaster, so I collected the money from the manager, gave each of the dancers what Whitey told me to—I think it was $75—and kept $25 for Whitey. At first, I wired Whitey's cut back to him like I was supposed to, but after a couple of weeks, even though I knew he wouldn't be crazy about the idea, I started holding onto it in case something happened.

There's a controversy because some people say Whitey made a whole lot of money off the Lindy hoppers. I think he made a good amount, but not all that much. Yes, he sometimes took 20 or 25 percent (or less if the job didn't pay that well), but he always paid us on time—in fact, he paid us even if he got scammed by a theater owner or booking agent—and he did *so* much for us. I knew some entertainers who never had any money because their agents took even more than Whitey, as much as 50 percent or more. Some of these guys had to borrow money from me!

When we were first coming up, Whitey did *everything* for us. In my opinion, the success of the group was due entirely to him and he deserved whatever he got. Other than Shorty Snowden, Whitey's groups were the only Lindy hoppers out there working professionally. Others attempted to make it but didn't do so well, and some of them eventually came back to Whitey.

Whitey pounded the pavement to find us work. He created opportunities for exposure by taking us to restaurants, bars, or nightclubs where they had social dancing between the shows and telling us to get up and dance. Sometimes we would get a job just from that. He arranged our schedule and made sure everybody got to rehearsals and jobs on time. If you were late, you paid a fine, but that's the only thing he ever took money out of our salaries for. Some managers also charged for transportation, costumes, photographs, and other stuff like that.

In the beginning, Whitey had costumes made for us. He drove us to all of our gigs in his Buick, or sent a chauffeur with his second Buick, or provided whatever kind of transportation we needed. He made sure we always looked sharp and arranged for publicity shots to be taken. He often took the whole bunch of us out to eat, especially at the Chinese restaurant across the street from the Savoy.

If there was a problem we couldn't solve, we knew we could call him and he'd try to fix it. Mac always stuck up for us and would talk to the management where we were working to get better conditions. I heard from some of the other dancers that he almost had a knock-down, drag-out fight with Michael Todd because he wasn't treating the Lindy hoppers as well as some of the other performers in *Hot Mikado*.

Yes, Whitey had a better lifestyle than us, but he didn't flash around a lot of money or live in a sumptuous home, just an apartment in Harlem. Billy and Willamae Ricker had discussions with Whitey about getting paid more because they were married and were living on their own (not with their parents like most of us), but the real complaining started with the dancers who joined in the late '30s. Before that, we didn't even think about Whitey's commission because we were so happy to be dancing *and* making money.

The Rickers handled it by speaking privately to Whitey, not griping in public, and they got a little more when they were in charge of a group. I did too sometimes, although if the salary wasn't all that great, I'd split it evenly with everybody else. The Rickers and I were alike in that we didn't mind taking on the responsibility for a group. (For instance, Willamae was the captain for the Ethel Waters tour.) If there was a problem, the kids knew they could come to us because we were willing to deal with whatever came up. We weren't looking for praise or thanks (although the dancers did appreciate what we did), it was just our way.

The younger crowd thought they should be getting more money for their hard work, and so did I, but I don't think they really knew how much Whitey was getting paid. They figured he was getting thousands and thousands of dollars, which wasn't true. I think the most money he ever made came from the bar he opened in upstate New York in the early '40s. The Lindy hoppers were working hard and stopping shows, but the money just wasn't there.

Whitey was a very charismatic leader and a smooth talker. That was one of the ways he held his command over the dancers. If he said we were going to dance on the Brooklyn Bridge in the hot sun all day long for nothing, he would have had plenty of people who would do it, even if some of them grumbled. He demanded respect from his dancers. He was also a bit of a ladies' man and, yes, he went after the girls, but there were a lot of women who were interested in Whitey; even the younger ones went for him. It might have been because of his image as a successful businessman and a powerful person in the dance community and in Harlem.

Actually, being in Whitey's Lindy Hoppers gave us all stature in the neighborhood. I was very proud to be part of the group. People would come up to us and say, "Aren't you one of Whitey's Lindy Hoppers? I saw you at the Savoy," or "I catch you every time you play the Apollo." Sometimes it took me a minute to realize why they were saying hello, because it wasn't like we were famous. As for getting the girls, that was more a matter of being a good dancer than being in Whitey's Lindy Hoppers. Girls didn't just fall all over you at the Savoy. You had to show them what you could do. Of course, every single one of us was a good social dancer, at least in the early days.

In my opinion, Whitey had a fatherly relationship with us as much as a professional one. He was also like a brother and a friend to me. I know a lot of the Lindy hoppers felt that way too, although of course, some didn't. I believe that he really cared for the dancers. He made us feel special and taught us to have self-respect. He knew that the Lindy was created in Harlem and felt it should be presented in a manner that would make people say, "This is a black art form, and a great part of American culture."

A Letter from Whitey

The Lindy hoppers who made *Day at the Races* were so good in it that the following year Whitey got a contract to make a movie called *Everybody Sing*.[2] In the fall of 1937, Dot Moses and Tiny Bunch, Eleanor "Stumpy" Watson and George Greenidge, Mildred Pollard and Eddie "Shorty" Davis, and Lucille Middleton and I drove out to the West Coast in Whitey's two automobiles, with Tiny at the wheel of one car and Ruben (I can't remember his last name) driving the other. Whitey loved his shiny black Buicks, but they were covered in dust by the end of the long trip. Stumpy remembers heating up cans of beans on the radiator for our dinner.

We had a great crew of dancers for *Everybody Sing*. Stumpy, who had short legs, was known for her footwork. She started dancing with Long-Legged George after Ella Gibson stopped. Eddie was a very exciting dancer who could also do acrobatics. One of his specialties was doing a flip using his partner as a support, which he often did with Gladys Crowder. It looked hard, but it wasn't that difficult if the dancers knew what they were doing. Gladys quit dancing after she won the 1937 Harvest Moon Ball with Eddie, which is when Whitey put him with Mildred, who was also very strong, enough so to hold him when he jumped into her arms for the cradle.[3]

Mildred had joined the Lindy hoppers earlier in the year with three other friends: Joyce James, Al Minns, and Joe Daniels. After he saw them dancing at the Savoy, Whitey invited them all to a little audition. When he asked my opinion, I said I thought they were pretty good. He agreed, but switched the partners around because he liked Mildred better with Al and Joyce with Joe, then started putting both couples into gigs right away.

Mildred danced with Eddie in *Everybody Sing* and in *Radio City Revels*. She was afraid of air steps, but you can see her do some with Eddie in the second movie. Her nickname was "Boogie" because she did that step so well, very low down and funky. She had a wonderful way of using her body.

Eventually Joyce and Joe got married. We used to call them Big Stupe and Little Stupe because in rehearsal they just couldn't replicate steps immediately, and didn't realize it. They would get it after a while, but they always looked funny at first. These were humorous nicknames, not meant to be ridiculing or degrading. All of our nicknames were affectionate, and no one ever resented having one.

I don't remember who gave me the nickname Musclehead, or when I got it, but it was because the muscles in my head bulged when I was concentrating on trying to get a step. I also clenched my fists with my thumbs sticking out, so they could just as well have called me Thumbs.

Shortly after we arrived in California, I received a letter from Whitey telling me about a new dance craze in New York called the big apple. As I've mentioned, he liked mixing the newest trends in with the Lindy so it would be more popular. I had never heard of the big apple, but he explained that it had various jazz steps like truckin', Suzie-Q, and boogies. It was done in a circle with a caller in the middle who called out the steps and was supposed to represent the core. That's all Whitey told me in his letter. He didn't say where or when to do each step, or anything about the music, which was swing, of course.

Whitey asked me to make up a big apple routine for the Lindy hoppers, so I got to work. At first, as I read the letter and tried visualizing the movements, I thought, *What the hell is he talking about?* Then I began playing some music and actually doing the steps. I used Count Basie's "John's Idea," initially, but then I switched to "One O'Clock Jump" because it was a little slower and more swinging.

I always brought my records when we traveled so we could rehearse. Most of the bands we worked with made recordings, although they didn't necessarily record a song exactly the same way they performed it. In those days, many bands didn't have a lot of written arrangements; they often just played head arrangements.[4] I played those records over and over again until they got so scratched I had to buy new ones.

After I put the steps that Whitey had mentioned into the big apple, I knew there had to be more than this for it to be a routine. I kept playing the music to get ideas about where to insert other jazz steps, some older ones that had been around, some I had made up but hadn't used in a routine yet, and some that I created on the spot.

Many jazz steps are characterizations of things in everyday life. For instance, someone might do flowing movements to show the wind, or imitate a chicken walking, and you've got peckin'. Seeing all those cornfields when we drove across the country inspired me to come up with a Charleston-based step that I called the scarecrow. I had already made up the Charlie Chaplin (another Charleston variation in which your right leg slides in front of you as if you just stepped on a banana peel) after seeing him do that in a movie, and I put that in. Gaze afar came from seeing cowboy-and-Indian movies.

While I was choreographing the big apple, a riff in "John's Idea" inspired a second version of the squat Charleston, which I called the quick squat. I had created the first version of the squat Charleston, which is not in the big apple, at the Savoy while listening to "One O'Clock Jump." The difference between these two steps is that in the first version you squat on counts one and two, then start the Charleston kicks with your right leg on count three. In the quick squat, you squat only on count eight, then start kicking on count one. Another riff in "John's Idea" suggested the jump Charleston, which I also used in the big apple. Both squat Charlestons and the jump Charleston were more swingy than the old-time Charlestons on which they were based. I continued adding steps, playing around with where they fit in, until I thought the big apple was ready.

On all three of my trips to California with Whitey's Lindy Hoppers, we stayed at the Hotel Torrance, which was on Central Avenue in a middle-class black neighborhood with a lively nightclub scene. Sometimes the Lindy hoppers practiced in the hotel lounge, which is where I worked on the big apple. We had also started performing in a nearby nightspot called Club Alabam, so I did some of the choreography there.

We were all so young and active back then that it only took me a few days to finish the big apple. The kids already knew many of the steps and they were very quick to learn the new ones, which were pretty simple. Remember, these were professional dancers. When I showed them a step, they got it. Plus, the sequence was in a set order, and since I was going to be the caller, they didn't even have to memorize it. I just had them repeat the routine over and over until everybody was doing it in the exact same rhythm.

····························· Jazz Dancing ····························

MANY JAZZ DANCE STEPS are based on African American "street" dance, originating as far back as the early 1800s, sometimes with a lineage that is traceable back to Africa.[5] Often gestural in nature and fancifully named, these vernacular movements (such as the shimmy, mess-around, pimp walk, fishtail, cakewalk, and strut, in addition to those mentioned in Frankie's description of the big apple) were incorporated into many swing era dances, including the Lindy hop.

During the 1930s, these movements weren't necessarily referred to as jazz steps. The term "jazz," commonly used in the '20s, was largely dropped in the '30s in favor of "swing," which was perceived as a new kind of music. At first, Frankie had no specific overall term for these movements, but by the late 1930s he began to call them jazz steps.

This family of steps has come to be known by the very apt term of authentic jazz dance. The origin of the phrase is obscure, but it appears to have emerged during the

1950s as protagonists of vernacular jazz dance tried to differentiate it from the style of jazz dance that was emerging on Broadway stages. The term was used by authors Marshall and Jean Stearns, filmmaker Mura Dehn, tap dancer Cholly Atkins, and Pepsi Bethel, a member of Whitey's Lindy Hoppers who in 1973 named his own dance troupe the American Authentic Jazz Dance Company.[6]

Authentic jazz dance steps have turned up again and again in numerous dance forms including tap, soft-shoe, vaudeville, chorus lines, social dances, fad dances, Broadway-style jazz, and hip hop, and have displayed remarkable resiliency as they are reincarnated with each new generation of dancers in a manner reflecting the current style. ●

The Big Apple

THE ROOTS OF THE BIG APPLE ARE NOT ENTIRELY CLEAR, but Katrina Hazzard-Gordon suggests that it may have developed out of the "ring shout," a form with "counterclockwise circling and high arm gestures" that "appeared on plantations in South Carolina and Georgia before 1860."[7] The ring shout, which has survived to this day among a small population in the South, and the African American tradition of improvisational dancing likely coalesced to influence the development of the swing era's big apple.[8]

By the mid-1930s, the dance that would come to be named the big apple had found a home at the Big Apple, a nightclub in Columbia, South Carolina.[9] There, to swing music, young African Americans performed a rousing ritual that featured dancers in a circle executing steps shouted out by a caller, alternating with an individual or couple "shining" as they improvised in the middle of the circle. A substantial vocabulary of steps consisted of popular vernacular jazz movements of the day, including truckin', Suzie-Q, shag, black bottom, peckin' Charleston, and praise Allah, the end figure in which participants rushed the middle of the circle, hands reaching to the sky.[10]

In 1936, three white University of South Carolina students driving by the Big Apple were drawn in by the jazzy music and became enthralled with the marvelous swing spectacle that they beheld from the nightclub's balcony. Billy Spivey, Donald Davis, and Harold "Goo-Goo" Wiles brought other friends to the club who eventually adopted the dance, named it after the club, and disseminated the big apple to the white community of dancers that congregated at local colleges and at clubs along the South Carolina shore.[11]

The dance took off, and in 1937, Gae Foster of New York City's Roxy Theatre came scouting for big applers to perform in the theater's famed stage show. Eight white couples, including Spivey, Davis, and Betty Henderson (who, under her married name, Betty Wood, would help revive the big apple in the 1990s by giving workshops internationally, often with dance historian Lance Benishek) introduced the big apple at a three-week engagement beginning on September 3. These sold-out shows greatly contributed to the dance's tremendous vogue between mid-1937 and mid-1938.[12]

Benishek considers the big apple to have been "the third biggest dance fad in American history, behind the Twist and the Charleston."[13] In December, in a four-page photo spread, Life predicted that 1937 would be remembered as the year of the big apple, as done by "nimble youngsters" and "puffing oldsters" at "colleges, country clubs, and private parties."[14] Like all popular trends, the big apple had its champions and detractors. The American Dancer reported in 1938 that Harriet James of Boston felt that the big apple "releases the folicsome instinct," and "has renewed people's enthusiasm for dancing. It is a perfect joy."[15] But a couple of months earlier, Bosley Crowther had quipped in the New York Times Magazine that the big apple "would seem to bear striking resemblance to some sort of mass convulsion, embracing as it does all the weird and assorted shakings of shoulders and shanks that modern 'Swing' music has provoked."[16]

In testament to its popularity, the big apple was covered extensively in the press, made appearances in feature films, short subjects, musicals, and nightclub acts, and inspired several songs. Arthur Murray simplified and codified the dance in order to teach it to large numbers of students at his popular studios. And, one Herbert "Whitey" White instructed his top choreographer, by letter, to tap into the trend and create, sight unseen, a big apple routine for his ace crew of Lindy hoppers. ●

Everybody Sing

Everybody Sing, starring Allan Jones and a young, up-and-coming Judy Garland, was filmed at the MGM studios in Hollywood. The producers wanted one routine, but I hadn't decided on the choreography for it by the time we got out to California because I had a lot of ideas swirling around in my brain.

I had initially planned on doing a Lindy hop number, but when we first met with the musical director, he wanted to see everything we had. In addition to writing and arranging original music for our routine so the producers wouldn't have to pay a royalty fee, he also oversaw our scene. We showed him several of our routines and Whitey, who had come out from New York, suggested we do the big apple because it had taken over in New York and was all the rage. Because the producers were looking for excitement and wanted to have a lot of jumping around and girls flying through the air, we also included plenty of Lindy hopping. We still weren't doing all that many air steps yet, but the ones we did were very thrilling.

Before I left for Europe, Whitey had rented out a basement at 101 West 140th Street that used to be a Chinese laundry, which he set up as a club for the Lindy hoppers so we could have a place to call our own. It was right across the street from the ballroom, so we could go back and forth whenever we wanted to. Sometimes we'd go there after the Savoy had closed and hang out until the wee hours, just exchanging stories, lounging around in the soft chairs, writing letters, and playing music. It had a pretty good floor, so we could practice if we wanted to. But it's funny—it was so relaxing that we didn't do all that much dancing there.

The big apple scene in *Everybody Sing* was supposed to be set in Harlem at this laundry.[17] Judy Garland and some other people are driving through Harlem on a tour bus on their way to the Savoy Ballroom. They see these kids in this club, get off the bus, and end up watching us dance. There were a whole bunch of extras in the background who were supposed to be folks from the neighborhood, but I didn't choreograph what they did. They were just told to move to the beat, so they did hand movements and rocked back and forth.[18]

There were a couple of articles in the newspaper about us being in *Everybody Sing*. I used to like to cut out stuff like that to put in my album, along with pictures that I took with my camera. It was always a thrill to see our name in the press (even though they always got something wrong), but I wasn't thinking about the future. It was just something I liked to do.

People think that the big apple in *Keep Punching*[19] is my original routine, but it's not, although it's similar to what we did in *Everybody Sing*. Actually, I've never re-created the first version of the big apple exactly, but the majority of the steps from it are still done. They form a solid base for the many different versions I've made over the years.

I used to change the big apple all the time, but there were some things that were always the same. I always started off with shouts,[20] stomp-offs, a leapfrog, and the rock step. Then, I usually included the standard jazz steps: Suzie-Qs, boogies, gaze afar, truckin', and spank-the-baby, not necessarily in that order. After that it could go anywhere. I might include fall-off-the-log, apple jacks, peckin', camel walk, scarecrow, Charlie Chaplin, jump Charleston, quick squat Charleston, or ride-the-pony (which I also made up).

Generally, we did London Bridge[21] at the end of the big apple. For performances (including in *Everybody Sing*), we followed that with Lindy solos, then exited with the horses, most of the time, or occasionally truckin' or break-a-leg.[22] The whole time that I was performing professionally, no matter what dance we started out doing, we always finished up with the Lindy hop because it was the most exciting and it was a real dance, not just a step, like truckin', or a bunch of steps, like the big apple.

We worked on *Everybody Sing* for about two weeks. Usually, we were on the set by six or seven in the morning and generally stayed until six in the evening. Of course, they weren't filming us all the time, but they wanted us to be available. Once they actually started focusing on our scene, we stayed until they told us we could leave, which was often close to midnight.

Now, we were wild kids, always carrying on. We didn't care where we were—music's playing, hey, man . . . dance time! As soon as we got to the studio, we'd put our records on and start dancing. Word got out around MGM, and people were telling each other they had to go see those crazy Lindy hoppers. Actors, actresses, stagehands, directors, producers, even some stars came by to watch us, but we hardly noticed them 'cause we were busy *dancing*!

I didn't even realize that Clark Gable was on the set when, one day, I decided to climb up a 15-foot-high scaffold that was used for the cameras. After I got to the platform on top, being very adventuresome (and young and stupid), I got an urge to run and jump over to another platform that was about 10 feet away . . . which I did without thinking anything about it.

As soon as I came on down, Clark Gable walked over to me and said, "What's your name, kid?"

I told him, and he said, "Well, I'm Clark Gable."

"Yeah, I know," I said.

Then he asked, "Can you do that again?"

"Do what?" I said. As far as I was concerned, I hadn't done anything.

"You know, jump from one scaffold to the other, like you just did."

I said, "If I did it once, I guess I can do it again."

"Good," he said. "I don't want you to do it now, but I'm going to bring Spencer Tracy and some of the gang to the set and bet him that one of you kids can jump from one scaffold to the other. Then I'm going to pick you out, but I don't want you to let on that we've already met. Okay?" I promised I would go along with the gag.

A couple of days later, he came by with Spencer Tracy, Charles Boyer, and Myrna Loy.[23] After they watched us practice for a while, Clark Gable suddenly said, "Hey, kid." We all looked around. I said, "Me?" "Yeah, you. Could you come over here for a minute?" I walked over, and he introduced me to all these stars. I asked Myrna if she'd like to dance . . . no, just kidding, but I wanted to.

Gable said, "You see those two scaffolds?" I turned and looked. Then he asked if I thought I could jump from the top of one to the other. I looked at them again and said, "I don't know . . . maybe I can. I think so."

Gable said, "I just bet Spencer Tracy that one of you guys could make this jump." The other Lindy hoppers, who were in on the setup, started egging me on so, as planned, I agreed to try it.

When I looked up at the towers this time, I thought, *Holy mackerel.* They seemed like they were a mile high. It was different now that I was doing this stunt for a purpose instead of just for the heck of it. I started climbing up, acting like I was scared, but when I looked down and the ground seemed so far away, I really was.

The platform wasn't very big, about 5 feet square, but this time, it seemed as small as a postage stamp! *Damn, I don't have any running room,* I thought. *What the hell did I get myself into?* I was beginning to wonder if I was going to be able to make the jump again. Now, the whole time, I had to put on an act and make believe that this was all a big surprise. I did such a good job, I think I could have won an Academy Award.

The moment had come, so I tried to remember that I had pulled this off before, said, "What the hell," took a deep breath and, as the dancers down below hollered, "Yeah, Frankie. Go ahead . . . jump! You can do it!" backed into the farthest corner of the platform. I took one last look at the ants on the ground, ran as hard as I could, and leaped over to the other side. When I was safely across, I got down on my knees, said, "Thank you, Lord!" then climbed down real fast.

A couple of hours later, Clark Gable came back. He had collected his bet from Spencer Tracy and, to my surprise, gave me the $25 and said, "Why don't you split it with the other Lindy hoppers?" which is exactly what I did.

Cut!

Judy Garland was often on the set with us because she was part of our scene, but there was always somebody hovering around her, as if the studio was protecting her, like they did all their contract stars. We were well into filming the big apple when the director decided to give her a rest break one afternoon. After she left, the director told Whitey that he wanted the Lindy hoppers to keep dancing so they could continue to shoot us. But Whitey felt that if they were going to give her a rest, we should get one too, since we had been working nonstop. He figured that if they were going to pay respect to Judy Garland, they should do the same for us kids. The director said no, and the two of them got into a fierce argument, at which point Whitey told us, "Y'all go sit down."

Even though we were tired, we would not have minded continuing to film the scene. If it was left to us, we'd have danced all day long. But Whitey was our boss, our mentor, father, mother, sister, brother; he was always looking out for us. We would do anything he asked, so when he told us to stop dancing, we stopped. We didn't even think about it.

The week went on and eventually we finished shooting the scene, but from what I understand the director was very, very angry with Whitey. When it came time to edit the movie, the Lindy hoppers were completely cut out of it. That's how he got back at Whitey. Instead of going to Harlem, Judy Garland went to Chinatown. Whitey, who found out about it from one of the editors after we got back to New York, was very upset. It wasn't that we didn't get paid—we did—but we really missed out on some big-time recognition. It was a very sad incident because everybody said it was a great dance scene, but I didn't dwell on it.

As I mentioned, while we were in Southern California, we also worked in a couple of clubs, Club Alabam and El Morocco, which was one of the biggest nightclubs out there. All the performers at Club Alabam were black and the audience was mostly black, about 85 percent, with some whites mixing in. It was actually me, not Whitey, who booked the Lindy hoppers at Club Alabam. We had gone social dancing there when we first got to town, and people went wild just watching us on the floor. Curtis Mosby, the manager (he had been a musician and band leader), knew about the Lindy hoppers because the group that did *Day at the Races* had performed there in 1936. He asked if we'd like to work to help pay for our trip. We ended up being in Hollywood for about a month because we didn't get called to the studio right away. Once we started shooting *Everybody Sing*, which took about two weeks, it didn't affect our performances at Club Alabam because we only did one routine and didn't go on until midnight.

Back at the Savoy

When the Lindy hoppers returned to New York, I taught the big apple to Whitey's other groups. (I still hadn't seen the big apple that had inspired his letter, although a little later on I got to see it being done by a group of white dancers at the Roxy. I don't know who they were, but even though we had some of the same movements, their version was very different from ours.) Everybody at the Savoy already knew most of the steps, and I showed them the ones I had made up. We started doing the big apple on Saturday nights at the ballroom, where it got to be quite popular. In fact, for a while it was such a hit that the management used it to draw people in by presenting it as a contest. My recollection is that the big apple was done about every other week (although I guess it went weekly at some point), and it included the Lindy hop but replaced the Lindy contest.

At a certain point in the evening, Buchanan would announce the big apple contest and clear the floor. We never asked for any particular tune, but the featured band would start playing something with a medium tempo so we could execute the steps. If Chick Webb was the house band, he usually played "Stompin' at the Savoy." Other bands, such as Teddy Hill, Erskine Hawkins, Buddy Johnson, or Lucky Millinder, generally chose "Christopher Columbus."

We staged the big apple at the Savoy differently from when we performed it in theaters and nightclubs, where it was always followed by Lindy solos and a group exit, and there usually wasn't a caller. I was the caller in *Everybody Sing* because it was the first time we had done the big apple, and Whitey's letter described it that way. Afterwards, I realized that we didn't really need a caller anymore because the order of the steps was choreographed and the dancers followed that.

At the Savoy, there generally was a caller. It might be Billy Ricker, Champ, Downes, or me. However, if Leon James was around it was usually him; sometimes Eunice Callen did the core with him. Whitey had designated Leon, who was one of his main men, for the job because of his outstanding personality. Leon stood out even in a group of top dancers because, among other things, there was something special about the way he used his face and hands. You can see what I'm talking about in his solo with Norma Miller in *Day at the Races*.

Even though the Savoy advertised it as a contest, the big apple was closed to the public. Only Whitey's dancers did it, and Buchanan never bothered to declare a winner. The caller danced around in the middle of the circle surrounded by about ten couples, hollering out the upcoming step just before the phrase in the music turned. He always started off with the basic steps, but then he would usually break it up by bringing up a team to do a Lindy solo.

The whole thing was very impromptu, which meant that nobody knew who their partner was going to be. The caller might say, "Frankie and Stumpy, show me whatcha got," or "Billy and Ann, it's your floor." You could end up with anybody, kind of like in a Jack & Jill contest.[24] Even though it was sort of a performance, the main couple just improvised while the other Lindy hoppers formed a semicircle behind them and egged them on.

After that, the caller might bring up another couple to shine or call out more jazz steps, which could be in any sequence he wanted. It was all at his discretion. The dance continued on like that, alternating the big apple with the Lindy, until the caller shouted, "Let's go home," and led us all off doing break-a-leg or truckin'.

At some point, the Savoy built a round wooden platform that the caller stood on and the solo teams danced on. It was about 7 feet in diameter,

2 feet high, and was supposed to be shaped like an apple. Once we had that, the other Lindy hoppers would stay in a circle during individual shines, but they kneeled down. Even though it was small, the couple on the drum was able to really cut loose because we were all pretty good at adjusting to different spaces. Some even did air steps.

Eventually, interest in the big apple died out and they got rid of the platform. The Savoy went back to doing just Lindy hop contests, but by the late 1930s Whitey had so many good dancers that not many members of the general public wanted to compete against them.

When I first showed Whitey the big apple out in California, he told me that he had bet Buchanan I could do a routine based on just a written description. Apparently, Whitey thought more of my talent than I did. He saw something in me that I didn't even see in myself. He just had that kind of insight. I never thought I was anything special. I just had a lot of ideas that I liked trying out.

Radio City Revels

Soon after we returned to New York, the same four couples from *Everybody Sing* were called back out to Hollywood to make another movie: RKO's *Radio City Revels* starring Ann Miller, Milton Berle, Bob Burns, and Jack Oakie. At this point, even though Whitey's Lindy Hoppers had made several movies, *Day at the Races*, *Everybody Sing*, and *Manhattan Merry-Go-Round*,[25] we still didn't have a sense of that being a bigger deal than appearing in a nightclub. We certainly didn't have any ideas about becoming stars. We were just following the money. It was only after the Nicholas Brothers started being in films that we saw the power in them.

Once again, we piled into Whitey's cars for the drive out. This time, he came with us, and occasionally arranged for performances along the way that were not booked ahead of time. Sometimes Whitey would tell us to dance to a jukebox at a restaurant in some little town. His main purpose was to spread the dance around, but sometimes we would get a gig out of it. Other times he'd talk to a nightclub owner and wrangle a spot for us. After days of sitting in a car, we'd loosen up, then run through our routine to test out the stage. For music, we'd just ask the band leader to play something swinging, beat out the tempo, and tell him to stop when we finished.

Late one night while we were going through Texas, Ruben, our driver, dozed off at the wheel, and our car veered briefly across the median line. Fortunately, there wasn't much traffic, except for one automobile coming toward us, which careened onto the shoulder for several yards. The driver and his passenger yelled at us as they whizzed by. We continued on, but after a couple of miles the other car came back, drove alongside us, then got in front of our vehicle, so we had to stop. Two white men got out and started cursing at us like crazy.

Whitey got out of the car with Ruben and started apologizing because, after all, we had been in the wrong. This is just speculation, but my take on the situation was that these guys wanted to make trouble for what they thought were just *two* black guys. At that point, I emerged from the back seat with another guy and two of the girls. Now they were looking at six of us.

Just then, the other Buick pulled up with the other three dancers and Tiny Bunch. This giant of a man, who was quiet but had a big voice, lumbered over and said, "Hey, Mac, having a little trouble?" You should have seen the expression on those guys when they saw all these people. Their attitude changed so fast. All of a sudden, they were *suggesting* that we should be more careful and saying that they didn't want to cause any trouble because they had a lot of black friends. One of them actually claimed that he knew Bojangles.

The Lindy hop section in *Radio City Revels* was part of a bigger production number, kind of a hoedown, with many other dancers and singers. Except for the end where we all fall down like dominoes, which was Whitey's idea, I choreographed the routine, but it wasn't one of our best. For one thing, the music, "Swingin' in the Corn," didn't swing, but it *was* corny.[26]

Our scene was shot separately from the eccentric dance solos that come before it. We never even saw them being done. Back then, they made films that way so that sequences with black performers could be cut when the movie played down South. My solo with Lucille was completely cut out of all versions, I think because we did a movement that was too provocative, that one where the girl boots the guy in the face with her behind.

It was a pretty uneventful shoot, except for the time Fred Astaire came by the set to see us dance. We were just clowning around like usual when we overheard him say to one of his companions, "I wish I could dance like that." We were so astonished that we all stopped what we were doing. We wished *we* could dance like *him*! Later, when I saw Astaire do a brief Lindy hop in one of his films, I thought, *Yeah, Fred, I know what you mean.*

Big Apple Dancers

A different group of Whitey's Lindy Hoppers went into the Roxy Theatre for a three-week engagement sometime in the early spring of 1938. Harry Howard, a theatrical producer, caught our act and liked it so much that he hired us, costumes and all, for *Hollywood Hotel Revue,* a big production that he had put together to go on tour to New Zealand and Australia.

Hollywood Hotel Revue had about sixty entertainers, including comedians, singers, acrobats, ballroom dancers, showgirls, and chorus girls, plus four teams of Lindy hoppers: Willamae Ricker and Snookie Beasley, Esther Washington and Jerome Williams, Eunice Callen and Billy Ricker, and Lucille Middleton and me. One team from the Roxy got cut, for financial reasons, I assume. We were the only black performers in the show.

Because Howard had seen us doing the big apple at the Roxy and the dance was still popular, we were billed as "The 8 Big Apple Dancers," or variations on that. I rehearsed the group very intensively for close to a month before we left New York in late July. We traveled by train to Vancouver, then continued via ocean liner, departing August 3. It was a very nice trip—we did a little performance with some of the other entertainers from the show at the captain's dinner for the first-class passengers—except for one incident.

Eunice was only about sixteen, so the board of education wouldn't allow her to travel unless she received tutoring (which she did from one of the cast members) *and* she had an official chaperone, which ended up being me. I always had to know what she was doing, but she didn't mind because I wasn't all that strict. While we were in Hawaii, Eunice and Lucille went off on their own and got high at this bar on some exotic drink. When they got back to the boat, Lucille discovered that she had lost her passport. We had to go all the way back to the bar to find it which, luckily, we were able to do. I laugh about it now, but at the time I was worried for Lucille because she wouldn't have been able to leave Hawaii without her passport. I didn't do anything other than tell them that they should have known better, but I was very upset.

I only had to step in one other time for Eunice. Later on in the trip, we met a trio of African American tap dancers called the Dancing Chefs who were working in a nightclub in Melbourne. We used to go see each other perform. One of them was trying to get to Eunice, so I intervened, even though she didn't want me to. She complained, "I can run my own life," but I told her, "This guy will be gone, and you could be walking around pregnant."

A Year Down Under

On August 21, the cast arrived in Auckland, New Zealand, where *Hollywood Hotel Revue* premiered at His Majesty's Theatre, then ran for two weeks. After a couple of nights in a hotel, the Lindy hoppers checked out and got our own flat. Since the seasons are reversed, it was cool, and firewood was supposed to be included in the rent, but we weren't getting it. So, as Eunice says, she and Lucille went into all the "tricks of the trade." Lucille greased her down with Vicks VapoRub, and when Eunice complained to the landlady about a cold and headache, we got stacks and stacks of kindling.

Our next stop was Sydney, where we played the Theatre Royal from September 23 through October and into November, before moving on to His Majesty's Theatre in Brisbane for two and a half weeks beginning in early December. Brisbane is close to the equator, so it was about 85 degrees each day. We then opened on Christmas Eve in Melbourne, where we had a month-long engagement at the Princess Theatre before closing for a brief layoff in early February 1939.

In Melbourne, we rented the whole downstairs of a house across the park from the theater, and actually had to break up a chest of drawers in order to have enough firewood. Billy and Willamae shared a room, because they were married. At first, so did Lucille and I since our romance was back on, but after we split up again, she roomed with Esther and Eunice and I moved in with Jerome and Snookie. Later, when Jerome broke it off with his showgirl girlfriend, he started living with an Australian woman he had begun seeing.

Opening night in each city was a major event that was often broadcast on the local radio station. Before the show began, some of the cast members would pull up in front of the theater in limousines and parade inside, decked out in evening gowns and tuxedos as if at a real Hollywood premiere, but also wearing lifelike masks that represented famous Hollywood stars such as Clark Gable, Myrna Loy, Greta Garbo, and Spencer Tracy. The male Lindy hoppers were the ushers holding the crowd back. As soon as these "stars" got inside, they'd go into the first number, which featured the Hollywood theme.

Everything about *Hollywood Hotel Revue* was spectacular: the sets, the costumes, the production numbers. The performers weren't famous because they hadn't starred in movies, but some of them were big on Broadway. I'd never heard of the comedian, Marty May, but he was hilarious. Unlike vaudeville shows, which are made up of a series of separate, unrelated acts, this was a real revue. It had a theme, each scene led into the next one, and each performing act was incorporated into their scene.[27] For example, before our first number, we were hidden under this huge set of stairs, which was the scenery for the act before ours. When our time came, the stairs separated and opened out to the sides of the stage, revealing the riverboat setting for our production number right in front of the audience. There we were, as if by magic. It always got a big hand.

We performed toward the end of the first act. Right after the lead female singer did a very tearful rendition of "Can't Help Lovin' Dat Man" from *Showboat,* we'd say, "Well, you're so sad, we're going to cheer you up," then start dancing. Our routine was similar to what we'd been doing since I'd first made up the big apple, except that for Australia I added an ensemble section at the end. During the Lindy solos, each couple might do specialty steps, jazz steps, or air steps. Of course, the audience thought our entire act was the big apple because that's the way we were billed, and they didn't know any better. They weren't doing the Lindy in Australia at the time.

I can't remember the music we used. They might have written some-thing just for this show, but it was hard to get the band to play at the right tempo. The revue's musical director had to hire local musicians, and the drummer wasn't used to playing as fast as we danced, so eventually he was replaced by someone they picked up in a nightclub. The other musicians also struggled. They'd say, "You expect us to play your music this fast. We can't even play it slowly!" They had these guys rehearsing for hours, until they got to the point where they could play fast enough for us to execute the choreography.

Everywhere we went, we got standing ovations and rave reviews. Here's a couple of examples from my albums:

> It is a revelation to watch the speed, dexterity, and symmetry of the eight original apple dancers . . . and the rounds of applause which follow the whirlwind finish prove without doubt its popularity with audiences.[28]

> But in this array of talent we almost overlooked the "sensation" of the show—those bounding colored bundles of terpsichorean energy, the Eight Apple Dancers, who flung themselves around the stage in an amazing dis-play of organized disorder and irresistible high spirits.[29]

Audiences and critics were so enthusiastic about our performances that I was asked to choreograph another number for the show. Eunice had the best voice in the group, and she used to like to sing Ella Fitzgerald's hit, "A-Tisket, A-Tasket" (which we had heard at the Savoy). This was the basis of our new jazz routine, which was a big success.

After an eight-bar introduction, during which we walked out onstage, Eunice would sing a chorus or two with the Lindy hoppers just moving in the background. When it got to the section where we sang, "Was it red?" and she answered, "No, no, no, no!" I had the dancers go out into the audience, and added some music so we could keep calling out different colors. If we came to somebody wearing a black sweater, we'd point to it and call out "Was it black?" to Eunice, who was still on stage, and she'd answer, "No, no, no, no!" It got a big hand. After we came back up onstage, we did a jazz routine for a chorus or two with all of us in a line behind Eunice. When she ended with, "Just a lit-tle yel-low bas-ket!" we all hit a final pose.

Even with the second routine added, this gig was a piece of cake for us. We did one show every night, including Sunday, and two matinees, so it was only nine shows a week. We didn't get paid extra, but we didn't give it a second thought. We were happy that they wanted to see more of us.

.... *Shines* ....

SHINES, ALSO KNOWN AS SPECIALTY OR SHOWOFF STEPS, are flashy moves with a strong character that makes them stand out from transitional steps like the basic Lindy swing-out. They can be inserted at any point, but often occur during a musical break and/or a separation between partners.

Shine steps may be gestural, acrobatic, or eccentric in nature. In the context of popular theatrical dance of the 1920s and 1930s, the term "eccentric" has a specific meaning. Eccentric dance, a subspecialty of some vaudevillian and jazz dancers, was a highly individualized, sometimes comical form, often with a distorted, grotesque, or acrobatic quality. Unusual physical abilities of the dancer were often exploited. In *Jazz Dance*, Stearns defines this genre as "a catchall for dancers who have their own nonstandard movements and sell themselves on their individual styles."[30]

One of the most famous demonstrations of eccentric dance is Ray Bolger's wobbly, seemingly out-of-control scarecrow fling in *The Wizard of Oz* to "If I Only Had a Brain." Less familiar, but equally wonderful examples are found in the two dance routines that precede the Lindy hop scene in *Radio City Revels*. Here, Melissa Mason's outrageously double-jointed hips allow her to do enormous, 360-degree leg circles. Buster West does anything and everything to entertain, including floor spins, now associated with break dancing, and oversized balletlike beats.

Individuals often became associated with certain shine steps. Frankie says, "Snookie was known for doing the lock, which he did in *Day at the Races* and on the Australia tour. Jerome did his comic thing where he gets booted in the face by Esther Washington. And Eunice shined on twists." (In the Lindy hop, twists are usually done by a woman, who might twitch her hips from side to side while circling her partner in a movement known as the twist-around, as well as during the basic swing-out.) "During our solo, Lucille and I generally focused on air steps." ●
....

Race Relations Down Under

Although I hardly saw any other African Americans in Australia except for the Dancing Chefs and this Golden Gloves boxer, we were very warmly received during our entire trip. We were the only black members of the cast, but we were completely accepted. Maybe it was because we were a novelty, but regardless of the reason, we were included in every cast party and dinner.

We used to have so many laughs with the singer, Magda Neeld, while we were waiting underneath the stairs before our scene. She'd be trying to get in the mood for this very sad song, and there we were throwing so many jokes at her that she'd have tears in her eyes from laughing so hard.

Each of us had a little line to say just before she started singing, and after a while we started changing it just to keep things from getting too monotonous. For instance, when she looked like she was crying, one of us was supposed to say, "Miss Julie, you don't have to do that. You can always get a man." Sometimes I would say my line and the next person's, so they'd be left with nothing and would have to make something up on the spot. If somebody stole my line, I'd just throw something else out. Sometimes we would mix the lines up and say stuff just to tease her. Like Eunice was supposed to say, "Don't cry, Miss Julie. He wasn't worth it anyway." But instead, she'd say, "Miss Julie, that guy was a bum. I don't see why you wanted him anyway." Poor Magda Neeld would be struggling not to crack up.

We were treated well in Australia, but I did see Aborigines being treated the same as we blacks were in America. They were excluded from places, and all that kind of stuff. In fact, it seemed like white folks there didn't want us associating with the Aborigines. No one ever came out and said it, but we were always kept apart. For example, one time I was standing in the theater lobby and this Aborigine walked in off the street and started talking to me. Right away, the manager came over, took me by the arm, and walked me away, saying that they needed me to do some publicity. Somebody always intervened. I think it was to keep the Aborigines from getting ideas from us, because we were doing better than they were.

As a matter of fact, I had a relationship with an Australian woman while I was on this tour. She was about ten years older than I was, and lived in a big apartment in Sydney. The producers sometimes gave parties with lots of society people, usually at some fabulous place. It was at one of these events that Anna Lee introduced herself and told me that she thought our act was terrific. After that night, she began to come backstage to watch the show from the wings, and each time we would chitchat.

A week later, she said she was throwing a party and all of the acts from the show were invited. We danced together at the party, a slow dance but a ballroom type of thing, not a slow drag, and I guess that's when I started feeling something for her. Soon after that, she said, "I'd like to see you sometime, but you know how it is here in Australia. I'm going to throw a big party out at my family's sheep ranch, and I want you and your group to come." She was saying that this was the only way we could see each other. We began spending time together at her parties, or sometimes by ourselves during the day. If anyone in the group had any suspicions, they never let on. There wasn't any problem with Lucille, because we had begun to drift apart after what happened in Paris, and by now it was completely over between us. After *Hollywood Hotel Revue* left Sydney, Anna Lee and I corresponded for a while, but I kind of let that fall off. She had talked to me about staying in Australia, but I couldn't have because, for one thing, I was bonded to leave by Australian regulations. (Only the black performers were; the producers put the money up.) And, of course, there wouldn't have been any future for us.

Throughout the tour, the producers made small changes to the show, but after our first engagement in Melbourne, they made some major ones. The biggest was that they replaced the headliners, comedians Willie and Eugene Howard, with two lesser-known veterans of Broadway, Bobby Morris and Murray Brisco, for much less money, I'm sure. This revamped version, billed as *Hollywood Hotel Review—Second Edition,* allowed the producers to book us for another month in Melbourne beginning on February 15, 1939, before we started touring again toward the end of March.

As I recall, *Hollywood Hotel Revue* returned to Sydney once more before heading back to America, but I didn't see Anna Lee this time. The cast had traveled to Australia in second class, but we sailed back in third class because the producers had begun to lose money toward the end. We arrived in New York harbor in spring 1939. After a year down under, when I got up to Harlem, it looked soooo dark . . . and soooo good!

10 • ON BROADWAY AND IN THE MOVIES

World's Fair

When we got back from Australia, Whitey had a bunch of dancers performing at the Savoy pavilion at the 1939 World's Fair in Flushing Meadows Park, Queens. I worked there for one day, but it was so grueling that I stopped. They were doing ten or twelve shows a day, plus ballyhoo for ten minutes before each show outside the theater, which was actually more like a tent.

People paid to see us, so we had to put on a full show, which included doing the cakewalk, Charleston, big apple, truckin', shim sham, Suzie-Q, boogies, and Lindy hop. It was exhausting, even though we didn't all perform every dance. It might have worked if we'd had morning and evening teams, as well as a separate crew to ballyhoo, but even though some of us protested, there was no way Whitey could do that. He would have had to turn work down, because by this time, he had more offers for jobs than he had dancers.

When I started out with Whitey, he would pick and choose his dancers based on how good they were, or on their potential. By late 1938 and into 1939, with eight of his top dancers touring Australia, it had gotten to where he needed a lot of bodies. People started asking to join the Lindy hoppers, and if you could swing out a little bit he'd put you in a group. There got to be a lot of people in Whitey's Lindy Hoppers who were not top-notch, although eventually many of them improved by performing with the better dancers and learning more steps and routines.

After I dropped out of the Savoy pavilion shows, I began filling in occasionally for some of the Lindy hoppers who were appearing in *Hot Mikado*, a swing version of Gilbert and Sullivan's operetta that was running at the Hall of Music, a huge theater at the World's Fair. It starred Bill Robinson in the title role. Michael Todd, the producer, had opened *Hot Mikado* on Broadway earlier in the year, but without any Lindy hoppers, I believe.[1]

The main Lindy number was part of a scene where the king (the Mikado) calls for his dancers. There were six couples.[2] Since I wasn't a regular—I just gave some of the Lindy hoppers a break if they wanted a night off—I don't remember the routine or know who choreographed it. I do remember that Bill Robinson said the Lindy hoppers could take care of the audience in the first act, and he would take care of them in the second half.

It was around this time that Chick Webb passed away. He had been in a lot of pain for much of his life. When he died of tuberculosis it was a very sad occasion because we all knew him.[3]

When Whitey's Lindy Hoppers had their first engagement at the Paramount Theater on Broadway, in the late '30s, they were on the bill with Chick Webb and Ella Fitzgerald. I created and staged a routine for this team of dancers, but didn't perform with them because I had another job. The stage at the Paramount was very wide, but it had a shallow apron, which is where the Lindy hoppers had to perform, and the band was set up in center stage, just behind this apron. Chick Webb, who had his drums right down in front, was scared that we were going to kick them while we were dancing, so he kept telling us, "Don't you kids touch my drum! Watch out for my drums!"

Because of this, I devised a way for the group to avoid him by traveling back and forth across the stage diagonally, rather than going upstage and downstage, front to back. While we were rehearsing the crossover Charleston, I would holler out, "Switch," to signal the dancers that they should change direction from one angle to the other. Yes, Chick could be salty at times, but he was fine.

Sometime in late 1939, while I was still dancing with Lucille, Whitey's Lindy Hoppers also made the movie *Keep Punching*,[4] but I don't remember doing it. Whitey must have said, "Come on with me, we've got a gig," and we just went. (I also don't remember making *Outline of Jitterbug History*, which we filmed in the early '40s, before *Hellzapoppin'*. It's the same dancers in both pictures.)

Swingin' the Dream

Next up for the Lindy hoppers was the Broadway production *Swingin' the Dream*, which opened on November 29, 1939 at the Center Theatre near Sixth Avenue on 49th Street.[5] This was a swing version of Shakespeare's *A Midsummer Night's Dream* with all these fabulous stars, and stars of the future: the Benny Goodman Sextet, Louis Armstrong, Maxine Sullivan, Dorothy Dandridge and her two sisters, and Butterfly McQueen, just to name some.

Whitey's Jitterbugs, as we were called, danced in three numbers. (Savoy dancers never used the term "jitterbug," although it had been around for a while and was coming out strong by the late '30s.) We did backup movements behind the Dandridge Sisters to "Swingin' A Dream," appeared in a production number with the chorus girls, and did a Lindy hop routine by ourselves to "Jumpin' at the Woodside," as played by the pit orchestra. We were wood fairies, little creatures of the forest. Our dark green costumes had small reflective patches sewn all over so we looked like little flickering bugs in the woods. When we hit the stage, we lit it up.

At the beginning of the big Lindy scene, we were all hidden behind hedges, bushes, and trees.[6] George Greenidge and I had the idea to position ourselves on these high platforms that were on opposite sides of the stage, so it looked as if we were actually up in the trees. When the curtain opened, we jumped to the ground, went right into rollovers, then did all these acrobatic moves like running up the sides of the trees and leaping back down. While we were doing all this crazy stuff, the others were flitting in and out of the forest. It was very exciting, and made for some sensational dancing.

There were so many couples, thirteen in all, that every team didn't get to have a solo.[7] Only about six of the most established teams did individual work, usually the same ones,[8] but some nights we gave others a chance. The rest, newcomers to Whitey's Lindy Hoppers, were in the background clapping, shouting, and jumping around. Everybody danced in the ensemble section at the end, but we had to stagger the lines to have enough room.

Dottiemae Johnson really wasn't an ideal partner for me, but Whitey told me to work with her anyway because she didn't have one. I hate to say this, but she almost ruined my career. I had just created the step where the girl kicks the fellow in the behind, kick-in-the-pants, which you see in *Hellzapoppin'* and *Hot Chocolate*. One day in rehearsal, she kicked me right in the crotch with the point of her foot. She must have ruptured something, because I practically had to crawl home that night. I was laid up for a few days afterwards, and it was a while before I could walk normally. When the show ended, I started dancing with someone else.

I remember that I really wanted to do *Swingin' the Dream* because it was a Broadway show that had a lot of great musicians, and also because one of my idols, Leroy "Stretch" Jones, was in it. Shorty Snowden's group had broken up, so Whitey invited Leroy and Little Bea to be in the show. Since I was the dance captain, it was my job to teach them the choreography, but it was very difficult. They had performed that one number for so long that it was hard for them to learn anything else. Little Bea did all right, but Leroy had trouble getting the ensemble section down because he wasn't used to dancing in unison with other couples. And he had a rough time adjusting to the new style of Lindy hopping with the bending over horizontally and the wildness. He and Little Bea danced more sedately. It was frustrating, because I looked up to Leroy. He had influenced my dancing so much that I wanted to help him switch over to our style. I worked with him a lot, but even though he had danced his whole life, he just couldn't change.

The program says, "Dances by Agnes de Mille" and "Jitterbugs by Herbert White," but I actually did all of the choreography for the Lindy hoppers. We came in knowing our specialty, but after we began rehearsals I had to choreograph the two jazz routines. Occasionally Agnes de Mille asked that the Lindy hoppers dance in a certain spot on the stage, but that was the only direction she gave us.

While we were still in rehearsal, she asked Whitey about giving this group of gospel singers in the show some movements to do while they were singing. Whitey sent her to me, and she explained that she wanted me to stage the scene with a religious feel to it. I said I needed to hear the song first.[9] I can't remember the title, but it had lyrics about climbing and climbing, so I choreographed some arm movements that went with that. I didn't give them any body movements because that would get them out of breath. After that, she started coming directly to me instead of Whitey.

Agnes de Mille was very nice to work with, as were a lot of other people in the cast. Most of the other dancers were ballet or modern dancers because that's the kind of choreography she did. They liked watching us rehearse and perform because we were always having so much fun that it was contagious.

I didn't see Benny Goodman around much, but Louis Armstrong was a very friendly guy, very loveable, with a wonderful personality. I'll just say that he was a great man. A lot of times, he would sit off in a corner by himself, just practicing on his horn. Slowly, some of the other musicians in the show would drift over to listen. They'd just stand there keeping time, and before you knew it they would take out their instruments and a jam session would begin that was something else. He also used to like to watch us rehearse. I remember him standing in the wings, trumpet in hand, patting his feet, with a big smile on his face, like he was really enjoying our dancing.

Swingin' the Dream was not a big hit. It lasted less than two weeks.[10] It must have been very expensive to produce since it was kind of top-heavy with stars, and people weren't filling up the place because we didn't get very good reviews. I thought it was a pretty good show and was disappointed when it closed but, what the heck, I just went on back up to the Savoy to dance.

My Last Harvest Moon Ball

Whitey's Lindy Hoppers worked constantly throughout 1940, including at Radio City Music Hall, where we performed at a benefit for Bundles for Britain.[11] This charitable event, billed as a night of four hundred movie stars, featured performers like Bill Robinson, Judy Garland, and Mickey Rooney, and was attended by a very moneyed, black-tie audience.

The first time a Lindy hop group had ever played Radio City Music Hall was shortly after we came back from France. The theater didn't hire many outside acts because they mostly used their own people. We were in a scene that came after the movie and was part of a full stage show with the Rockettes and corps de ballet. I hadn't started dancing regularly with Lucille yet, so I may have worked with Ann Johnson for this. Willamae and Russell Williams were the other couple. The end of our routine was a cue for the next performer, Robert Merrill (I think), to come out. When we landed the last step, ace-in-the-hole, he was supposed to step onstage and say, "Stop! Stop! Do you want to go to heaven or do you want to go to hell?!"

On opening day, we did our routine as planned. Merrill came out at the end and said, "Stop!" but he couldn't get to the next line because the audience was still applauding. He must have said it about four times. Eventually, he just backed offstage and waited in the wings. In the meantime, the stage manager was signaling us to keep dancing, so we did an encore. We made sure to end with the same step, so that Merrill would know when to come back on. This time, he looked right at the audience as he said, "Stop!" which made them laugh. It was the only way he could get through his lines. Finally, he was able to start singing, and we drifted off the stage.

After the first show, the producer gathered his staff and all of the performers together, like they usually do on opening day, to tell everybody what was wrong or what they wanted to change. When he got to the Lindy hoppers, he said, "We don't have anything to say to you guys. It was wonderful."

It's so funny, because when we first started rehearsing at Radio City Music Hall, all these muckety-muck ballet dancers would hardly speak to us lowly Lindy hoppers. But after the opening, whenever we rode up in the elevators with them to our dressing rooms, they would congratulate us on the show and applaud silently. In fact, we became very friendly with some of the classical dancers, and even took several of them up to the Savoy because they wanted to learn how to Lindy hop.

One thing that stands out in 1940 was the Harvest Moon Ball, my last. (The program for the 1939 Harvest Moon Ball lists me as a competitor, but I didn't enter that year. Whitey sometimes made last-minute substitutions and did not or could not change the names with the competition authorities, so those programs weren't always completely accurate.) He had to talk me into competing in 1940 because by then I thought I was a professional. But Whitey felt that even though he had about fifty Lindy hoppers by this time, they weren't all up to par. He was adamant that the only way to win was to send in his best dancers.

Whitey had already gotten two of his top teams to enter: Norma and Billy Ricker, and Wilda Crawford and Thomas "Tops" Lee. He was able to convince me that he really needed me by pointing out that the other ballrooms were gaining on us like crazy, so I agreed to compete with Ann Johnson, who I'd started partnering with after *Swingin' the Dream*.

Ann had been dancing for quite a while. From the beginning, she was considered a good, although not spectacular, dancer, but she had really come along by the time we started working together. Ann was like a cat. You could throw her in the air all kinds of ways, but she would always land solid and come down right on the beat. And it didn't matter what step I did, she was always right there with me. Ann quickly became my favorite partner of all time.

As luck would have it, the six of us ended up in the same heat at the Harvest Moon Ball. As planned, we started out doing our own individual thing, but then, just like in 1936, instead of every man for himself, we did an ensemble routine together. I don't remember which routine because there were so many by then, but we tore up the house! The Lindy hoppers had been allowed to do whatever they wanted at the Harvest Moon Ball since 1937, so we included air steps and acrobatics and even formed a horse at the end. Tops and Wilda won first place. Ann and I came in second. Norma and Billy took third.

Every year after the Harvest Moon Ball, Ed Sullivan featured the winning couple from each type of dance in a one-week engagement at Loew's State Theatre in Times Square. All of the winners except us (I have no idea why) were seated at tables along the back of the stage, as if they were the audience in a nightclub. Each team went out and performed their particular dance, then sat down. The Lindy hoppers performed last.

Instead of taking just Tops and Wilda, Ed Sullivan invited all six of us because he had seen us compete as an ensemble. We did the same routine, but had Billy and Norma solo first, followed by Ann and me. Tops and Wilda went last because they had taken first place. Now, they were very good dancers, but we were more spectacular. Ann and I did air steps and comedy, and when Billy got through doing the shake-around with Norma (a movement they made up), it was tough for anybody to come behind that.[12] So after the first show, Ed Sullivan said that Tops and Wilda should go first. We put Billy and Norma second and, as usual, my partner and I closed the act because our finishing step went smoothly into the ensemble section and, being more athletic than the other dancers, I had very good wind.

After the Loew's gig was over, the Lindy hoppers went on the road with Ed Sullivan for a few weekends around New York and New Jersey. I remember that it was just us because the advertising for the gig said "Harvest Moon Ball champions," and the couple who had won the title of All-Around Champions for that year and performed with us at Loew's got confused and turned up at the first show.

The Daring Young Dancers

I've always felt that ballroom dancing is very male-oriented because the man leads and the woman follows. It was pretty much the same thing with the Lindy hop, especially in the beginning. You always heard how good the guy was, never the girl. She was in the supporting role while the man got to take more liberties. He got to do a lot of footwork, but her feet just kept time as if she was his rhythm section. It was kind of a macho thing.

I had started learning the girl's part way back with Herman and, personally, I always felt that the women should be able to do exactly what the guys did. At some point, I discovered that if you did the same steps *with* your partner, it would actually make a bigger statement, so I began asking whoever I was dancing with if they could mimic me. Mickey Jones was one of the better dancers and quick at catching steps before the other girls, so I often called her over to try doing the guy's footwork, like the scissors, heels, and the kick-away.

Maybe because there's always been more individualism in the Lindy hop than in other ballroom dances, I also realized that my partner could perform the steps we had both been doing on her own. As an experiment, I told Mickey to do the slipslop, but I didn't do it in order to see what happened. It worked, and the other girls started to pick up on this and improvise more movements on their own. I also started to make up variations on steps that I thought would show off the girls, so they weren't just doing swing-outs, in order to give them a chance to shine on their own.

There's a big difference between dancing in a ballroom and getting up on stage. When you're dancing socially, you can do whatever you want.

Professional dancing is all about entertaining people. As an entertainer, I was always trying to please the audience, to make them laugh or bring them up out of their seats.

The Lindy hoppers would do almost anything to make our act look wild and excite people, but we still had to be excellent and know what we were doing, just like a clown who belly flops off a diving board has to be an excellent diver first. Or like Victor Borge, who does all those funny things at the piano, but can play seriously if someone asks him to.

The late '30s was my most adventurous period. Although I had tried to make the act exciting from the beginning, by that time I was coming up with all kinds of crazy things. One of my ideas turned out to be very embarrassing, but what the heck—I'll tell you anyway.

When we were working at the Cotton Club with the Berry Brothers, they did this stunt where they jumped off a platform, leaped over the whole band, and landed in a split on the stage. It was sensational! Later that year, while we were appearing at the Apollo Theatre, I got the bright idea to try doing the same thing with the Erskine Hawkins band. The Apollo didn't have a platform that I could leap off of, but I had noticed that there was a bit of space on the bench that Avery Parrish, the piano player, sat on. I figured that if I ran from the backstage area to build some momentum, then used the bench for leverage, I could vault over the piano and the band.

I didn't tell anybody about my plan, or rehearse it, but at the next performance when Erskine Hawkins brought his hand down at the beginning of our song, I came running onstage, hit that bench, and flew above the piano . . . but I didn't quite make it over the band. No, I landed on top of the saxophone players' music stands! I scattered their books all over the stage! *Uh-ohh*, I thought, and frantically started scrounging around for their music, putting it anywhere I could—on the wrong stands, in the hands of the wrong players—while the audience was laughing their heads off.

At first the band was in shock because they didn't realize what had happened, but once they did they thought it was hilarious. They were used to playing in clubs and weren't actually reading the sheet music anyway, so they just kept blowing and cracking up at the same time. The Lindy hoppers, who were cutting up, tried to stay out of my way and keep going while I ran all over the place grabbing papers and hollering, "Keep dancing! Keep dancing!" After the show, Mr. Schiffman, who owned the Apollo, came over and said, "That was great. Are you going to keep it in?" "Hell, no!" I said. I was lucky I didn't break my neck.

Sometimes, even if I thought the antics I had come up with were good, they didn't get the reaction I hoped for. After all, people didn't always like the same things that I did. Occasionally, one audience might go for a certain step, but another on the same day at the same theater might not be as enthusiastic. At first, I would keep doing the movement whether everyone liked it or not, but after a while, if the majority didn't respond, I would drop the step.

Around 1937 or '38, I developed another step that I continued doing right through my time with the Congaroos. The idea came from seeing comedian Dusty Fletcher, who was the king of pratfalls and always got a lot of laughs. The stage at the Apollo was low enough and close enough to the audience that the people sitting in the front row could easily see what was happening up there and, unlike in most theaters, there weren't any footlights at the front. At the end of one show, when the Lindy hoppers came running out for our second or third curtain call, I suddenly decided that I would purposely trip and slide off the stage. I had noticed this young lady sitting in the first row, and I designed my movements so that I landed right at her feet. I sat there for a moment looking into her eyes, while the guy who was sitting next to her glared at me. Then I said, "Excuse me, ma'am," slowly climbed back up, waved good-bye, and walked across the stage with a limp as if I were injured. Just before I got to the wings, I straightened up, eyeballed the audience with a big smile on my face, and ran off . . . all just to get a laugh, which it did.

I didn't do that bit every time I played the Apollo, but I did it there quite often, and occasionally at the Royal Theatre in Baltimore. It all depended on the stage setup and whether I saw a woman in the audience who was acceptable. I'd have to size her up and decide if I thought she wouldn't be offended.

Another move I introduced at the Apollo was "the swim." It resembled something I'd seen a couple do during a movie scene with lots of people enjoying themselves at a picnic in a park. The movement I came up with is actually a floor step. The girl lays face down on top of the guy's knees so her head is over his feet. While he slides along the floor on his back, she does a breaststroke movement, so it looks like she's swimming up and down through the waves.

Before Lucille and I did it for first time, I asked her if she could hold some water in her mouth for a few bars. She wasn't too sure, but agreed to try. As soon as we started swinging out, the water began leaking out of her mouth! I could see that she was trying to tell me she couldn't hold it any longer, but she couldn't talk, so I said, "Let's do the step *now*." Lucille tried to spew out what was left in her mouth as we slid along the floor bobbing up and down, but we just got the stage all wet. It was hilarious!

Later on, we did the swim in a contest over at the Savoy, but without the water, which we never used again. Naturally, all the other Lindy hoppers wanted to learn this new movement since it was something different. We only used the swim a few more times. It seemed like a finishing step to me, so I always put it at the end of our solo, but it didn't really work as a lead-in to the ensemble section because it was hard to get up and start dancing after doing the swim.

Many of the other dancers developed specialties to distinguish themselves and wow the crowd. As Dawn Hampton, my good friend and one of my favorite dance partners today, likes to point out, "All of the Lindy hoppers at the Savoy had their own individual style. It's not like everyone was going to class and learning someone else's way of dancing." A lot of the girls came up with their own way of swinging out. Some would back away from their partner; others would go out facing away from him, then flip around—whatever fit their fancy. No one ever told them they weren't doing the Lindy just because their swing-out was different.

Joyce and Joe Daniels developed a swing-out that became known as "the submarine." He'd bend down so low that his left arm was coming up from the floor as he pushed her so forcibly that she'd shoot out. It was almost like what we call the whip today. We'd say, "Man, you submarining that girl!"

Eunice Callen had a very low-down and funky twist. She would twist down to the ground into almost a sitting position, and keep on twisting from there. She used to do that with Billy Ricker, so we always gave them steps that would show off her twisting ability.

I don't know who created cradle-round-the-back,[13] but Tops and Wilda added to it when they invented a step called the "wrap-around," where the guy continues wrapping the girl around him a couple of times.[14]

As I've mentioned, Snookie Beasley's specialty was a step he called "the lock," in which he twists his legs around each other like a pretzel very quickly while leaning against his partner for support.[15] We all tried it, but none of us had the finesse that Snookie did. He would hit that step—SHOMP!—hold it for a beat or two, then come out of it and start dancing.

Al Minns had a talent for doing what we called "rubber legs." Because his legs were so flexible, he could twist them all kinds of ways and toss them this way and that while doing high kicks. The term came from an eccentric dancer named Rubberlegs Williams, who would flash his legs around and do all kinds of stuff with them.[16]

Sometimes, we used to say that a person doing rubber legs had "crazy legs," which wasn't always a compliment. If you did rubber legs, you did it on purpose. It was a more specific phrase and it was always a compliment. Saying someone had crazy legs might also mean that he didn't have any control over them. We applied the name crazy legs to Al because he was a very talented dancer with fantastic rhythm. He could wiggle his legs around and stretch them out until they seemed longer than they really were, what we used to call legomania. Whitey suggested that I work with Al to encourage him to use his special ability, so I gave him routines where he could really express himself with his legs, really show them off. I'd say, "Use those legs! Don't keep 'em down." It kind of changed his style of dancing.[17]

Billy Ricker, who was an idea man, was known for a routine he created with Esther Washington for a contest at the Savoy after we came back from Australia. One Saturday night, the two of them swung out onto the floor, and that was the *only* swing-out they did during the entire routine. There were quite a few air steps by this time, and Billy and Esther did all of them, one after another. He was throwing her up and down, through his legs, around his back . . . everywhere! They must have rehearsed the routine off in a corner by themselves someplace, because nobody knew about it.

It took them about a minute and a half to go through all those air steps, which they were both great at. Esther was so light and buoyant she could do air steps with anybody. The whole time, people were screaming. Even the other Lindy hoppers were hollering, "Look at Billy and Esther go, man! Wow!" When they came off the floor, the house roared.

As soon as he came over to me, I said, "Billy, that's *mutiny!*" It was a joke. I meant that it was mutiny to the Lindy hop because they didn't do any Lindy hopping, just air steps. Everybody else picked up on it and started calling the routine "mutiny" also. It was one of the few that actually had a name. The big apple and my first routine, the stops, were two others. Usually, we would just say "the number one group's routine" or "the number three group's routine." (It wasn't until the 1980s that I discovered that when Al Minns returned to New York after touring Rio with Whitey's Lindy Hoppers in the early '40s, he began calling the routine we did for *Hellzapoppin'* the "California routine," and the name stuck with Lindy hoppers at the Savoy.)

When Billy and Esther repeated mutiny the following Saturday, it didn't get as big a response, which is very interesting. That second time didn't excite me as much either because I began to feel like it needed more swinging out. Even so, after that most of the dancers who entered Lindy contests started looping more than one air step together, with swing-outs or floor steps in between.

Billy, George Greenidge, and I turned mutiny into an ensemble dance by working out the girls' parts so we could show it to them, and adding some very intricately choreographed spots where we switched partners *while* doing air steps. I only performed mutiny once or twice. To be honest, I wasn't crazy about going out there and just doing air steps. I wanted to swing.

On Choreography

In mid-1941, Whitey got a contract to send a group of Lindy hoppers to California to be in the movie version of *Hellzapoppin'*.[18] The Broadway play was written by and had starred the comedy team Olsen and Johnson. Even though the show didn't get very good reviews, it had a pretty good run.[19] The group Norma was in had performed in *Hellzapoppin'* in Boston, but they were cut before it came to New York.[20] So the producers already knew about the Lindy hoppers when they began casting the movie.

Whitey chose the three 1940 Harvest Moon Ball winners to make *Hellzapoppin'*. Since the contract was for four teams, he added Mickey Jones and William Downes. Before we started rehearsing, Whitey told the group that I was in charge and gave me complete authority right in front of them. We had two weeks until we had to leave, so we all sat down and had a talk. I told everybody that I didn't want to make something up on the spot when we got out to California, like with the first two movies. I didn't want Hollywood looking down on Lindy hoppers the way so much of show business did, so I had decided it would be more professional if we had a routine ready by the time we hit the coast. I wanted to show the producers the best we had. Everyone agreed to practice every day, and that they better have a *damn* good excuse if they missed a rehearsal. I made it clear that if they didn't, they were out ... period. We were all excited about being in the movie, and started practicing for three or four hours a day.

I had decided to make up a routine, but didn't want to show up at the first rehearsal totally blank, so before we started I listened to the music I was planning to use and pictured the steps that I thought would go with each particular sound. When I'm choreographing, the first thing I think about is the music. It's my inspiration. Usually I work from a recording. On rare occasions, I might make up a step to a swing tune that I'm humming.

My goal is for the audience to see the dancers and musicians working in synch. The majority of what I do is accent certain beats, phrases, or sounds with a movement. Like, I might kick my leg out just as the drummer hits a downbeat. I'm pretty good at phrasing steps into musical rhythms, and I'm partial to movements that go smoothly into the next one or end with a break. Most of all, I want to emphasize riffs that the band is playing.

Choreography should match the style, time period, setting, and mood of the music. If the song has words, I try to come up with movements that are suggested by the lyrics. For example, when Chazz and I do the shim sham to "'Tain't What You Do," we act out the words in the song as sung by Trummy Young and the Jimmie Lunceford Orchestra.

Sometimes I want to portray a particular attitude that's suggested by a spot in the music. When I was a teenager, I used to see these pimps hanging out behind the Apollo Theatre who had this special rhythmic stride that seemed almost natural to them. As they walked, they actually bent over at the waist, with one hand laid on their back and the other swinging in rhythm. It looked like they were doing it for show, maybe when they were walking up to a group of friends or to their girlfriend, but it got to be a habit with some of them. All the kids thought it was so cool.

Eventually, I injected the pimp walk (as we called it) into the Lindy hop. I usually have my partner face me and do the fishtail backward with her arm extended so her hand is pushing on my forehead. It's as if she's saying, "No, I don't want you that close to me," and I'm saying, "Oh, baby . . . c'mon." We try to perform it in such a way that the audience can understand our unspoken conversation.

At other times, I want to express a certain feeling to the audience. There's a step I made up in recent years in which my partner strolls behind me and runs her hand down my back, as I shuffle forward. My arms are stretched way out to the sides, and I roll my head from side to side, as if I'm laying on a beach enjoying the cool breeze trickling down my spine. I like to call that step "ecstasy."

For *Hellzapoppin'*, I started from the beginning of "Jumpin' at the Woodside" and worked with about sixteen bars at a time, choreographing both the solos and the ensemble section as we went along. (Basie used to stay at the Woodside Hotel on 142nd Street when he played at the Savoy, and some of the jam sessions there inspired the song.) I hate to keep saying *I* choreographed this and *I* choreographed that because it makes me seem egotistical, but for *Hellzapoppin'* I set up a routine for each team. Even though we all knew the same steps, I wanted each couple's solo to look different from the others. If you watch the scene, you'll see that nobody repeats what anyone else does.

It's important to start out with an exciting entrance so you catch the audience from the beginning, and I always try to save the most spectacular movement for the climax of each specialty because you want to keep the excitement up and finish strong. Downes and Mickey, the first couple to dance, start off with several steps they already knew, but they finish with the foot pitch, where he lies on the floor and flips her over by pitching her with his foot into a somersault. I think *Hellzapoppin'* was the first time this very spectacular step was performed. George Greenidge and I had seen a balancing act do the foot pitch and we had recently adapted it. As soon as we perfected it, I gave it to Downes and Mickey because I knew it would be a good climax to their solo.

The upside-down step that I told Willamae and Al (the third team) to do, where she holds him in a handstand, was a very exciting ending for their specialty. (Al and Mildred Pollard made that one up.) I also gave them the movement that Norma and George made up (it doesn't have a name) where the guy spins around with his leg held out horizontal to the floor while the girl ducks down under him each time he pivots.[21]

I wasn't that particular about which move Ann and I ended our routine with, because a lot of ours made good finishing steps. The important thing was that we be in a position to go right into the ensemble section since we went last. Much of Ann's and my routine had already been choreographed by the time we started rehearsing for *Hellzapoppin'*.[22]

Toward the end of our routine, we did the snatch, which is where Ann jumps up toward me as I pull her to my right shoulder. It doesn't work if she actually aims for my shoulder. She has to leap upward, and at that moment I snatch her toward me. I always took two steps back to make her movement cover more distance, so the shape of the picture we were making was elongated and more exciting. The snatch (which I made up, but I think was inspired by the head snatch) was one of the few air steps that nobody else could do. They tried, but it never seemed to come out exactly right.

Right after the snatch, we did the slide-through. I had gotten the idea for it from the slide-through-and-pull-back (now known as the shoot-through), which I did not make up and was already being done. I thought it would be comical for the girl to pop through my legs and keep sliding. Lucille had done the slide-through briefly in a contest, but Ann was the first one to perform it professionally. When she did this move for thirty shows a week at theaters like the Apollo, which had a very rough floor, she wore out so many pairs of panties that she tried sewing a leather patch onto the bottom of her costume. Later, she started having extra sets of underpants made to go with each costume.

To finish our routine, we did the head snatch, which is different from the snatch, like I said. I'm pretty sure that Russell Williams originated the head snatch with Connie Hill. They were fantastic at it.[23] The girl stands behind the fellow, who reaches over his shoulder with his right hand and grabs her by the back of her neck. Then she pushes off the floor as he flips her forward, causing her to land in front with her back to him. To make it more comical, I changed the head snatch around so that Ann snatched me, which is generally how Lindy hoppers do the step today.

When I'm making up a routine, the movements that I picture in my head often don't look good or feel right when I actually do them, so I mess around until I work things out or come up with something else. If there are still problems when I have other dancers try out the steps, I'll make more adjustments. For *Hellzapoppin'*, we tried lots of things one way, then another to see if we could make them work a little better. And at this early stage, when everyone was still learning the choreography, people made suggestions which I'd either accept, reject, or use elsewhere.

Each solo had to be exactly one chorus long, thirty-two bars. The Lindy hoppers knew rhythm and beats, but they didn't know much about choruses, so I made them repeat their specialty over and over until they became familiar with the amount of time they had. That way, they wouldn't have to worry about it. All they had to do was dance.

Showdown with Tops

One day, Tops and Wilda didn't show up for rehearsal. They didn't call to say they were sick or give any other reason, so I went to Whitey and told him that I wanted to replace them. He asked who I had in mind. After thinking it over, I suggested Willamae and Al. They were both great dancers, they looked good together, and I thought that it would be nice for the Rickers to be together in California since they were married. Mac said that was fine.

Now, Tops and I were not very friendly, for two reasons. First of all, Tops thought he was king of the hill for winning the Harvest Moon Ball. Only a couple of the winners acted like this because most of us felt we were just representing the Savoy. We rarely looked upon any one person as the very best, since there were a lot of good dancers and any of them might cut into another's lead on a given night. Tops's head had gotten so swelled that he figured he could do whatever he wanted, and he resented that I was in charge of the group.

In general, I didn't envy the other Lindy hoppers, but I was very competitive. For example, I always wanted to be able to do all the steps that everybody else did. One time, Norma, who always had a knack for comedy, was clowning around while she was dancing, and Whitey said, "Girl, you're good *and* you're funny." I remember thinking, *I can be funny too so Whitey will say that about me.* He must have sensed how I felt, because he said, "Oh, yeah, you're funny too, Frankie."

The other reason Tops and I didn't get along too well was because of Lucille. Tops met Lucille right after we got back from Australia and was attracted to her immediately. At first, she rejected him because she wanted to marry me, but I just wasn't ready for that. Tops wanted to fight me for her, but I explained that I didn't fight over girls. My feeling was that even if you win, it doesn't mean she'll go with you. I told him that if he wanted to have a personal fight just to see who was the best, we could do that anytime.

Eventually Lucille and Tops became involved, and she and I stopped performing with each other because he didn't like us dancing together. By the time we started working on *Hellzapoppin'*, they had gotten married, but I don't think it worked out in the end. I don't know why Lucille and Tops never performed together, but Lucille didn't do that much dancing after we got back from Australia.

The day after Tops and Wilda missed practice, they showed up at the Savoy and just started dancing as if nothing had happened. I said, "You're not going to California, so you don't need to rehearse." Tops wanted to know why, and when I reminded him about our agreement, he got very angry. But my feeling was that if I let them back in, everyone else would think they could miss rehearsal.

Right away, Tops went to Mr. Buchanan to protest. I guess he thought the Savoy's manager had more clout than Whitey, and he knew Buchanan liked him. Buchanan went to Whitey, who said that he had put me in charge and that if I decided Tops couldn't go, that was it. Mac told him that since I was taking the group to Hollywood, I was the one who was going to have to contend with them.

The next day, Tops showed up at the Savoy with his two brothers. The three of them wanted to gang up on me. I said, "Look, Tops, if you want to fight, that's okay. But if you think you can't handle me alone, then I'll just have to tangle with all three of you. You guys might kick my ass, but you're going to know you were in a fight." In the meantime, somebody had gone and gotten Whitey, who came running to the ballroom and wanted to know what was going on. He told the brothers to get their butts out of there, then sat down to talk with Tops and Wilda, who started pleading to come back in. But Whitey explained that the rules were the rules. Tops continued to work for Whitey, but we never reconciled. In fact, I don't think that I ever saw him again after I came back from California.

It didn't take Willamae and Al very long to catch up with the rest of the group. I had put the routine together in a few days, but getting it down precisely, getting everybody to hear the same music, to think together, was the difficult part. One of the biggest challenges was that we had more air steps in the ensemble section of *Hellzapoppin'* than we had ever done in unison before. Although air steps had become a staple in the group section, up until this point we usually just did one or two as a way to finish. Most were done by couples in their solos.

Air steps shouldn't be thrown in just anywhere. They should be emphasized and should always be done *with* the music, like any other step. For example, if a musician is taking a hot solo with a lot of high notes and you can hear a high C coming up, you might want to throw the girl over your head so she hits that note at the same time. You can also cap off a step, a Charleston for example, by finishing up a musical phrase with an air step.

In those days, unlike nowadays, when we rehearsed a routine we executed all of the air steps every single time. There was no faking it. It's okay to learn them first, but when you're running the choreography, the air steps *have* to go in there, otherwise you're not really doing the routine. I think one of the reasons so many people get injured doing air steps today is that they practice them separately.

Even with Whitey's Lindy Hoppers, it was a challenge to get the air steps synchronized because each couple did them a little differently than the others. Some anticipated the beat, landed at the wrong time, or threw or pulled their partner too hard. If there was a problem, I made everyone repeat the movement until they were doing it the same way. Of course, there were little arguments, but we worked things out. I guess I was being a bit of a perfectionist—we rehearsed very, very hard—but we all wanted to get it down pat for the movie.

Hellzapoppin'

In early fall 1941, we headed out to California again. It was my third trip there in four years. This time we took the train. On our first day at the studio, Nick Castle, a great tap dancer who had worked with the Nicholas Brothers and was now Universal's dance director, came by to meet us. When he asked if we had a routine ready, I felt proud to be able to say that we did. I knew the kids were ready, so I put on "Jumpin' at the Woodside" and we ran through it.

Afterwards, Castle said, "That's good. Leave it as it is." Then, almost as an afterthought, he said, "Do you guys know how to do the splits?" Fortunately, I had foreseen that this might happen because, at the time, a lot of dance teams were including splits, knee drops, and that sort of thing in their acts. I had actually made up two endings. The first finished with the horses, which is what we had just done. The other ended with the guys jumping over the girls and landing in splits, followed by the girls doing the same thing over the guys, which we showed him the second time around. He told us it looked great and chose that because the other group had ended with horses in *Day at the Races*.

Although Castle visited the set occasionally after that, he never stayed long, and that was the only thing he suggested to me besides showing us the boundaries of the area we would be dancing in. Naturally, he got credit for staging the dances, but at the time, I never even thought about it. As far as I was concerned, it was wonderful just to be making a movie.

By the second day, the musical director at Universal started sitting in on rehearsals to listen to the music and watch us dance. His job was to create a composition for our number so the studio wouldn't have to get permission to use Count Basie's song. As we went through the routine repeatedly, he started writing an original score that fit the choreography and really emphasized certain movements we did. Within a week, he had finished, and the studio band made a recording of his composition, which is what we rehearsed to from then on. We used that when we filmed the scene and, as far as I can tell, that's what's on the soundtrack of the movie.

All in all, it took two weeks to make *Hellzapoppin'*. We rehearsed four or five hours a day for over a week in a studio at Universal, but we actually filmed the Lindy hop scene in just three days. It took the director and the cameraman much of that time to figure out the best way to film us, since they had no experience with the kind of dancing we did, which was fast and traveled across the stage.

What you see in the movie was not a straight run-through. In those days, filmmakers didn't have multiple cameras that move all over the place on dollies and lifts or are strapped onto a cameraman who travels around you. Back then, they used only one camera. The crew set it up in a certain position, then looked through the lens while we just stood there. When they found a shot they liked, they put on the music and filmed us doing the whole routine. The entire process was repeated over and over, with the camera situated in different places, until they got all of the angles they wanted. When the film was edited, they used the best shots in the final cut.

Even though we were exhausted from so many takes, we somehow summoned up our energy to get through the last shots at the end of each day. By the way, the movements we did in the background were not choreographed and they were not repeated exactly for each take.

The only part of the shoot that was really difficult for me was executing the step Ann and I did near the end of our routine, where she kicks me in the pants and I go flying across the floor. When we first practiced it at the

Savoy, Ann was very tentative about kicking me. She would hesitate and then just push lightly. Once we got to California and started rehearsing at Universal, I said, "Look, Ann, we're making the movie now, so I want you to really haul off and kick me."

She didn't want to: "Frankie, I'm going to hurt you."

"It's only one take," I told her, "so make it look real, and do it in time with the music." The next time we went through the routine, I really felt her foot on my butt, and I went flying. The force of it actually helped propel me forward, more so than from what I was doing on my own. At first, I thought, *That's great.* Then the director asked us to do the scene over. We had to do the same step again . . . and again and again! I don't know how many takes they ended up doing, but it seemed like a million. Each time it felt like Ann was kicking me harder, as if to say, "Okay, he wants me to kick him, so I'm going to kick him." I didn't want to tell her to lighten up, because I was afraid she'd go back to doing it the old way. I kept telling myself, *Well, I'll just stand it one more time,* thinking each take would be the last. I don't think I sat down for a month!

Hellzapoppin' was a zany movie with a lot of slapstick and other kinds of comedy. We had fun making it and enjoyed the opportunity to work with quite a few stars, including Martha Raye, who was in the film and used to sing on the set and fool around with the dancers. I never did meet Dean Collins, who briefly dances with Martha Raye in another musical number in *Hellzapoppin'*. He ended up performing in a lot of other films and has become known as the father of West Coast swing.

I usually didn't see the movies we were in until they came out, but we were out of the country when *Hellzapoppin'* was released. I didn't actually see it until the 1980s, when Ernie Smith, a well-known collector of jazz dancing on film, showed me the Lindy scene on a projector in his apartment. A lot of the original Lindy hoppers got to see these old movies because of Ernie, and I give him all the credit for collecting and preserving them for the younger generation.

My first thought when I saw *Hellzapoppin'* was that it was pretty good, considering that we were a bunch of tired people when we made it. Not that we looked tired, but I remembered that we were. But the more I looked at *Hellzapoppin'*, the more I started marveling at it. I had choreographed the routine so that the dancers could fully execute the steps—not cut or chop them, which can happen if the music is too fast—and I think we accomplished this. Each of the dancers was so rhythmically attuned to the others; we all hit the same beat at the same moment. Part of the credit for this has to go to Freddy Martin's score. He had really wanted to come up with something that was as lively as "Jumpin' at the Woodside," and although I can't even hum the tune, I think he was right on the money.

Of course, there were some things that I thought could have been improved. Maybe I'm being too critical, but I wish that the camera could have gotten a *full* shot of the whole group dancing. We had limited space (which Nick Castle or the director had marked out with us), so I think they couldn't get back far enough to show everyone lined up for the waterfall. That's too bad, since that was the first time we'd ever done it. And when Ann and I separated during the slide-through, the camera could only follow one of us, so they lost me.

I also thought there were moments when we could have done a better job on the dancing, like when Ann and I do the snatch, or when I do the handspring over her back before she kicks me. Actually, there were other times when we did that routine a lot better, but unfortunately they weren't filmed. Still, I have to say that I think *Hellzapoppin'* had the best timing and was the most precise routine that Whitey's Lindy Hoppers ever did.

When I'm performing, I want the audience to know that I'm enjoying myself, not just by my facial expressions, but from my body movements too. I try to dance in a way that expresses how good I feel moving to great swing music. There's a saying: "Smile, and the world smiles with you; cry, and you cry alone." When people watch me dance, I hope they feel as joyous as I do. *Hellzapoppin'* exemplified how we felt while we were dancing. Yup, we were having a helluva time.

11 • DOWN RIO WAY

Hot Chocolate

We had a contract to do two movies for Universal, but since they didn't have another vehicle for us right away, we ended up being in Hollywood for a couple of months. In the interim, I asked the manager at Club Alabam if he'd hire the group. The salary wasn't all that great, but it was enough to sustain us while we were waiting around.

Whitey's Lindy Hoppers were such a big draw at Club Alabam—whenever they put us on the bill, the place was packed every night—that we were the stars for this engagement. They built the entire show around us and asked me to stage the whole thing. It was the first time I'd ever been in charge of a whole production. I created routines for the chorus girls, decided on the order of the acts, and was responsible for the length of the show, as well as choreographed three numbers for the Lindy hoppers: a medium-tempo Lindy, a floor routine with the chorus girls, and a flashy Lindy routine at the end.

There was one night at Club Alabam during this trip that I will never forget. The Lindy hoppers weren't appearing, but T-Bone Walker, the well-known blues singer, was one of the featured acts in the show. While he was performing, we heard this booming voice coming from one side of the balcony. It was Joe Turner, answering him. All of a sudden, someone else started singing from the other side of the balcony—Wynonie Harris! The two of them came downstairs to the stage, singing the whole time, and started shouting the blues with T-Bone Walker. It was fantastic! They did this challenge, making up the words as they went along, where one would sing a verse, the next would try to top it, then the third would try to top the first two. Man, they tore the house apart! Everybody in the audience was screaming!

We'd been performing at Club Alabam for about a month when I got a telegram from Whitey saying that he had a contract from William Morris for us to go on tour to South America. Universal agreed to release us from our commitment to do another feature if we would dance in a soundie they were making with Duke Ellington's band playing "Cotton Tail."[1]

We never actually worked with the band, just to the recording. The recorded music and the movie were made separately, then put together, but it was dubbed poorly so the music doesn't quite jive with our dancing. Actually, it doesn't match what the musicians, who were faking it for the camera, are playing either. At one point, you can see Ben Webster looking around as if he's wondering what's going on.

To me, *Hot Chocolate*[2] was a throwaway kind of thing that we had to do. We used the same routine we had done in *Hellzapoppin'*, except we ended with the horses and did the shoot-through instead of the slide-through because the soundstage floor was concrete. It was November and it was cold in there, which is why some of us wore coats. As soon as we finished filming, we got on a train and went back home.

The new contract required Whitey to trim the group down to three couples. Since the job fell to me, I chose to eliminate Downes and Mickey. I didn't want to split up the Rickers, but I couldn't put them together as partners because Whitey had separated them from the beginning, and Norma's style was perfect for Billy. (In fact, they ended up dancing together for twenty years.) These three teams had styles so varied they were almost entirely different from each other. Billy and Norma were wild, almost roughneck. Willamae and Al were more smooth. Ann and I were acrobatic. It was left to me to tell Downes and Mickey. Fortunately, Whitey put them to work elsewhere right away.

We had to restage the routine for three couples, so after a day or two in the city, the six of us went upstate to practice at this new bar that Whitey had opened in Oswego. Earlier in the year, an Army facility on the outskirts of Oswego had taken in a group of African American soldiers for training. There were white restaurants and bars in town, but blacks were not welcome in them. When Whitey heard about this, he decided to open a lounge where the guys could go to relax and not be discriminated against. He had been scouting around for a location since before we left for California. Mr. Buchanan went in on it as a backer, but he let Whitey manage it. It turned out to be a real moneymaker because there wasn't anyplace else for the soldiers to go.[3]

Some of the female Lindy hoppers, including Lucille, were waitresses in the lounge and acted as hostesses, which meant that the soldiers could come in and dance with them. Whitey asked us to come up there to rehearse because he figured having us out on the floor social dancing would be an attraction. After five or six days in Oswego, we went down to Washington to get passports because it was faster there than in Manhattan, then set sail from New York for South America the next day. We celebrated

Norma's December 2 birthday on board, and docked in Rio de Janeiro on December 5, 1941.

Stranded in Rio

Two days after we arrived, while we were out sightseeing, there was this big hullabaloo going on in the streets. We noticed people gesturing excitedly and talking loudly about the Americans, the Japanese, and Pearl Harbor. Since we didn't understand Portuguese, we didn't know what they were talking about. "What's a Pearl Harbor?" we asked. I had hired this guy Harry (a fellow I knew from Paris and had run into right after settling into our hotel on the beach) to be our guide and interpreter because he spoke the language, so he read the newspapers to us and explained that the Japanese had bombed an American naval base in Hawaii. We were shocked because we didn't have any idea that there were hostilities with Japan, although of course we knew about Germany. So there we were in South America, with the United States at war! At the time, we didn't have any notion that it would affect our work. Hawaii seemed so far away.

Casino da Urca was owned by one of the richest men in Rio de Janeiro. He also owned two other casinos, including Casino Icaraí, which was across the harbor from Casino da Urca. These two casinos had the most beautiful nightclubs I had ever seen in my life. The only thing that even came close was the sets for those fabulous movie musicals from the 1930s where the stages rise up out of the floor, come down from the ceiling, or slide together.

There were *three* bands at Casino da Urca. The stars of the show, Orquestra Ray Ventura, had twenty pieces and occupied center stage. They were not a swing band for dancing, but played jazz, contemporary, classical, everything, just for listening. Two local bands, Gao Kollman and Vicente Paiva (who had all the music from the big American swing bands and played for our act) held spots on either side of the stage.

We were billed just under Ray Ventura as "Whitey Congeroo Dancers." The name actually came from two different sources. Around this time, the conga was a popular Latin dance, and "swingaroo" was slang for a good swing dancer or musician. I combined the two terms and decided to call the group the Congaroo Dancers (that's the correct spelling) for *Hellzapoppin'*.[4] Universal Pictures added "Harlem" to the billing, and when we went to South America, we substituted Whitey's name. I don't know why I changed the name in the first place. In hindsight, we should have kept Whitey's Lindy Hoppers so people would know it was the same group that had done the earlier movies.

There were a bunch of other acts in the show, including Linda Battista, a Brazilian singer who a lot of people thought was better than Carmen Miranda, and I kind of agree. Grande Otélo was a very funny comedian and we became very good friends. When I visited Brazil in the '80s, he had gotten to be such a big star that he was grand master of Carnival. I couldn't even get near him.

Our entire act lasted ten minutes. To fill out the time, we started with a jazz routine that was longer, slower, jazzier, and more swingy than our Lindy hop number, which we always closed with. We used the same routine from *Hellzapoppin'*, more or less, except that we ended with the horses.

On opening night, when we'd finished, the audience started throwing their fists in the air and chanting something that sounded like, "Boo! Boo! Boo! Boo! Boo! Boo!" We were so discouraged because we thought they didn't like us. As we started walking back to our dressing rooms with our heads hanging low, the stage manager came running after us. "Hey kids! Get back on the stage!" "What for?" we asked. "They don't like us." "Yes, they do!" he said. "That's what they're saying. Now get back out there!" We went running back on stage while the people were still yelling. It turned out that this was their way of saying, "More! More! More!" We did an encore, and after that, every time we finished our routine, the audience "booed" us.

We did two shows a night, five nights a week, with Sunday and Monday off. (There was plenty of time to enjoy ourselves because we had such a good work schedule, but this is when the dancers started calling me Simon Legree since they couldn't go to the beach until after we practiced.) After the first show at Casino da Urca, the entire cast would walk out onto the dock behind the casino without even changing costumes and board these two yachts for the half-hour ride to Casino Icaraí, where we'd repeat the whole show at about three in the morning. In the meantime, all of the performers from Casino Icaraí would switch over to Casino da Urca and do their acts there.

Our contract was for six weeks, with an option to renew for six more. There was a tradition in American nightclubs called "burying the show," which meant that on the last night of a long engagement, some of the acts would imitate each other's performances. At the end of the twelve weeks, for our last show at Casino da Urca, Grande Otélo dressed up like Ann and clowned around in the Lindy hop routine as my partner. We had rehearsed a little to make sure he could do the air steps, which wasn't hard because he was a very talented youngster, and I threw him around like he was a rag doll. The audience loved it!

We were so successful in Rio that the contract was extended in order for us to tour other cities in Brazil, including São Paulo, São Vincente, and

Bahia. The nightclubs were smaller, but some of them were fabulous. There was an incredible casino in Belo Horizonte (owned by the same person as the two in Rio) that sat on a hillside above a man-made lake. The whole place was made of glass, and at night it was lit from inside by lights that changed colors all the time, purple, orange, green. . . . From the bottom of the path leading up the hill, it looked like a fairy-tale castle.

Even the dance floor was made of very thick glass. There was a small wooden stage where we'd start our jazz routine, but then we'd jump down onto the main floor for the Lindy hop section. One night, Norma landed kind of heavy and broke the glass! Luckily, she was fine, so we continued dancing, but we had to get back up on the stage in order to avoid the crack. We were all laughing so hard. The management repaired the crack, but from then on, we did both routines on the main floor.

After six weeks on the road, we were ready to go home, but the Germans were sinking ships traveling between the United States and South America. It was too dangerous for passenger boats to go back and forth, so we had to stay longer—much longer than we expected, as it turned out.

We went back into Casino da Urca for another six weeks. For this run, I reworked the solos and ensemble section of the *Hellzapoppin'* routine. I based the solos on steps each couple already knew how to do, and sometimes they played around with the choreography. I also choreographed two new numbers for our repertoire. We didn't know of anyplace in Rio to go out Lindy hopping, but these people did their own dancing everywhere, in ballrooms, on the streets, in nightclubs, at bars. They did the hell out of the samba. I'd never seen anything like it. They were much better than any professional in America that we'd ever seen on the stage. One of the new routines was based on the Frevo Pernambucano, a Brazilian social dance similar to a samba, very sexy, that we had seen in Belo Horizonte and that was very popular in towns outside of Rio. I combined movements we were already doing with some new ones that imitated the folk steps of this dance and fit the local music it was done to. We wore native costumes and performed it in a separate section of the show. Carlos Machado's Brazilian band, which was very, very good, played for us. The other new piece was a jazz routine. I used a few of the same steps from the first routine, worked in a bunch of different ones, and added some splits and handsprings.

Meanwhile, I was still trying to figure out how to get home. The only way to get out of Brazil was on a commercial flight. I spent the next five months trying to book our passage, but it was very difficult to arrange because Americans were buying up all the seats. In addition to the exorbitant fares, I had to slip all this money under the table to travel agents just to get the proper papers. The planes couldn't fly over the Atlantic because of the war, so they had to cross over Peru, Colombia, and Panama, and we had to have a visa for each country.

The whole thing was very corrupt and took a lot of jiving and finagling. You had to know somebody, who knew somebody, who knew somebody. I would go around and ask, "We want to get back home. Can you do anything for us?" then pay this person off, so they could pay off someone else, who paid a third guy off. What an ordeal! Fortunately, after our first six weeks in Rio, once I started hearing that transportation out of the country was getting difficult, I had stopped sending Whitey his commission. That was the only reason I was able to pay for everything. During this whole period, we gigged around wherever and whenever we could—sometimes at Casino da Urca or a theater in Rio, sometimes at nightclubs in other cities— and bided our time.

One evening, in Belo Horizonte (I believe), while we were in the square in front of our hotel boarding a bus to go to work, this Brazilian man grabbed Willamae and pulled her back down the steps. Naturally, Billy tried to protect his wife. He pushed the fellow, who swung at him, so Billy hit the guy, which caused him to fall back into my arms. Then this cat turned to hit me, so I fought him off. The incident caused a little disturbance, but eventually we got on the bus and went to the nightclub.

That night, when we got back to the hotel, there was a commotion going on in the street. Some man was up on a platform preaching to a crowd and rousing them up. Since we didn't know what it was about, although we heard him mention Americanos several times, we didn't pay it any mind and went on upstairs.

As the night progressed, we could tell by peeking out the window that the crowd was getting larger and larger. The police came and tried to disperse them, but there was some pushing and shoving. At that point, the hotel manager came to our room and told us we shouldn't go out there because they were fascists and were against Americans. It was a political demonstration, but apparently the incident that afternoon had started the whole thing, and the leader was inciting the mob against Americans to the point where the situation was unruly and getting worse. There started to be fighting between the police, some of whom were on horseback, and people in the street. Several detectives came to our room and told us that they didn't know what was going to happen, and decided it was best to get us out of the city.

We were all so scared, we could hardly move. When Ann got nervous, she used to stutter: "The-the-they're scaring the sh-sh-shit out of me, F-f-f-f-f-Frankie. W-w-we got to get our asses out of here!" Only this time when she said it, she let out a loud fart. This broke the tension and we started cracking up, and got going. We threw our stuff in our bags, and the police hurried us out the back door into a couple of cars and drove us to a railroad station outside the town, not the main terminal. Before they put us on the train to Rio, these officers started talking about how they had saved our lives. They were hinting around, so naturally I had to slip them a few bucks. *There goes a little bit more of Whitey's dough*, I thought.

Finally, after ten months in South America, I was able to get three dancers back to Florida. We sent Ann, Norma, and Al first because they were the youngest. A week later, Willamae, Billy, and I joined them.

Florida

By the time we finally got to the States, we were flat broke, so we had to stop over in Miami long enough to earn money to return to New York. Except for Al; he got drafted right away, so his parents sent him some money to take a train up North.

At first we couldn't get any work as Lindy hoppers, so we all took other jobs. Norma, Ann, and Willamae got employment as maids in a hotel. I worked nights mopping and cleaning the kitchen of an Army PX (a facility that sells food and Army goods to soldiers) on the beach. Billy took the day shift. I didn't even consider calling Whitey to ask him to send us anything. I'm not sure why. Maybe I was a little bit afraid that he would be angry because I used his money to get us back home. Or possibly it was a pride thing. I figured we'd do it on our own.

Shortly after we arrived, *Hot Chocolate* came out and was playing on the jukeboxes around Miami. There was an article in the paper saying that those same Lindy hoppers were in town, which got us some gigs in a couple of nightclubs and at a ballroom called the Rockland Palace. We picked up a kid down there as a replacement for Al, a pretty good dancer. I don't remember his name, but I taught him what he needed to know and he caught on quickly.

We were in Florida for quite a while before we were able to leave, but the group had a good time. As a matter of fact, we didn't just pick up and go once we had the money. After some time, Ann and Norma went home, then Willamae, then me; Billy came back a week after I did.

The truth was I had to leave. While I was in Brazil, my mother had received my draft papers, which she'd sent down to me. There was nothing I could do at that point, but when she mailed a second notice to Miami and I replied to the Army, they told me to report to Fort Bragg in North

Carolina. I had heard a lot about this camp, that there was terrible prejudice and they treated blacks very badly, and I did not want to go there. I told Billy, "I'm going back up North. Let them draft me from there," and got on a train.

As I had anticipated, when I got back to New York, Whitey confronted me about his commission. At first he didn't buy my explanation, and when he said I owed him the money, we got into a heated argument. There was no way I could have paid him back. At that point, some of the dancers from the trip who were there chimed in to back me up, and Whitey calmed down. I felt bad about the whole situation, but I knew I had done the right thing. After the discussion, it was over. It wasn't like Whitey and I came to blows or parted company. We actually worked together again on a couple of gigs, and he even tried to get me to come up to perform in Oswego, but I wasn't interested.

I notified the military that I was back in town, and while I was waiting to get drafted, Whitey helped arrange a date for a group of Lindy hoppers at the Roxy Theatre. This was now summer 1943. (We may also have done a few performances in Washington and Baltimore before this.) Since Whitey wasn't really around that much anymore, we were hired directly by Sammy Rausch, the Roxy's booking agent, and the contract was with each individual dancer, not with Whitey's Lindy Hoppers. By this time, Whitey's groups had pretty much disbanded. Most of his best male dancers—Al, Billy Ricker, and George Greenidge—had gone into the Army. Whitey had moved his headquarters up to Oswego, and his interests had turned to making a success of his place there. I never asked why he relocated. Maybe he had the foresight to realize that all the guys were going into the Army and he couldn't count on having the Lindy hoppers anymore. He was able to keep things going for a little while with the new crop of dancers that was coming up, but, looking back, I'd say this was the beginning of the end.

We opened at the Roxy for a three-week engagement in late July 1943, playing with *Stormy Weather* on the bill.[5] My son Chazz, who was almost eleven, came to see the show with his mother. It was the first time he'd ever seen me perform. He says he loved the dazzling lights, the colorful costumes, the exciting music, watching me throw all these girls around like crazy, and seeing everybody in the audience smiling. By the end of the show, when his mother asked if he thought he'd like to be on stage, he said yes! Chazz says he knew he wanted to be an entertainer right then. Dorothy put him in the Mary Bruce Dance Studio in Harlem, where he began to study tap, acrobatics, a little ballet, modern, interpretative, social dancing, and the basic Lindy.

After a week in the theater, I got my draft papers again, telling me to report for duty in a couple of days or they were going to come and get me. I didn't want to leave in the middle of the run, so I spoke to Sammy Rausch, who decided to write a letter to an official at Camp Upton saying that I was essential to the show. Their response: "That's too bad. We need him worse than you do."

PART IV
WAR AND HOME
$\left(1943-1984\right)$

Frankie Manning and buddies in Los Angeles in 1946
shortly after World War II had ended.

12 • DANCER INTERRUPTED

Sad Sack

Before we went down to Rio, the Lindy hoppers had been getting some very good jobs. After we got back, the William Morris Agency, which had exclusive booking rights for some big-time nightclubs, started booking us into spots like Club Mocambo in Hollywood. Only big stars like Sammy Davis Jr. and Frank Sinatra were playing there, but before we could get near the place, just about all of Whitey's best male dancers got drafted. I did not want to go into the Army. My reason was simple: I wouldn't be able to dance anymore.

Initially, I was ordered to report to Camp Upton, a training base in Yaphank, Long Island. I was supposed to catch a train there early in the morning, but being reluctant to join the Army, I didn't care what time I got to the station. I was up till all hours the night before, so I was about two hours late. To be honest, I was hoping they would forget about me, but they had people there who told me to hop on the next train.

Once I got to Camp Upton, some of the guys I knew from show business suggested that I try to get into the Special Services, a section of the Army that was for big-time entertainers—musicians, singers, and dancers. I asked my commanding officer to request my transfer, and I reminded him a couple of times, but nothing came of it. I didn't know the right people, and I wasn't up to the level of some of the other entertainers like Stump and Stumpy.[1] Whitey's Lindy Hoppers just wasn't a household name.

At Upton, a lot of the guys I knew, and met, were trying to get out of there, so along with the rest of them, I became something of a sad sack. For instance, when we first got to the camp, they put us through different exercises for our physical exam. Some of the guys told us about a hearing test where a sergeant whispered something to you softly. If you turned around, he'd know that you were okay, so I pretended that I didn't hear him. Then he called my name loudly, and I responded. Also, somebody had discovered that if you put a penny under your tongue, you'd get a fever. We'd go to sick call, where the doctor in the dispensary would take our temperature, then tell us to take the day off. And sometimes when we

•

were drilling and the sergeant would say "Left, right," I'd do right, left purposely.

Looking back, I knew what I was doing, but I wasn't very happy with the way I behaved, because it was just not *me*. Usually, if I got a job or was supposed to do something, I always tried to do my best. I'm not saying I'm proud of myself, but in the end, I did go through all of the training and the drills.

... World War II and African American Soldiers ...

UPON ENTERING THE ARMY, Frankie tried to put his unique talents to use. Many performers, both famous and lesser known, supported the war effort by providing troops with morale-boosting entertainment designed to provoke memories of home and daydreams of better times to come. Swing music, with its upbeat persona, energized rhythms, clean-cut romanticism, and ubiquitous popularity, was the perfect medium for the message.

Glenn Miller formed his Army Air Force Orchestra upon enlisting in 1942. Artie Shaw led a Navy band that toured the South Pacific war zone during 1943–44. Dave Brubeck's Wolf Pack Band entertained soldiers in the European theater. There were fewer opportunities open to black entertainers. Despite their military service, blacks were subjected to discrimination in housing, mess halls, service clubs, and endless other circumstances. Black GIs were often relegated to positions of menial labor or, conversely, to the most dangerous front-line battle missions. Tensions between black and white soldiers were high; respect for servicemen of color was low. Rising through the ranks was difficult, if not impossible.

According to *Invisible Soldiers: Unheard Voices*, a documentary on African Americans serving in World War II, "Not only did the African American soldier have to watch his back for the enemy, he had to watch his back for the ally also, which was Uncle Sam."[2] Despite adverse conditions, African Americans made tremendous contributions, distinguishing themselves on all fronts, in all branches of the service, and throughout the course of the war.

Reflecting the broader military environment, "Several top black bands—including those of Ellington, Calloway, Hampton, and Waller—were not asked to go abroad to entertain troops," and "black musicians had a harder time being admitted to service bands than their white counterparts."[3] Nevertheless, a number of African American band leaders, determined to do their part for the country, presented their orchestras in USO shows and war bond rallies on the home front. Tap dancers Cholly Atkins and Fayard Nicholas also performed in stateside military shows.[4] ●

Poster for the All American feature production of *Killer Diller* with Four Congaroos in lower right corner, 1948. *Left to right:* Frankie Manning, Willamae Ricker, Ann Johnson, Russell Williams.

Frankie Manning *(far right)* and army buddies at Club Alabam in Los Angeles after returning from war, early 1946. COURTESY OF FRANKIE MANNING.

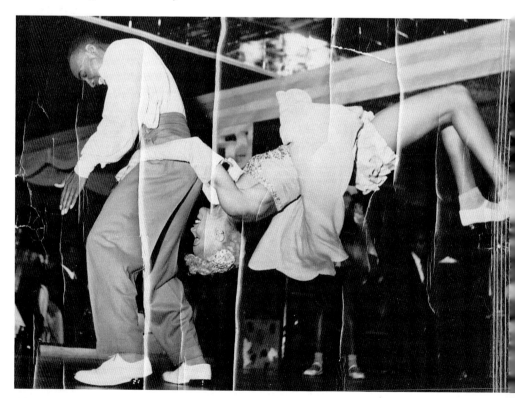

Congaroo Dancers Helen Daniels and Frankie Manning performing handspring-down-the-back at Sugar Hill Nightclub, 1952. PHOTOGRAPH CREDITED TO H. KELL. COURTESY OF FRANKIE MANNING.

RAY Robinson & Mrs. Robinson WALTER WINCHELL
Jackie Robinson & WIFE

Celebrities in audience for Miami performances of *Smart Affairs of 1952,* featuring the Congaroo Dancers. *Left to right:* unknown, unknown, unknown, Sugar Ray Robinson, unknown, Walter Winchell, Jackie Robinson, Mrs. Jackie Robinson (Rachel), Mrs. Sugar Ray Robinson (Edna Mae).

COURTESY OF FRANKIE MANNING.

Frankie's family at a Harlem church event honoring his mother, 1970s. Front row *(left to right)*: Michael Manning (Vincent's son), Gloria Manning, Lucille Durant (Frankie's mother remarried in the early 1950s), Frankie Manning Jr. Back row *(left to right)*: Chazz Young, Vincent Manning, Frankie Manning.

PHOTOGRAPH CREDITED TO MISS LUCKETT. COURTESY OF FRANKIE MANNING.

Dancers from California, London, and New York meet at the Cat Club, New York City, March 23, 1986. Front row *(left to right)*: Jonathan Bixby, Sylvia Sykes, Steven Mitchell, Erin Stevens. Back row *(left to right)*: Bob Crease, Claudia Gintersdorfer, Warren Heyes, Angie Selby, Frankie Manning, Norma Miller, Laurel Watson *(singing on stage)*, Jeanefer Jean-Charles, Yvonne Washington, Pepsi Bethel, Ryan Francois.

PHOTOGRAPH BY PAUL ARMSTRONG.

Frankie Manning teaching in Oakland, California, at a Northern California Lindy Society event, assisted by Laurie Ann Lepoff, 1998.

ABOVE: Dancers performing a
jazz movement called the scarecrow
in "Wednesday Night Hop," a routine
choreographed by Frankie Manning
for *Black and Blue,* 1989.

COURTESY OF MEL HOWARD.

RIGHT: 1989 Tony Award Winners for Best
Choreography. *Left to right:* Henry
LeTang, Fayard Nicholas, Cholly Atkins,
Frankie Manning.

PHOTOGRAPH BY ANITA AND STEVE SHEVETT.

Otis Salid, Frankie Manning, and Spike
Lee at a pre-production rehearsal for
Malcolm X, New York City, mid-1991.

PHOTOGRAPH BY DAVID LEE.

Frankie Manning *(in tuxedo in lower left corner)* leading the shim sham at his eightieth birthday celebration, New York City, May 29, 1994.

Norma Miller and Frankie Manning performing
at the Cat Club, New York City, circa 1987–88.

Frankie Manning and Judy Pritchett at unveiling
of commemorative plaque where the Savoy
Ballroom once stood, May 26, 2002.

Chazz Young and
Frankie Manning
performing the shim
sham onboard
Frankie's eighty-
ninth birthday
Caribbean cruise,
2003.

Tanked

After a short time at Upton, I was assigned to a tank corps and sent to Camp Hood, a training camp south of Waco, Texas. I was in a black company nicknamed "Tiger," with white officers. All of the other soldiers in the camp were white. It was in Texas that my attitude changed. Our officers took us around to visit all these hospitals where we saw veterans who had fought in the South Pacific and lost an arm or leg, were maimed, or were delirious. It was just pitiful. Then we had a lecture about what it was like to fight on the front lines, which is when I decided that I'd better know what I was doing. Tank corps was pretty tough. They trained you just like they would train a marine. I did every drill full out and began studying all of these books. Soon I became a private first class, then a corporal.

We trained in Texas for three or four months, so we're into late 1943 now. While I was down there, a friend and I had a little run-in with Jim Crow. All of the buses had signs about three-quarters of the way down the aisle that said "colored." One day my buddy, Claude, and I got on a bus that was practically empty and, for a joke, moved the sign up to the front, so there were only about three rows left for white people. Rather than go into the colored section with just the two of us, these folks kept getting on the bus, crowding themselves into the little front area. It was hilarious to see them packing in like sardines.

After a few stops, the bus driver noticed the crowd, saw the sign, and figured it out. He didn't do anything himself, but he stopped the bus when we went by some MPs. As they were getting on the front of the bus, Claude and I hopped out the back door. They chased us, but we lost them pretty quickly. We ran all the way back to camp, then laughed our butts off.

When we finished up in Waco, they sent us out to Camp Hunter Liggett, just outside of San Francisco, for another few months. They had taught us the basics of operating a tank on the flat ground in Texas, but now they wanted us to practice on a hilly landscape, more like where we were going to be shipped to, which I assumed was North Africa.

After our training was completed, they gave us a three-day pass, so a bunch of us went into San Francisco. The guys wanted to let their hair down, so we all went to this bar where I ordered a Singapore sling. I was *not* a drinker. In fact, that was my first drink ever. The waiter advised me not to have more than two because they were pretty strong, and I said sure, figuring I'd only drink one. But when he brought this big tall glass with strawberries in it, it tasted so delicious that I ordered another one, then a third one. I figured the bartender didn't know what he was talking about.

Later, my buddies told me that I was talking a mile a minute, which was how they knew I was high, but I don't remember any of that. Apparently I stood up and BAM!—I just collapsed. They had to pick me up and carry me back to the Y. When I woke up, the guys said, "Come on Frankie, we have to go." "Go where, man? I don't feel like going anywhere." They answered that we had to go back to camp. "Wait a minute, what are you talking about? We don't have to go back until Monday." They said, "This *is* Monday!" I thought they were kidding, but I had slept for two days!

Whatcha Know Joe?

Before being shipped overseas, I was given a two-week furlough to go home, but I had such a good time dancing at the Savoy, visiting with my buddies, and seeing my girlfriend that I wasn't in any rush to get back, and ended up returning to California a few days late. In the meantime, my battalion had left! My commander immediately reassigned me to the 650th Ordnance Ammunition Company, which was going to a very nice spot—the jungles of New Guinea.

After some more training, we sailed on a troop ship, the *Lurline*, in late June 1944. There were four or five female Red Cross workers on board, and one of them used to play the piano and sing in the lounge every evening. Many of the soldiers would come around to listen to her. It was a mixed crowd, black and white. One of the songs she did every night was "Whatcha Know Joe?" a Jimmie Lunceford tune with a gag. When the lead singer asks, "Whatcha know Joe?" the band members respond with "I don't know nothin'." When he repeats, "Whatcha know Joe?" they come back with, "Tell me somethin'." Since this lady was singing the whole song by herself, she did both parts.

One night, for some ungodly reason, when she sang the first line, I stood up and did the next one. It cracked her and the crowd up, so we kept that going back and forth for the rest of the song. From then on, she always looked to me to help her out whenever she did that number. It got to be a thing every night with the soldiers. Some of them even started joining in.

Right after she sang, "Whatcha know Joe?" one evening, the alarm suddenly sounded, which meant that there was a submarine in the area. The ship went dark, and everybody had to keep deathly quiet so we wouldn't be detected. We were so nervous, sitting there in the darkness waiting to see if the Japanese submarine was going to sink us. It probably only lasted for fifteen or twenty minutes, but we were so scared that it seemed like hours.

As soon as the lights came back on, I stood up and hollered, "I DON'T KNOW NOTHIN'." Everybody just craaaacked up! I mean, all the tension that had built up just let out. It was hilarious! After that, this lady asked if I'd help her put on a show for the GIs. There was a fellow named Martin who could sing a little bit, and another guy who played guitar, so we got together. We played and sang Tommy Dorsey's arrangement of "Marie," which was very popular at the time, and I did a tap dance number. There was no real Lindy hopping, but Martin and I did some fooling around. He would play the man, while I'd swing out and do some twists.

Tales of the South Pacific

Nothing could have prepared us for invading New Guinea. The United States wanted to take back the island from Japanese control, because it was a very strategic spot since it wasn't far from Australia. When we first arrived, the guns on our ships shelled the shoreline of the island so that we could get some kind of foothold. It took about three days before we could even begin to advance inland because the enemy was shooting and killing our boys as we landed on the beach. I was scared as a mother.

When we finally did start to advance, it was pretty rapid. We were really moving through the jungle, even though it was terribly muddy and bogged down because it was the rainy season. There was a lot of fighting going on, and even though I was in an ordnance company, we got put into combat. I don't know that I actually killed anyone because I didn't stick around to check if they were dead or not, but I shot at some guys and some of them went down.

In New Guinea, you had to fight three elements: the Japanese, Mother Nature (because they have dry and wet seasons), and wild animals, including snakes and wild boars. We had to put our tents up off the ground because of the snakes, but even so some guys would wake up with snakes in bed beside them.

Once, after the island was secured and they brought in some female USO workers, one of them was driving with this MP outside of the base. When he stopped the car and went around to her side to open the door, a boa constrictor dropped down from a tree, wrapped itself around him, and began crushing his body. He struggled with the snake and tried to shoot it in the head, while she screamed hysterically. Some soldiers ran to the scene and tried to shoot the snake while this guy was fighting for his life. They finally killed it, but it was too late. Word got around, and by the time a bunch of us got there to see what had happened, this cat was dead and so was the snake. It was really terrible, just awful.

While I was in New Guinea, I made sergeant. As a sergeant, I had a squad of men who were all black, and I tried to be the kind of leader they could trust. I never asked them to do anything I wouldn't do, and I tried to pull out all the protection to help them accomplish their mission. I treated them well, and I think I was well-liked.

I guess I did a pretty good job because I got several medals while I was in the service. A couple were given to everyone in the battalion for fighting in the South Pacific, but some were for specific incidents. One time, I volunteered for a dangerous mission to get explosives during a bombing raid by the Japanese. About five of us got medals that time. It was a commendation for bravery, but it was just something that needed to be done. It wouldn't have bothered me if I didn't get anything. To me, it was about trying to stay alive and to protect the people in my command.

Sergeant Montgomery

I'm sorry to have to say this, but I experienced more prejudice, and worse prejudice, in the military than at any other time in my life. I was in a battalion that had one black company, but most of the other soldiers were white, and all of the officers were. There was tension because the white soldiers resented our being in New Guinea, or in the Army, period. They didn't think we could fight well enough or had the necessary courage.

There was one fellow in particular, Sergeant Montgomery, a noncom (noncommissioned officer) who was very prejudiced and hateful toward blacks. Even though he was not in charge of any men in my company, just his own squad, if he met a black soldier, he would always expect you to get out of his way, and he called us "nigger this" and "black so-and-so." The guys in my company resented it, and some of them would get into arguments with him, but I never did.

One day, during a skirmish with the Japanese, we got orders to advance down the line. I couldn't see the enemy, but I could see the fire from their guns. Montgomery's squad was stationed close to mine. He would get orders from the top and snap them at me when he passed them on: "Tell them black motherfuckers they have to do this or do that." Whatever the orders were, however he said them, I tried to carry them out. I'd pass them on to my men so they'd know what we were supposed to be doing.

As we started to move out, both of our squads in one line, Montgomery took a bullet. He was on the ground hollering and crying something awful, so I told my corporal, "You move on with the guys; I'm going to get him." My corporal wanted me to leave him there, but I said "Man, I can't do that." The enemy was shooting at anything that moved, so I crawled over to where Montgomery was lying and asked where he was hit. He pointed to his leg, gasped that he couldn't move, then told me to get one of his guys. When I said that I would take him back, he didn't want me to. He was bleeding so badly that he was beginning to pass out, so I just rolled him onto my back and started crawling through the undergrowth. When we got back to a gathering spot where there wasn't so much fire, I called for a medic and returned to my men.

A few days later, I went over to the hospital to see how Montgomery was coming along. He told me that he was doing fine. Then he said, "I don't know how to say this, but I come from a small, backcountry town in Mississippi. I never had much encounter with colored people. The only things I knew about them was what I heard from other white folks, and what I heard was that they were no good, and cowards, and always up to this or that. But after being with you guys, my attitude has changed. I want to thank you very much for saving my life. I never thought a colored man would do that for me. When I get back to my hometown, if I have the opportunity, I'm going to try to educate as many people as I can about colored people. I'm going to tell them that we've been wrong. Well, that's how I feel, because I really appreciate that you saved my life."

I just stood there, not knowing what to say. I had mixed feelings. I didn't like it—people being ignorant and going along with what everybody else said—but I was kind of touched by what he said, and appreciated that he was man enough to admit it.

After we had all moved on to the Philippine Islands in '45, I ran into Montgomery at a little local nightclub. He called all of us over—I was with four or five buddies, all African American—and we sat down with him and talked for a while.

There's one more chapter to this story. When I was discharged from the Army in early 1946, it so happened that Montgomery was too. We were on the same boat back to California, and flew from there to New Jersey with three other soldiers to be mustered out. All five of us were master sergeants. Claude, the same guy I'd trained with in Waco, and I were black; the other three were white. When our plane stopped for servicing in West Virginia, we decided to walk to a diner just off the base in order to get something to eat.

As soon as we walked in and sat down, the waiter came right over and announced, "We're not serving any niggers in here. We'll serve you guys, but you niggers have to go someplace else." Well, that pissed off Montgomery and the other two white guys. They jumped up out of their seats and said, "If you don't serve them, we're going to tear this fucking place apart, and we mean it. We just came back from fighting with these guys in New Guinea and the Philippines. They were fighting for your life and you're saying you're not going to serve them?! Well, you better. If you don't, prepare to have this place wrecked." The waiter started stammering and went to get the manager.

Claude and I were scared as hell. We said, "Look, man, let's forget it. We'll just go someplace else." I knew that they really would have leveled the place, and if they did the police would have thrown us all in jail. Then these rednecks would probably have separated Claude and me from the others, beaten the hell out of us just for going in there, and lynched us. I just wanted to get the hell out, but they insisted on staying, so Claude and I shrugged our shoulders and sat down.

The manager came over and explained that the policy of the diner was not to serve niggers, but Montgomery told him, "They're not niggers— they're Negroes, American Negroes. They've been fighting for America. Now, do you want Americans fighting against Americans? Because we're going to ruin this joint if you don't serve them."

Well, it all turned out okay. The manager agreed to serve us, so we sat down and ate everything in sight. That was a pretty incredible incident. It was a big turnaround for Montgomery from when he went into the Army. And it proves what I always say: People who are prejudiced aren't educated about other human beings. They're like that because they hear things about people and take it to heart, as if it were true.

Legs Grable

My years in the Army included some really horrible experiences. When it was over, I tried to put some of the things that happened out of my mind, and wasn't able to speak about them for years. But there were also some lighter moments. After most of the fighting in New Guinea was over, my unit was assigned to build bases and roads. I spent most of my off-duty time sitting on my bunk writing to my girlfriend. I wrote some very intimate things.

One day, my commanding officer called me into his office. Lieutenant Bednik pulled out some letters with a lot of holes cut out of them, and said, "Manning, these are yours, and I must say, you write some very interesting letters." I was caught completely off guard because I had no idea that our mail was being read by Army censors. It was because they didn't want us giving away strategic information and having it get into enemy hands. He told me that this kind of correspondence could not be allowed, and asked me to send more subdued letters in the future. I wrote my girlfriend that I was going to have to calm it down a little from now on.

I guess I missed swing dancing while I was in the Army, although I didn't think about it all that much. But I did try to take every opportunity to put on a little show. There was a fellow in my company who played guitar, another who played piano, and a third who played saxophone. I played drums and sang a bit, so we formed a little band. Sometimes Martin joined us. We usually did songs that I remembered the words for, although there weren't too many of those, mostly ballads and popular songs. I discovered that if you put a swinging tempo to it, you didn't have to be that good a singer. Out there in the middle of the jungle, these soldiers didn't care that much.

We played at the officers' club and also put on a show for the battalion. Usually I'd do some jazz steps or a tap dance routine, just in my Army suit and boots, but I managed to do some handsprings and splits. Sometimes I'd also do a parody with Martin where I'd put on a rag mop for a wig and act out the female part of a song. There was this one white fellow who also used to sing and dance. He was very Broadway, but even with his tails, high hat, and cane, he wasn't that good. The guys would be like, "What's with this cat?" but when I would come out and do this down-to-earth boogeying, they loved it.

Another very good memory happened toward the end of my time in New Guinea. The government had started sending in USO shows, and word went out that Jack Benny was going to bring in a show featuring two starlets, Betty Grable and Carol Landis, comedian Jerry Colonna, and a big band. You should have seen the guys when they heard that Betty Grable was coming over. Everybody was washing out their khakis and sprucing up. Man, we were sharp!

Now, we knew that whenever these USO productions came through, they invariably asked some of the soldiers to come up onstage and dance with the girls. It was a real morale booster. A whole gang of about ten of us finished up our chores and went to the amphitheater very early in order to get seats in the front row.

By the time the performance started, the sun had gone down. Jack Benny came out and announced, "Let's put out the lights on the stage." Once everything was dark, he said, "All of you guys that have cigarette lighters or a match, light them." Man, you should have seen it! It was like this huge bowl filled with lights. Then everybody started singing "God Bless America," while they were swaying back and forth. It was such a wonderful sight. He kept it like that for about a couple of minutes, then started the show.

Betty Grable and Carol Landis sang and danced. Jerry Colonna did his jokes. The band played. Finally, Jack Benny said, "It's time to get acquainted with these young ladies. Some of you fellows can come up onstage." Before he could even finish his sentence, we were up there. I was among the first. I think everybody would have gone up there if they could have. When Jack Benny signaled the MPs, they stopped the rest of the guys, who reluctantly went back to their seats.

It would have worn Carol Landis and Betty Grable out if they both danced at the same time because there were about twenty-five men, so they alternated. After each dance, Jack Benny would give the actresses a little break by talking to one of the soldiers for a minute or two. I didn't want to dance until the end, so I just wandered around the stage, talking and joking with the musicians in the band, buttering them up. I told them that I used to dance at the Savoy Ballroom, which they thought was great.

I wanted to dance with Betty Grable and, as luck would have it, when everybody else had had their chance, I was the last soldier left on the stage and it was her turn. Jack Benny started asking me where I was from and all that stuff. Then he said, "Okay, you want to dance?" so I said, "Yeah!" and turned to the band: "Hey fellas, give me something really swinging, something like . . ." and I stomped out the time.

The musicians started playing something that was jumping, and when I turned around, there was Betty Grable standing in front of me, just smiling. All I could think was, *I'm going to be putting my arms around Betty Grable. Oh, man! Wow!*

The band was giving me a nice, easy swing, so I started dancing with her. Her Lindy hop wasn't all that great, but what did I care? I was dancing with Betty Grable! She was following me pretty well, so I threw in some of my tricks like boogies and Shorty Georges, footwork like that. She told me that I danced pretty nice and I said, "Well, thank you. You dance pretty good too."

The crowd was with me, clapping and laughing and egging me on. Although most of the guys in the company had seen me dance, they had never seen me swing out with a woman. When the band got near the end of the song and I was ready to finish, I picked Betty Grable up in my arms and walked off the stage. Well, the house just roared. I mean, these cats were cracking up!

After I put her down, she ran back onstage and took a bow. Then she pointed to me and called, "Come on soldier, take a bow. Soldier, you were good." I took a bow and everybody kept applauding and applauding. Jack Benny, who was laughing, said, "You all want more?" The whole place exploded, "Yeah, let him dance again. Let him dance again," so I shrugged my shoulders and started dancing. At the end of the song, I picked her up and walked off a second time. Everybody just howled, and Betty Grable was laughing to beat the band! Oh man, it was really something! I felt so great, so wonderful.

The next day, the guys kept asking me how it felt to dance with Betty Grable. I told them that she was so soft and she wore this perfume that was intoxicating. I was in heaven, heaven-n-n. They wanted to shake my hand, but I said, "Not this hand." I joked that I wasn't going to wash it, but to tell you the truth, I had to take a cold shower that night.

The Philippines and Japan

In mid-1945, my battalion was deployed to the Philippines. For the next several months, we just waited around for something to happen. It was very tedious, except for a few occasions. My buddy Claude and I secretly adopted a pair of Filipino orphans, a brother and sister about fourteen and ten, who we caught eating out of a garbage bucket. We started sneaking them food and clothing, and one evening they surprised us with a delicious native dinner of fish wrapped in leaves and cooked on hot rocks.

Another time, I was riding in a truck, and as we were passing another truck full of soldiers, I suddenly recognized Billy Ricker, who was standing in the back. "BILLY!" I yelled, and he called out, "FRANKIE!" but that was it. That was the only time I saw him during the war. I hadn't even known he was over there.

In Panay, we were training for an invasion, so the Army commanders wanted us to keep that edge. (At the time, we didn't know if it was for the invasion of Japan. It could have been for any of the islands held by the Japanese.) They would take us out on a ship and have us go through the motions, but we never actually knew whether it was for real or not. Week after week, we kept going through the same procedures. Then one morning, we came up on deck and saw what looked like thousands and thousands of ships, every kind of warship—battleships, torpedo boats, carriers. You could hardly see the water for the ships. All the guys started rushing up on deck. We were like, "Uh-oh, this is it"; we were going to invade Japan.

As it turned out, we were actually preparing to occupy the country after the bomb was dropped. Before we got our orders, we were stuck outside Yokohama for a helluva long time, at least a month. Eventually, we went ashore in Yokohama as part of the occupying troops. I was there for over six months, and this is when I became a master sergeant.

While I was in Japan, I went to see a USO show that was touring the country. One of the acts was Apus and Estrellita, a comedy team that I knew from the entertainment world. When I went backstage to say hello, Apus urged me to do something for the next show, so he called me from the audience and I got up and sang "Honeysuckle Rose" and did a tap dance number. At the end of it, I jumped off the stage and landed in the aisle in a split, then got up and walked right on out. The soldiers *roared*! It was such a hit that Apus went to my commander and asked him if I could travel around with the show, which he agreed to. I ended up doing about five shows with them, and we always staged it as an impromptu thing with that same ending.

When the Army finally sent my company home, we stayed in a little town outside of Los Angeles for quite a while. One night, a whole bunch of us guys went to Club Alabam, and who should be there but Norma Miller! She had staged the dances for the chorus girls in the show. What a thrill to run into an old pal from Whitey's Lindy Hoppers on my way back home from the war.

13 • THE CONGAROO DANCERS AND A DAY JOB

Me Bop?

By the time I came out of the Army, the music scene had changed. Many bands, mostly small, like Charlie Parker, but some large ones, like Dizzy Gillespie, were playing bebop, which was such a strange sound to my ears that I could not understand it. I went to Minton's Playhouse to hear some jazz, and I said, "What the *heck* is going on?"

On my first night back at the Savoy, they had a swing band (the big orchestras continued to work, although not as much as before) and a smaller bebop combo. People were trying to adapt the Lindy to bebop, trying to mix the two, but they ended up doing this jerky kind of dance, almost like going back to the Charleston. It was like they were beboppin' instead of Lindy hopping. We actually called that kind of dancing bebop or boppin'. Even though the dancers were trying to change over to this new music, they hadn't gotten rid of the Lindy, just as we never completely got rid of the Charleston when we began dancing to swing.

I was used to music for dancing, but this new sound was only for listening. At first, I was devastated because it was such a big change for me. I just could not get the feel of bebop, and I couldn't dance to it. But *eventually*—and it took some time and a lot of listening—I learned to understand it better. Everything changed when the music did. There was a different crowd at the Savoy, a new crop of dancers, and the place just didn't have the same feel to it. There were still a few Lindy hoppers around, but I didn't recognize too many of them.

Some of Whitey's Lindy Hoppers had talked about working together again after we returned from the Army, at least those of us who made it through, and the whole time I was in the service I assumed I'd be coming back to that, but after the war we never really got ourselves together as a cohesive group. I guess it was because Whitey wasn't around much anymore to organize us, although he still had some involvement with the Savoy.

Since I wanted to get back into performing, I decided that I would start my own group. I was living back home with my mother and Aunt Marie at

230 West 140th Street, and had a little money saved up. It wasn't from the Army, which only paid a small salary. I had made it while sailing back from Japan. A lot of the men were shooting craps and some asked to borrow money from me, so I got the idea to charge a very small interest fee. It's the only time I ever did this.

Willamae Ricker and Ann Johnson were still dancing (Willamae had kept a small group going for a while during the war), and the two of them agreed to work with me. For the second man, I wanted someone who was a very good Lindy hopper, but who could also tap a bit. Keeping the group small was an artistic decision because there weren't that many dancers around who could do both styles. I tried out a couple of guys, but wasn't satisfied until I invited Russell Williams to join us. Russell could *dance*. He had been in Whitey's Lindy Hoppers, and had won the 1939 Harvest Moon Ball with Connie Hill. I put him with Willamae and, once again, I worked with Ann.

While the Four Congaroos (as I decided to call the act) were rehearsing at the Savoy, I heard that the Roxy Theatre wanted some teams of Lindy hoppers, so we went down there. Sammy Rausch (the Roxy's booking agent) knew the Lindy hoppers, but Gae Foster, the dance director, wanted everybody to audition. Even though I had performed there so many times, we had to try out just like all the other couples, which was a little annoying. She picked my group and three other teams, and asked me to do the choreography for everybody.

At the end of our two weeks at the Roxy, Mr. Rausch asked my group if we'd like to go into Club Zanzibar (on West 49th and Broadway) for a couple of months to be in a show starring Cab Calloway, Pearl Bailey, and the Charioteers (a gospel singing group). This nightclub was set up like the Cotton Club, with a big band, a fast-paced floor show, a chorus line, fine dining, and social dancing, so we jumped at the opportunity.

This was our first gig as the Four Congaroos. Our act started with a fast number, which was a combination of Lindy hop and the conga, a Cuban social dance with lively hip movements and footwork that's similar to what you'd do in a conga line.[1] I actually made up the music for this routine, which I called "Congaroo," by working with an arranger named Tom Whaley.[2] I would hum my idea, and he would write it out and arrange it to match the choreography, which alternated eight bars of conga with eight bars of Lindy, and included air steps.

I've said music was the inspiration for my dancing, but in this case dancing was the inspiration for my music. I got that idea from movies with the Nicholas Brothers, Fred Astaire, and Gene Kelly where the song and choreography fit together perfectly because a musical director wrote or arranged something to match their movements. It was the first time I'd done anything like that, except when I adapted "Jam Session" for the tour with Cab. From then on, I thought up most of the music for the Congaroos, and worked with Tom to get it written and arranged.

"Congaroo" was followed by a jazz routine that included the usual steps, and some additional ones like kick-ball-change, corkscrew steps, and some sexy moves like the mess-around. I also tried to include some funny bits that would give the audience a laugh.

Before this, whenever we did jazz routines, we always played right to the audience, facing out to the front of the house in a line. I never thought about doing it differently, but now that we were working in a nightclub where we could be seen on all sides, I broke the lines, so the girls went forward while the guys went back, then reversed it. I also had the two lines face each other for crosses, where we'd dance across the stage trading places. Naturally, we finished out our program with the Lindy hop,[3] which we did to an arrangement of "Jumpin' at the Woodside" that I worked out with Tom.

While we were appearing at the Zanzibar, my father died of a stroke. He was fifty-nine, I think. Cab offered to give me the evening off, but I said no, and the other dancers said it was one of the best shows I ever did. I didn't want people feeling sorry for me, so I guess I put more energy into my dancing that night. Butterbeans (of the comedy act Butterbeans and Suzie), who was a good friend and had come to see us perform, joked about it: "You should have somebody die every night, because you just did a hell of a show." Afterwards, I wanted to be by myself, but by the next night I was right back in there.

Although I lost my father, I had begun to see more of my son, who would come by the apartment to visit when I wasn't working. Chazz had been taking dance classes the whole time I was away, and had started doing some little shows at his high school. He even had an act called Hot Sauce and Ketchup with another kid, Nathan Alonzo, and they were on the television show *Teen Topper Revue* many times. I went to see him in several annual recitals at Carnegie Hall with the Starbuds, Mary Bruce's student dancers, and he was fantastic. In fact, he was so good that he started teaching at her studio when he was just fifteen.

The Zanzibar was followed by a short run at the Apollo Theatre, then an extended engagement, between six and twelve weeks, that I arranged at Club 845 in the Bronx. We shared the bill with Betti Mays and her band, Ray Sneed Jr. (a modern ballet dancer), and Juanita Pitts (one of the top-notch female tap dancers around), among others.

This was a period when we really grew as an act, and a time of experimentation. Depending on what the audience liked, or what I liked, I changed things around a lot and fine-tuned the act as far as staging, costumes, music, etc. For example, I added sections into the jazz routine where each dancer had about sixteen bars to come out in front of the group and do their thing. I also had some new costumes made, and over the next few years we built up our wardrobe enough that we didn't have to wear the same outfit for three days. In fact, we inspired other acts to follow suit.

All four of us began to study gymnastics at the acrobatic school of Max Powers, which was downtown, in order to improve how we executed some of the more demanding steps. I wanted to be sure we all understood the dynamics of the movements. Russell and I learned the correct way to perform our front flips, back flips, no-hand flips, splits, and handsprings, and it helped the girls do their air steps better. Doing our act night after night became easier on all of us.

This was the only time I ever took lessons for my dancing—except, that is, one time when I was in Whitey's Lindy Hoppers. I had read that they were giving Lindy hop classes at an Arthur Murray dance studio downtown. Out of curiosity I decided to check it out. When I walked in, the teacher was counting out the steps and doing I don't know what, but it wasn't the Lindy hop. It took me just a few minutes to say, "Oh man," and start to leave. The teacher asked, "Where are you going?" "This is a little bit too hard for me," I said, and cut out.

For the Club 845 engagement, we developed a new program that lasted a full ten to twelve minutes. My goal was to vary our act, so we weren't doing just the Lindy hop. I wanted to add a tap number for Russell and me, but I was not a tap dancer (although I could pick up a few steps), so I hired a professional tap choreographer, whose name was Buddy Bradley, I believe.[4] He made up a great routine, which he taught without using music. One day I was listening to the Artie Shaw recording of "Begin the Beguine" and realized that it fit the choreography perfectly. That happened sometimes. I'd hear something and think, *That's our routine right there!* Tom and I rearranged the song to fit the cartwheels, turns, splits, and other flourishes that Russell and I did. I also added an introduction, and had Juanita Pitts put together a few tap steps for the middle of the routine.

In 1952, we were on a bill with Teddy Hale for about four months. He also tapped to "Begin the Beguine," but to Eddie Heywood's version. When Teddy Hale danced to that song . . . ooooh! He tore up the stage! There was no way we could compare with him or follow it, so I switched our music to Sy Oliver's arrangement for Tommy Dorsey's band of "Swanee River."

Of course, I had to rearrange the choreography to fit the new song. When Buddy Bradley came to see us perform at the Apollo Theatre, he said, "That's not the same routine I taught you guys." "Yeah, well, after seeing Teddy Hale, we're not going to be dancing to that song anymore," I told him. "That's okay. I like it," he said, and smiled because he knew Teddy Hale.

The tap routine was followed by a new, medium-tempo floor routine I developed for just the two girls. We called it flash because it was done to "Flash" by Harry James. While the girls were doing their duet, Russell and I changed out of our tap shoes. They were okay for the conga number, but we couldn't wear them during the Lindy hop.

Soon after closing at Club 845, I think we're in mid-1947 now, we did the circuit, and I will never forget something that happened at the Howard Theatre in Washington, where we were on the bill with the Will Mastin Trio with Sammy Davis Jr. (before he was a big name) and Dizzy Gillespie's big bebop band. Dizzy had a drummer the Congaroos used to call Foots because his feet were so bad. He could hardly walk, but he'd kick it on the drums, very heavy on the beats. I had given Dizzy our music, but when we got out on stage and started dancing, it sounded *terrible*. "Jumpin' at the Woodside" is a swinging tune, but this drummer was dropping all these bebop bombs on us. We were up there trying to do our routine, but because of the way the music felt, we kept doing all these jerky movements. We just could not swing to what he was playing.

When we came off the stage, Dizzy was standing in the wings. "What the fuck was that?" I said. He just smiled at me, turned, and walked away. I'd known him since he was a youngster in Teddy Hill's band, but he could tell that I didn't understand the music. For the rest of the week, we had to struggle through the way that drummer played our charts. I remember thinking, *I guess this is the kind of music we're going to have to try to dance to.*

We went on tour with Dizzy another time while he still had his big band, and his drummer at that point, Kenny Clarke, who was more old school and could play bop *and* swing, managed to give the band a beat behind the bop. It was supposed to be a bebop band, but these cats could *swing.* I thought it was one of the best big bands around. I enjoyed this engagement much more than that week at the Howard Theatre!

It was in 1947 that I met Gloria Holloway, the woman I would eventually marry. We were introduced by a mutual friend at the Savoy, where Gloria went every Saturday night with a group of friends. She loved dancing, but was not a professional. Since I had just formed the Congaroos, I was out on the road a lot and didn't see her very often, but I did write. We began dating when I was in town, and over time got closer and closer. After a while, we started spending most of my time in New York together.

Smart Affairs

The Congaroos worked in St. Louis in the spring of 1948, for a production called The "Y" Circus Boosters. Everybody was in this show—Peg Leg Bates, Arthur Prysock, George Kirby, Buddy Johnson, Ella Johnson, and many others—and every act was a tremendous success. We all had to do encore after encore!

Around this time, Willamae found out that she needed major surgery. While she was laid up recuperating for about six weeks, the Congaroos didn't work at all. We just stayed around New York and practiced, although I worked as an ice man. Well, actually, I was really a numbers runner. The ice man part was kind of a cover for me to go around to people's apartments and collect their bets. I became very efficient at this, to the point where I could remember the numbers without writing them down. But it's a funny thing: I guess I was so courteous to my customers that some of their neighbors wanted me to be their ice man too. That part of the business grew, which pissed off my boss because he wanted me to spend all my time picking up the bets.

Hortense Allen (who I'd recently met in St. Louis, where she was the head of the chorus girls) got a job as the assistant choreographer for a production at Club Harlem in Atlantic City, and told Pops Williams about us. He remembered the Lindy hoppers from 1936 when he was running the Paradise Club. There had been a competition between the two nightspots back then. Eventually, the Paradise Club closed, and now Pops was running Club Harlem.

He was hiring entertainers for a show that he was planning for the summer called Larry Steele's "Smart Affairs." Larry Steele was a producer and entertainer who staged the revue, emceed, and sang in it. The show was done every year for a while and always had a great lineup. For instance, the 1952 revue included Butterbeans and Susie, and The Chocolateers. The Congaroos were not the stars of "Smart Affairs," but we were always the closing act, and we always stopped the show. We drew such a good crowd that we got booked into Club Harlem as part of "Smart Affairs" every summer from 1948 through 1954. People would recognize us when we walked down Kentucky Avenue. Gloria came to visit for a weekend and she thought we were wonderful.

Willamae wasn't ready to dance yet, so we hired Helen Daniels, who I knew from the Savoy and Whitey's Lindy Hoppers, to replace her until

Willamae could take over again. A few years later, Ann decided to get married and stop dancing. I tried out another dancer briefly, but she was very unreliable. Helen, who had been working elsewhere, became available, so we brought her back as my partner.

Russell stayed with the Congaroos the entire time. There was a short period when he couldn't dance because he was injured, which was a problem because we had some contracts for the Four Congaroos, and only three of us could perform. From then on, whenever I could, I had the act billed as just the Congaroos or the Congaroo Dancers.

Since everybody was listening to bebop, even though I didn't like it very much, I decided to try to create a number around it for "Smart Affairs." I made up a new Lindy routine and created a tune with Tom. We could dance to it, but the song just didn't have the flow of swing. We ended up only performing this piece once in a while.

Using different jazz routines was a way of varying our act a little bit for the patrons who sometimes stayed on from the first to the second show. We had another number called "Bibeau" (the nickname of the guy who created it for us), and one that I choreographed and named in tribute to the chorus girl who inspired it. I knew Tranky Doo (her nickname) from the Club DeLisa in Chicago, and she could really get down. Oftentimes, in show business, as the chorus girls were exiting the stage, one of the best dancers would be featured at the end of the line doing a couple of special steps before going into the wings. Tranky Doo held that spot. I used her exit steps, fall-off-the-log, shuffle, and bogeys, for the beginning of a moderate-tempo, two-chorus routine, made up of a bunch of other jazz steps that I put in a certain order. We sometimes did the Tranky Doo for an encore.

The Congaroos used to do the Tranky Doo in the corner of the ballroom when we stopped by the Savoy, which was only occasionally at this point. People who watched us picked it up, and it got spread around that way. I still teach the Tranky Doo, using "Tuxedo Junction" for music, although I've lengthened the choreography. The Rhythm Hot Shots, a Swedish jazz dance company, do it faster and have added some steps, which is fine with me. I don't mind if people change my choreography, as long as they stay in the same groove. In my opinion, that's what's kept the Lindy hop going all these years.

Most of the other Lindy hoppers had stopped dancing by now, but Norma had started her own group, the Del Rio Trio, with Billy Ricker as her partner and Mike Silva on drums. A few years later she formed a larger group, the Norma Miller Dancers, with several other men and women including my son, who was about seventeen at the time. The Congaroos went on tour with them to Venezuela and Colombia, and this is when Chazz and I really started to get to know each other. After that tour, the two dance groups often ended up performing in the same cities, at different spots, and he and I would have a ball hanging out between shows. On the rare occasions that I was appearing in New York, Chazz would come to the performances, and I'd drop by his rehearsals with Norma. I think this is when he really began to understand how much travel and hard work was involved in being a professional entertainer.

I thought Chazz was a wonderful dancer, so good, in fact, that I had suggested him when Norma was putting her company together. I was flattered that people often said they could tell he was my son by his dancing. He performed with Norma for about fourteen years, and went all over the world with her. Chazz had a helluva career, and I'm very proud of him.

I had arranged the Club Harlem spot on my own, and Sammy Rausch was still getting gigs for us (he was also handling Norma's group), but by a certain point the Congaroos had gotten big enough to have an agent who took over the booking. We were represented briefly by United Artists before going over to the William Morris Agency, which was better connected and was able to get us some very good engagements, including with Martha Ray, and Martin and Lewis. Through the agency, we worked six weeks at the Latin Casino in Philadelphia, the first two as the opening act for headliner Tony Bennett. He was a newly discovered star, but after we tore the house up, they changed the order around so he went first. A few years ago, when Chazz and I were staying at the Grand Hotel in Stockholm, we saw Tony Bennett in the dining room at breakfast. I went over, introduced myself, and said, "I doubt if you remember us, but I performed with you," and went on to tell him about the Latin Casino. He looked at me, started laughing, and said, "Yeah, you were the dance act that wouldn't let me on stage."

I also hired a publicist to help get our names and announcements and reviews about our performances into the press, including in trade publications like *Variety* and smaller local papers. My hope was that booking agents would see it and we'd get work.

We were invited to be part of *The Biggest Show of '52*, a revue that was produced and booked by Moe Gale. It was a big deal. The headliners were Nat King Cole, Stan Kenton and His Orchestra, and Sarah Vaughan. During that fall, we performed in Canada and toured all over the United States. We even played Carnegie Hall.

Working with the likes of these stars was a big thrill. One night, Sarah Vaughan, who was a wonderful singer, said, "I'm feeling really good tonight, and I'm going out there and sing my ass off." And she did! She was so great, even the musicians were smiling and applauding. She and I became very good friends and sometime social danced together.

With the Congaroos, I always provided the band—even if it was Basie, Dizzy, Hawkins, whoever—with our charts. On the first day of rehearsal with *The Biggest Show of '52*, I gave Stan Kenton our music. He took one look at it and said to the band, "Okay, fellas, I want you to play this straight. Just stay out of it." He meant he didn't want the guys improvising. He had very good musicians, and that's exactly what they did . . . for the first show. But as soon as we started the second show, Shelly Mann, the drummer, began adding extra beats to the conga and swing rhythms that were in the charts for our first number. His playing was so rhythmically Spanish that he got us really grooving to the music. It sounded so cool that, right in the middle of the routine, I yelled out, "Hey, Shelly! MAAAAAN!!!"

Just adding that little extra something to his drumming made us feel so good while we were dancing that I asked him to write out the rhythm for me. "That's hard," he said. "Drummers don't write down what they're feeling, they beat it out." But later on he did put something on paper. He played the same thing for the rest of the tour, and I called out the same thing on stage every night: "Shelly! MAAAAAN!"

Most of our time with *The Biggest Show of '52* was wonderful, but there were some very unpleasant incidents too. Except for Nat King Cole, who had his own limousine, the cast traveled by bus if we were only going a short distance. All of the black entertainers, including Nat Cole's musicians and Sarah Vaughan, rode together. We didn't mind. It was like one big family. Same thing for all of Stan Kenton's musicians. Of course, we also stayed in different hotels from the white musicians. We had to go to places that allowed blacks.

We were in the South, Virginia I think, when we pulled into this little town and said, "Okay, who's going out tonight?" That meant, who was going to find out which restaurant would serve us. It was my turn so, very reluctantly, I got off the bus and walked into this diner. As soon as I went through the door, this fellow said, "Hey, hey, hey, buddy. Where do you think you're going?" I told him that we had a busload of people outside and I wanted to see if I could get some sandwiches for them. "Sorry," he said, very tersely, "we don't serve you people." He didn't even care when I told him it was for takeout. Man, I thought, we've got Sarah Vaughan on this bus and he won't serve us!

As I was trudging back to break the news, this white cop who had overheard our conversation walked out behind me. "If you're looking for someplace to eat, you can follow me," he said. He led us on his motorcycle to an African American-run restaurant across town.

Once, when we were touring with *"Smart Affairs of 1952,"* the cast stopped into a restaurant that was divided by a partition, with whites on one side, blacks on the other. Helen Daniels was very light-skinned, so we dared her and another young lady from the chorus line to go into the white side. As we later found out, when a waitress asked them if they were with the show, they said they were the managers, so she let them sit there. We were over on the other side laughing so hard because they were passing.

When we were in Miami with *"Smart Affairs,"* we found out that cab drivers were discouraging people from going to the show because they didn't like a mixed audience going to see black performers. Attendance was so poor that the PR people for the club we were in got Walter Winchell to come. He started promoting it, but the management still had to let some of the more expensive acts go and hire cheaper, local entertainers. We stayed on because we were one of the more affordable acts, and were a staple of the show since we always got such a good hand.

These stories aren't really about the dancing, but people should know that this kind of thing went on all over the country. At the time, we looked at this stuff as just another one of those things, and we tried to laugh it off.

Act-ion

For six or seven years, the Congaroos did very well. We worked almost non-stop and we were making good money. We performed with Alvino Rey, Lucky Millinder, Illinois Jacquet, Ella Fitzgerald, with Basie two or three times, and with Erskine Hawkins on several occasions. We worked at the Apollo and the Palace Theatre quite often. In Chicago, we appeared at the Rhumboogie in 1947 and were the headliners at the Club DeLisa for several years, including in 1947, when Fletcher Henderson was the band.

In 1948, we made the movie *Killer Diller*, although I honestly can't remember doing it. Our performance was supposed to take place on the stage of the Lincoln Theatre, but I think it was filmed somewhere else. My one comment on the scene is that Andy Kirk's band played our music too damn fast.

We went to London in 1953 with a show called *A New Folies Bergère Revue: "Pardon My French,"* and appeared with Dinah Washington at the Apollo in 1954. We also did a couple of television shows: Ed Sullivan's *Toast of the Town* and Milton Berle's *Texaco Star Theater* (in 1951, I think).

When I was with Whitey's Lindy Hoppers, we were always changing our routines around and improvising. The Congaroos repeated the same show, more or less, every night for seven or eight years. Everything was choreographed, right down to the bows. Another difference was that Whitey's Lindy Hoppers only did Lindy routines—I don't separate the big apple and jazz routines from the Lindy—whereas the Congaroos were a complete act that performed comedy, tap, jazz, Latin dancing, *and* Lindy.

We could do anywhere from ten minutes to an hour if the management asked us to, although that rarely happened. The first time was in Providence, Rhode Island. We figured we were one of many acts, but when we showed up for rehearsal, we found out there wasn't anybody else on the bill. I don't know if this was because the nightclub was so small-time or it was just their policy. We protested that we couldn't do a whole hour, but the manager insisted. I didn't know what to do! We couldn't dance the whole time, so we sweated through a rehearsal and somehow came up with enough material to fill out the bill. I worked out some jokes, and practiced "Honeysuckle Rose," which I used to do in the Army. Of course, I didn't have the music, but the band, which was just a small combo, threw something together.

We opened with our conga routine to get the audience's attention. In between the dance numbers, I clowned around, desperately trying to keep the audience entertained. I had gotten some jokes from the band, and I could hear those cats laughing in the background even if I bombed with the audience.

When I sang "Honeysuckle Rose," I played it for comedy. I'd walk out into the audience, sit on some fellow's lap, and sing, "Honey, ssssuck my rose." Then I'd clown with his girl as if I'd made her jealous. Usually, it got a big laugh, but one night this guy got really mad and pushed me away. At the end of the show, I apologized to the whole audience, saying that I didn't mean any offense and was just kidding around.

Every night, I tried something different, attempting to find out what worked. I also found out what didn't work. It was rough, but people mostly seemed to like what we did and kept coming back. Some of them even requested "Honeysuckle Rose."

When I was with Whitey's Lindy Hoppers, we were very inexperienced. The only thing we knew was Lindy hopping. My hope had always been to elevate Lindy hopping to the point where the entertainment world wouldn't look down on us. Even with the Congaroos, it was a battle. I remember overhearing a conversation between my agent and the manager at a resort in the Poconos. My agent was telling this guy what a great act we were, and I heard him reply, "They're only Lindy hoppers. I can get them for a dime a dozen." He wanted Lindy hoppers because they were so exciting, but didn't want to pay our full fee. I got very annoyed because we had really perfected our act, so I told my agent to forget it. The manager went and got himself a dime-a-dozen group of dancers, and they stunk up the place so badly that he had to come back and ask if we were still available. I said, "Yes, but the price has gone up."

What I would have liked for Whitey's Lindy Hoppers and the Congaroos was to have achieved the status of a group like the Nicholas Brothers. Usually, when they were in a show, they were headliners. But we never got to that point. Although we appeared with many great stars, it was always in a supporting role. We might tear the joint apart and be the best thing in the house, but when we came back to that theater or nightclub, our names were in the same place on the marquee.

During all my years of dancing, I never really knew if I was successful or not . . . until one of the Congaroos' last gigs. We were appearing with Cab Calloway, one of the greatest entertainers in the world, at the Apollo Theatre. At the first show, and every night from then on, Cab introduced us by saying, "The Congaroos have become one of the finest acts in the entertainment world." It was a tremendous pleasure to me that we were finally getting credit as an act, and had come to be considered one of the best in the business.

End of the Beguine

The last time I saw Whitey was while we were performing at Club 845 in 1947. He was in the audience and came backstage afterwards to tell us how much he'd enjoyed the show. "You guys were great!" he said. "I love the act."

We made plans to meet at the Savoy the next day, which we did. After congratulating me again, he started asking if I would teach him the Congaroos' tap routine. I didn't know why he was interested, but my thoughts were that maybe he was trying to get me back into his fold. Or, always the con man, maybe he was going to show it to some of the better dancers who were still around and try to build a group back up. I said sure, and got up to show it to him, thinking, *he'll never remember the steps*, which is exactly what happened. In fact, he never really got them at all. When we parted, I said, "See you around." Whitey's last words to me were, "Good luck with the act."

I was on the road with the Congaroos when I heard that Whitey had passed away in September 1950. I think Pal Andrews, an ex-Lindy hopper who was Whitey's gal Friday before he left the city and moved up to Oswego, told Billy Ricker, and he let us know. I felt *really* sad about it. Here was a person who had almost brought me up. In fact, it was kind of rough on all of us.

Around 1953, 1954, things started slowing down a little as far as jobs for the Congaroos. In New York especially, a lot of the nightclubs started closing and the only place we could find work was in theaters. There were only a few big bands playing swing anymore, like Duke and Cab, and they were really trying to hang in there, mostly by doing concerts. Some of the musicians were still playing swing or bop in small combos, but many had gone over to R&B to make more money, or just to keep working. As I watched the whole scene dissipate, I wondered how much longer the Congaroos could hold ourselves together.

With This Ring

Believe it or not, I proposed in Klein's Department Store on Fourteenth Street at Union Square, where Gloria was working as a cashier. This was 1953. We had been dating for about six years, and I had begun to think about marrying her. One day I bought an engagement ring, and stood in line with the rest of the customers. She was so busy that she didn't notice me. When I got to her cash register, I put the box on the counter. She noticed the box, looked up and saw me, then opened it and almost fainted when she saw the ring! I said, "Will you accept?" and she said, "Yes!"

All these people were standing around laughing and saying what a nice thing it was. Gloria was worried that she would get in trouble, but her supervisor told her to take some time off, so we stepped off to the side to be alone for a few minutes.

We didn't get married until June 26, 1954 because I was still going out of town a lot with the Congaroos. Our wedding was in a church in the Bronx, followed by a four-day honeymoon to Atlantic City. Then we both had to get back to work.

I kept things going with the Congaroos for a while, but the work wasn't too steady, and things really started to slow down. Eventually, Gloria suggested that I get a job, something for just a year or so. We were trying to bring up a family—we had a baby daughter, Marion, by then—and that's difficult if you're on the road all the time.

Applications for policemen and postal workers were being accepted. Gloria didn't want me to apply for the police job because it was too dangerous, so I opted for the post office. This was before they had a good union, so you had to work long hours in order to make any kind of money. There we were again with me not home very much.

Gloria, who had become a nurse by now, worked during the day, while I stayed home with Marion. My first job in the post office was from 6 p.m.

until 2:30 in the morning, so as she was walking in the door, I'd be walking out to catch the bus to work. I'd get home early in the morning, catch 40 winks, and start all over again.

By 1960, Gloria was pregnant again, and we were able to purchase a home in Jamaica, Queens. Since I wasn't making that much money, I took a couple of part-time jobs and Gloria's mother helped out with child care when Frankie Jr. was born. The schedule was tough on all of us, but we also had some very nice times as a family.

Right after I started working in the post office at Lexington Avenue and Forty-fifth Street in late 1954, I got a call from my agent at William Morris saying that he had a one-week job for the Congaroos at the Palace Theatre, if I wanted it. I couldn't keep working because this gig was for four shows a day. So, not knowing the rules of the post office, I just left without even notifying them.

After we opened at the Palace, I got a letter from the post office about not showing up. When I went back to talk to my supervisor, he told me that I should have informed them. In the meantime, we had gotten a few more dates, so I told a little white lie. I said I had to go down South to take care of some family matters, but that I would like to come back at a future date. They told me to write a letter explaining all of this, which I did.

The Congaroos went out on some more dates, but during the next six months things started to get slower and slower, until we weren't working much at all. One gig was a special benefit in Philadelphia with Lionel Hampton's orchestra. There were a lot of different acts in the show, and we gave him our music at rehearsal along with everybody else. He played everyone's music for their run-through, but when it came to our turn, he said, "We don't have to use their music for the Lindy hoppers. We can just play anything." It was as if he looked down on us, like we were dirt.

I said, "No, you can't play just anything. We're an act," but he wouldn't listen. We didn't get to rehearse and, because of him, we couldn't even do our act; we had to improvise our way through. I haven't forgiven Lionel Hampton to this day. As it turned out, that was the Congaroos' last performance.

Neither Snow nor Rain nor Heat nor Gloom . . .

I decided it was time to return to the post office. Fortunately, they took me back. I think I had made a good impression on them because I was a hard worker and willing to learn, and it probably helped that I was a war vet. This time, I was sent to the main post office on Thirty-third Street and Eighth Avenue. I thought I was going to be a clerk at a window where people bought stamps, so I went in looking sharp in my white shirt, white tie, and suit. Instead, the supervisor herded a bunch of us over to this long table with a chute over it. When they opened it up, all this mail and dust came pouring out. I got filthy.

When they gave us a break from standing there and separating the bulk mail from the plain letters, I said to myself, *I'm going to quit this place right now!* I walked into the lunchroom, and who should I run into but Samuel Scott, or Scotty, as we called him. We had met at the Savoy before the war and become close friends from being on the road together when I was with the Congaroos and he was the valet for the Gerald Wilson Band. Scotty had been at the post office for three years. We swore to each other that we'd be out of there in a minute, but we both needed the job, so we stayed . . . for thirty years.

During the next decade, I jumped at every opportunity to learn new jobs. I worked a number of different details, including as a distributor and at the time desk, where I was one of only two African Americans in an otherwise all-white, male department. When I was occasionally given the privilege of picking out people to help at the time desk, I was able to bring in some other blacks and some women. I helped get them into that department, and I'm kind of proud of that. After about ten years, I passed the test to become a supervisor, which meant that I oversaw an entire mail processing unit. Before the end of my time in the post office, I also worked on selecting sites for new stations, and trained in the earliest forms of computerization that the post office had begun to use.

Working at the post office was difficult at times because I missed being in show business, but I did all right because I was busy raising a family, and I was able to adapt to my surroundings and made a lot of new friends. The job could be monotonous, but I managed to have a very good time during my years there. A group of six or seven co-workers and I often found ways to make things more interesting. For example, we came up with a numbers game that kept us from getting bored while we were sorting mail. The stakes were very high—a cup of coffee or a bottle of soda. We got to be so fast that the higher-ups often called on us to break in new supervisors and foremen.

I also became part of a very tight group of fun-loving people. In the mid-1970s, I began working the 3:30 p.m. to midnight tour, and we'd go out dancing after work (the time for Cinderella *and* for me), have barbecues or go to the beach on our day off, and go on cruises down to Bermuda and Nassau for vacations. Scotty, his companion, Delores Spencer (who also worked in the post office), me, and some others even formed our own social club called the Seven Friends, because that's how many of us started it.

Lots of postal workers belonged to social clubs. The main activity of all these groups was attending parties and dances. When one club threw a dance, they would invite all the other ones, and my crowd would always go together. The Diplomat Hotel on Forty-third Street off Sixth Avenue was a popular spot because it had a beautiful ballroom and wasn't all that expensive to rent. One time, we put on a dance at the Audubon Ballroom, and hired Norma's group (with Chazz) to perform and Buddy Tate's group to play. We got a big crowd for that.

In general, people stayed within their own ethnic groups in the post office, but we also got to be friends with everybody. You must remember that people were working in close contact. We hung out together, and when there was a dance or a retirement party, it would be a mixed crowd. I'm not saying it's the answer to all racial problems but, in general, whatever color you are, when you get to know somebody, it's a different story altogether.

I always agreed with Martin Luther King's point of view. In 1963, a whole group of us from the Postal Workers Union went down by bus to the rally in Washington, D.C. to support him. When I heard him give his famous "I have a dream" speech, I was very moved. He didn't preach against any one group. He preached that everybody could get along, which is how I look at it.

During my early years in the post office, I still thought about dancing professionally. Once, while I was listening to a Count Basie record, I got all excited because I could really envision a routine from just that. I called Russell Williams on the telephone and said, "Hey, man! I want you to hear this." He listened over the phone and said, "Yeah, that sounds great." I said, "Man, I could really make a fantastic routine to this," but I never did.

Hardly any of my co-workers knew about my previous career, and I didn't discuss it with anybody. When we went out dancing in the '60s, they were playing music for dances like the twist, the jerk, and the monkey, so I just did those along with everybody else. Well, okay, I admit I stood out a little. At some point, I met a postal worker named Shirley who could swing dance pretty well. If we were at a party, someone would always ask, "Frankie, why don't you and Shirley dance?" They'd put on some swing music, and when we got out on the floor, people would just stand around and watch.

The Savoy was open until 1958, but I only got up there about once a month because of my work schedule. It wasn't anything like the old days, anyway. There was a whole new batch of Lindy hoppers up there. Some of them knew me from the Congaroos, but I didn't see too many guys from the old gang.

IN 1968, *Jazz Dance: The Story of American Vernacular Dance* by Marshall and Jean Stearns was published. As the first comprehensive, academic history of African American social and theatrical dance, *Jazz Dance* heralded an emerging interest in vernacular black culture that would accelerate in the following years. At the time of publication, no one could have predicted the ardent resurgence of interest in swing dancing that would take root in the early 1980s and build to a more widespread popular cultural movement by the late 1990s.

Prior to the re-release of a second edition of *Jazz Dance* in 1994, newly minted Lindy hoppers were paying out-of-print prices to score copies. Imagine their disappointment when, upon reading the three chapters on the jitterbug (including one titled "The Savoy Ballroom," which refers to the introduction of air steps and ensemble dancing into the Lindy hop vocabulary), they found no mention of their adored Frankie Manning. (He is in two group pictures of Whitey's Lindy Hoppers, but the dancers portrayed are not credited.)

Many swing dancers were, and remain, bewildered by the excision of Frankie's role in Lindy hop history, especially considering the Stearnses' major sources of information for these chapters. The authors relied almost entirely on accounts by two prime members of Whitey's Lindy Hoppers, Al Minns and Leon James, men with whom Frankie had thrilled audiences and shared an incredible decade.

Frankie didn't know about *Jazz Dance* until Chazz gave him a copy in 1971. Despite the fact that, at the time, *Jazz Dance* must have seemed like the first and last word on the subject, Frankie didn't blame his colleagues, although he was surprised. When pressed to divulge if he felt anger or bitterness over the book's unwitting revisionist history, he swears he didn't. "I just felt puzzled. I didn't know why they told it like that."

Frankie will point out that neither Leon James nor Al Minns was on the scene when he created the Lindy air step and synchronized ensemble Lindy routines in 1935. And he disputes some other statements in the book, most notably the account of a brawl that took place at the Renaissance Ballroom in the mid-'30s. As described, the incident ended with the beating to death of a rival gang member by one of the Jolly Fellows (Whitey's social club), with Whitey present and in command.[5]

Frankie remembers the event a little differently: "I was at the Savoy Ballroom when we heard that there was a fight at the Renaissance. A bunch of us went over to see what was happening, including Whitey, and there had been a fight, but nobody got thrown off the balcony or killed. When I confronted Al about his version, I said, 'Man, you hadn't even started coming to the Savoy at the time, so how could you know what happened?' It's possible that by the time Al heard the story, it had already been exaggerated, but he told me, 'I just made it sound exciting.'"

Swing dance historian Terry Monaghan's research into the writing of *Jazz Dance* leads him to suggest that dissatisfaction on the part of some readers may be due to the fact that Marshall Stearns, having suffered a series of heart problems, knew he was in a race against time to complete the project. "The basic manuscript was ready by the summer of 1966, by which time Stearns had reworked the testimony of some two hundred, often strongly opinionated artists into a rich exploration of the many types of jazz dance. His research was hampered by a range of problems, including being shunned by some dancers, being fed self-serving information by others, a widespread indifference by academia, and difficulties finding a publisher. Inevitably, some people were left unhappy with the result. Stearns died on December 18 of that year, leaving his widow and co-author to see to the final details of publication, which took place two years later."[6]

Judy Pritchett, creator of the "Archives of Early Lindy Hop" at Savoystyle.com, also points out that "Frankie had retired from professional dancing in 1955. From the mid 1950s into the early 1960s, Stearns, Minns, and James toured colleges and jazz festivals, and made several television appearances presenting their lecture/demonstration on the history of jazz dance. I don't think it occurred to Stearns to seek other sources."[7] ●

In 1975, my mother passed away at the age of seventy-six. The whole family mourned her. Fortunately, she didn't linger long once she became ill. I might not have shown it outwardly, but at the time I was really bleeding inside because I loved my mother and I missed her. She had been my guiding star and my inspiration for the way that I lived.

A year later, after twenty-two years of marriage, Gloria and I split up. To this day, I think the problem was that our heavy work schedules eventually took a toll on us. We tried to keep it together, at least for the sake of the kids, but it just didn't work out. I left with just my clothes and records and moved in with Chazz, who was also separated from his wife, and living in Harlem at the time. A few months later, we got an apartment together in Lefrak City. The records got an entire walk-in closet.

This was a pretty tough time for me. I had thought Gloria and I would be together for the rest of our lives, and our marriage ending made me feel like a failure. I felt pretty low and worthless for a long time.

Chazz had stopped performing with Norma in the mid-'60s when the work began to dry up, and had been driving a cab for a while, so I helped him get a job in the post office. He managed to keep up some dancing by teaching tap to kids at the Austin Dance Academy (where he still teaches in their new Las Vegas location), but his professional performing career came to a halt. Once he started working in the same place as me and we began living together, we became very, very close, best friends, really.

Gloria and I officially divorced in 1989, but by then we had developed a very wonderful friendship based on our concern for our children.

Whenever anything would happen with them, good or bad, Gloria would call to let me know and we'd talk about it. These days, if there's a family affair, we all try to gather at someone's house—Gloria, Chazz, Frankie Jr. and his wife Debbie, Marion, my seven grandchildren, my four great-grandchildren, sometimes Vincent (my half-brother) and his family—and we have a wonderful time. The family is closer now than we've ever been before.

PART V
SECOND
ACT
$\left(1984-2007\right)$

14 • REVIVAL

Back in the Swing of Things

In 1984, just about thirty years after I'd gone to work in the post office, Norma Miller called to tell me that Smalls' Paradise, an old nightclub in Harlem, had begun holding swing dances on Monday nights to live music with Al Cobbs' C&J Big Band.[1] I was still working, so I couldn't go very often, but I went up there a couple of times to check it out. The crowd wasn't all that big, but it was a good mix of colors and ages. I didn't dance much, partly because I didn't know many people. I mostly just watched and listened to the music.

There were other things going on around this time. The year before, I had judged one of the Harvest Moon Ball contests that Mama Lu Parks was still putting on. In April 1983, at Norma's suggestion, Larry Schulz and his wife, Sandra Cameron, had invited about thirty Savoy Lindy hoppers to a little get-together at their dance studio.[2] It was wonderful to see everybody, and we had a ball catching up and dancing with each other. We were all out there clowning around, trying to remember our old routines.

In my opinion, Larry and Sandra deserve a lot of credit for getting the older Lindy hoppers back out there and helping to introduce their style to a new generation. In 1982, they had hired Al Minns (who had been introduced to them by Sally Sommer, a dance critic and historian) to teach at the Sandra Cameron Dance Center, which, to my knowledge, was the first time that a dance studio brought in one of the original Savoy Lindy hoppers as a teacher.

Norma put together a show for the Village Gate in April 1984 that was produced by Larry Schulz and starred Harold Nicholas (of the Nicholas Brothers). She served as master of ceremonies, did some comedy, and performed in the dance numbers (a big apple, shim sham, Lindy hop, and jazz routine) with the Norma Miller Jazz Dancers.[3]

Al Minns, Billy Ricker, and I were all in the audience, and at the end of the show Norma invited us to come up on the stage. She told the crowd that this was the first time we four had been together since we came back from Brazil in 1941. (Willamae Ricker and Ann Johnson had passed away by

•

this time.) Then, each of us danced with Norma. We just fooled around, but it was very exhilarating, and the audience, which had quite a few of Al's students in it, responded enthusiastically.

I really enjoyed all of these occasions, but none of them gave me the feeling that swing dancing was coming back. It wasn't until I walked into one of the New York Swing Dance Society's dances at the Cat Club in 1985 that I first had the thought, *Wow! Maybe something is happening.* When I saw all these people out on the floor dancing to a live big band and having such a good time, I said, "*Look* at this!" It was like being in a smaller version of the Savoy all over again. *That's* when I first thought, *Okay, it's coming back.*[4]

The NYSDS has been holding dances continuously since May 1985, and I still go to them as often as I can. I think this organization has done a tremendous amount for swing dancing in general, and Lindy hopping in particular. I credit them for giving orchestras the opportunity to perform for dancers and giving Lindy hoppers a chance to dance to live swing music. They've also hired many of the Savoy dancers to teach authentic Lindy hop at their events.

Over the years, I've taught quite a few workshops for the NYSDS, and pretty early on, I introduced the shim sham at their dances. A few of us, like Norma, Buster, Betty Brisbane (an ex-chorus girl), and I began doing it, and people started to catch on even before I taught any shim sham workshops. I created a special version of the shim sham for swing dancers with freezes instead of breaks in the second chorus, and a third chorus of boogies and Shorty Georges. Somehow, we got into doing it every week (which we did not do at the Savoy), always at the top of the third set. Over time I've added some special features, such as swinging out after the third chorus, with slow motion, freezes, and itches. The shim sham has really caught on, and it's now done at swing dances all over the world.

There was also some good dancing going on at these parties that Bryant DuPré, a musician, started throwing every weekend in spring 1986 in the basement of a building in TriBeCa. Sometimes he played tapes, and sometimes his band, the Swing Now Trio, performed.[5]

A Teacher Is Born

One evening, I got a phone call, and when I picked up the receiver, a young lady asked if this was Frankie Manning the dancer.

"No," I answered, "this is Frankie Manning the postal worker."

Then she said, "But did you used to dance?"

"Yes," I said, "but I don't anymore."

She explained that she and her partner, who were dance teachers and Lindy hop enthusiasts, had been studying with Al Minns before he passed away.[6] She said she had gotten my name from Bob Crease, a board member of the NYSDS, and looked me up in the phone book. She was calling all the way from California, and wanted to know if I would work with them when they came to New York in a couple weeks. At first, I said no, but this lady was very persistent, and asked if I would just look at them dance.

I was sitting with Norma at one of Bryant's parties when Erin Stevens and Steven Mitchell came over and introduced themselves. As I had agreed, I watched them swing out, and right away I could see that these two had soul. They were very good dancers, had wonderful rhythm, and carried themselves well. Even though the Lindy hop is a partner dance, some people dance it like they're on their own. But these two were real partner dancers. As I watched them, I thought, *Maybe I can help them get a little better.*

The next day, I picked them up in the city and drove them out to my apartment in Queens. We worked a little in my living room, which was carpeted, and I showed them my old photo albums, but after that they rented space at Fazil's, a studio in Midtown Manhattan. The first thing I did when we got there was ask them to dance again. Erin and Steven had studied the Lindy scene in *Day at the Races,* and they were into fast dancing in California.

When you dance fast, you tend to compensate by cutting the steps so that they fit into the amount of time you have. "Wait a minute," I said, "I can't even see what you're doing." I wanted them to dance to something slower so I could see how they actually executed the steps. I put on "Shiny Stockings," but it was hard for them to slow it down, and I hadn't developed any teaching skills yet. At that point, Steven said, "Frankie, can you please just dance with Erin for me." He wanted to see what *I* did with Erin, so I started dancing with her, moving with the music, working with the beat. I wanted them to express what they were hearing in the music through their dancing, which is what I tried to show them. They have since both told me that this was the moment things started to click for them.

We worked for about three or four hours a day for the rest of the week, going through a lot of material. I showed them how to do some of the movements they had seen in movies but didn't know the name for, and I know we worked on the basic swing-out. Erin and Steven showed a lot of improvement. By the end of the week, she knew she was going back to California to teach the Lindy, and he now teaches all over the world. They say that week changed their lives; well, it changed mine too. This was my first real teaching experience, and I have to say that it was their abilities and enthusiasm that got me juiced up again.

Some of the dance spots in New York had different groups give little demonstrations. While Erin and Steven were here, they did an exhibition at the Cat Club, along with the Jiving Lindy Hoppers from London, and Sylvia Sykes and Jonathan Bixby from Santa Barbara (who had worked with Dean Collins and Maxie Dorf). I guess it was kind of a big deal for all of these cats to meet each other, to find out there were people getting into swing dancing in different places.[7]

The swing dance scene continued to grow. Bryant's parties had stopped, but the Swing Now Trio had started playing at the North River Bar, also in TriBeCa, every Wednesday. They had some very good guest musicians, like Buddy Tate, Doc Cheatham, Max Kaminsky, and Panama Francis. I used to like going there because it was such a small, intimate place that people could really cut loose, and I got to dance with some of the best dancers in New York at the time.

More and more people also seemed to be interested in having me teach them. Around late 1986, early 1987, Monica Coe and Pat McLaughlin started the Big Apple Lindy Hoppers, the official dance company of the NYSDS. Their purpose was to preserve and present the performance side of Lindy hop, to learn how to do air steps, and to work with me. It had taken them a while to talk me into training with the group because I didn't think I was a good enough teacher, but when I realized how serious they were, I agreed to choreograph some routines for them. Monica and Margaret Batiuchok (an original board member of the NYSDS, its current president, and a dance teacher), used to help me teach by breaking down the choreography for the other dancers. I got into working with the BALH so much that I began performing with them when I was in town. I continued to coach them until about 2001, and still do occasionally.

Larry Schulz had been asking me to replace Al at Sandra Cameron's for some time, but I was kind of reluctant because I wasn't sure how to teach the Lindy at a dance studio. By May 1987, I felt a little more confident in my teaching skills from working with the Big Apple Lindy Hoppers, so I started giving group classes at Sandra's, which I've been doing there ever since.

Sometime in the first half of the year, I also began performing in school shows all over New York City with Norma Miller's latest group, the Savoy Swingers, which I continued doing until early 1991.[8] I thought it was wonderful that all these kids were getting to see this program about swing dance and music, and they really seemed to like it.

Mid-1987 was an important period for me because, among other things, it was the beginning of my long association with a Swedish dance group, The Rhythm Hot Shots. I think they had heard about me in London from Erin and Steven. I guess my name was beginning to get out there among swing dancers. A few of the Swedes[9] had come to New York in 1984 trying to find some of the dancers they'd read about in *Jazz Dance* and seen perform in films.[10] They met Al on that trip, studied with him in New York, and invited him to work with them in Sweden later that year, which he told me all about. In early 1987, The Rhythm Hot Shots contacted me about coming to Sweden to teach them, and in late June I flew over for two weeks. I brought clothes that were right for the nice weather we were having in New York, but it was so cold there that I had to wear three or four layers all the time!

I worked with six dancers: Eva Lagerqvist and Eddie Jansson, Catrine Ljunggren and Lennart Westerlund, and Ewa Staremo (who I nicknamed W because her name was pronounced the same as Eva's) and Anders Lind. For my first week, we practiced in Stockholm every day for several hours after they finished their jobs. After that we went out to Herräng, a little town about two hours north of the city where the Swedish Swing Society had been running small dance camps since 1982. We stayed at Folkets Hus, the community center, which has a big main room that we used for rehearsing and rooms on the second floor for sleeping.

I was amazed to discover that The Rhythm Hot Shots had learned to Lindy by watching *Hellzapoppin'* and *A Day at the Races* over and over in slow motion on a VCR. They would sit in front of the television for hours trying to get a step. These dancers really wanted to learn what the Lindy was all about, and we worked very intensely once we got to Herräng. For starters, I showed them the difference between social dancing and stage dancing. It was only after we spent time on social dancing that I showed them the authentic way to do the air steps, which they were very good at catching on to. They even improved on some of them.

I also taught them jazz steps and the shim sham. I would say: "Throw your hips out of joint because this is a down-to-the-ground, nitty-gritty dance," or "Really get down low for the Suzie-Q," then show them what I meant. I would have them do a step over and over, until I thought they had it down well enough to go on to something else.

One day, we spent a lot of time practicing the pimp walk, trying to get the right attitude. After rehearsal, I went to bed. When I woke up, my clock said four o'clock, the sun was shining, and I could hear music playing downstairs. I thought, *Man! I've been sleeping all day long!* jumped up, threw on some clothes, and ran downstairs. Anders was in the hall practicing the pimp walk over and over, trying to do it exactly the way I had been doing it. I said, "Why did you all let me sleep all day?!" Then I looked around. "Where's the rest of the group?" "Frankie," he said, "it's four o'clock in the *morning*. Everyone else is sleeping."

The Rhythm Hot Shots (which was reorganized as the Harlem Hot Shots several years ago) developed into very good teachers and a very exciting performing group. I didn't go back to Sweden until 1989, but I've taught at their camp every year since then. Herräng Dance Camp started out with about 30 people who were all Swedish, but it's grown every year. Now, camp lasts for all of July, and in 2006 they had more than 50 of the best instructors in the world teaching over 3,500 people from more than 40 different countries.

Herräng is a haven of Lindy hopping, and I think it's really helped the swing dance revival in a lot of ways. First, The Rhythm Hot Shots have done a lot to pass on the dance traditions of the 1930s and 1940s to the next generation. Second, when people take back all that they've learned in Sweden to their country, it's helped keep the dance evolving. Finally, Herräng has inspired a lot of other people to start camps and weekends all over the world, many of which I've been privileged to teach at.

The Only Count I Know

Figuring out how to teach people who didn't learn to Lindy hop by going to the Savoy has been a strange experience for me. At first, I found teaching to be very difficult, and it took some time for me to develop into what I call a studio teacher. I remember when David Wend, one of my students at Sandra Cameron's, asked if the step I was demonstrating in class was in six counts. I had no idea what the heck he was talking about. I knew how to count out bars, but I had never counted how many beats there were in a step. I'd never even thought about whether the Lindy is made up of eight-count *and* six-count steps, which it is. It's not that you decide how many counts a step should be. Some steps are just naturally one or the other. For instance, the basic step is eight counts, but the overhead turn and the jig walk just work out to be six counts.

A lot of my students want me to count for them, and I sometimes joke that the only count I know is Count Basie. I prefer to sound the rhythm out (which can sound like scatting or a word rhyme), and I think a lot of swing dance teachers do that. But I do think that counting can be valuable because some people are just not going to pick up a step without it. When I was first trying to learn how to count, I'd tell my students, "I'll do the step and you count it out." But over time, I developed the skill to do it myself. Once they have the movement, I tell dancers to start listening to the music *while* they're counting, because if they do they'll hear that the music is counting *for* them. Then they can stop counting and just dance.

Going Pro 2

I had been planning on retiring from the post office, although I didn't have any idea what the heck I'd be doing with all that free time. In early June, right after I got back from Sweden, I finally did. Several months later, when Scotty also left the post office, he and I shared a wonderful retirement party. There were two bands and dancing, and I performed a routine with the Big Apple Lindy Hoppers.

Many wonderful things continued to happen on the swing dance scene, and for me, during the next few years. In April 1988, I went to England to work with the Jiving Lindy Hoppers and help choreograph and perform in a show that their manager and researcher, Terry Monaghan, cooked up and produced called *The Cotton Club Revue (Re-Visited)*, which celebrated my first visit to London in 1937. Warren Heyes was the artistic director (it's Carolene Hinds now). They're a very good group that performs and teaches the Lindy and jazz dancing. I had done a two-day workshop with them in New York in spring 1986, with Norma joining for one of those days, and I give them a lot of credit for training with some of the other older dancers, like Mama Lu Parks, Pepsi Bethel, and George and Sugar Sullivan.

Ryan Francois and Julie Oram were also an integral part of the London scene. In 1987 they had begun teaching at a weekly swing dance night called Jitterbugs.[11] Sing Lim helped run Jitterbugs for a time and contributed many wonderful ideas to the event, before moving back to Singapore and getting swing dancing going there. And, beginning in 1988, Simon Selmon started hosting weekly swing dances to live music at The 100 Club in London.

Toward the end of 1988, Alvin Ailey invited Norma to choreograph a Lindy hop routine for a new piece he was planning for the Alvin Ailey American Dance Theater called "Opus McShann," which was based on the music of Jay McShann. Norma asked me to collaborate with her on the choreography, which was to "Jumpin' the Blues," and to help teach the dancers. Here were professionals trained in modern and ballet who were taught to be very upright, and we were telling them to get down! But, you know, they kind of liked the idea, at least for this one number. They tried to the best of their ability, and I think they did a very good job. Norma and I actually danced in the piece at its New York premier in December, which was a special fund-raiser for the company hosted by Bill Cosby.

Broadway Black and Blues

While I was teaching a private class at Sandra Cameron's in early 1987, Larry brought somebody in to watch the class who he introduced as Héctor Orezzoli. Héctor and his partner, Claudio Segovia, were theater producers who had conceived and directed *Flamenco Puro* and *Tango Argentina* (both of which had played in Europe before opening on Broadway), as well as a Parisian revue called *Black and Blue*. Sally Sommer had been hired by the producers to locate people who could help train the dancers from *Black and Blue* for a new version that they hoped to take to Broadway. Larry later told me that during my class Héctor leaned over and said, "This is the man I've been looking for!"

At that point, Héctor and Claudio were planning to open *Black and Blue* in 1987, but it was delayed because they got involved in some other projects. A year went by before I heard from them, at which point they contacted me to set up a little audition. When they put the music on, I just got up and did my thing. Afterwards, they asked if I would train some of their core dancers in the authentic style of jazz dancing, which I started doing for the next few months.

I think Héctor and Claudio had been planning to let the dancers improvise and create most of their own choreography, which is how it was done in their other shows, but after we got going, they sat me down one day and said they wanted me to actually choreograph a routine for *Black and Blue*. As usual, at first I was a little reluctant, but I agreed and began rehearsals with all of the dancers in mid-1988.

I was given freedom to choose the music, so I selected an Andy Kirk tune. Even though you can Lindy to "Wednesday Night Hop," I made a decision not to put too much Lindy hopping in the routine because the dancers were in a lot of other numbers and they would have gotten exhausted. And I would have wanted to give them a lot of air steps, which might have caused some injuries. Besides, none of them knew how to Lindy, and by then I knew how hard it would be to teach them to do it with the right style.

So what I did was put something together with a lot of jazz steps from the big apple, mixed in with a few Charleston and Lindy steps, then worked with them on getting the right feeling for the choreography. Now, these kids were real professionals. Sometimes, while they were relaxing on their union breaks,

I'd be in the front of the studio trying to figure out a step by myself. I'd look up and be surprised to see many of them out on the floor doing the step right along with me. They were that quick to catch on. They really got into the spirit of it, and I think I was able to help them bridge the gap between Broadway jazz and the older style. In fact, I thought they did a hell of a job.

The producers were so happy with "Wednesday Night Hop" that they asked me to choreograph another number, in this case to Duke Ellington's "Black and Tan Fantasy." This time I said nope, period. There were a couple of reasons. The first was that this song is a slow blues, and I didn't have enough confidence in my abilities to do a routine in that style. Dancing to the blues, which I do socially, is one thing, but teaching it to people and choreographing the blues was something else. I wasn't sure I—not the dancers, but me—could do it justice.

The second reason was that, although I had had complete freedom for the first routine, Héctor and Claudio had a concept in mind for "Black and Tan Fantasy." Even though they kept trying to explain their idea to me, I just couldn't picture what they were saying. The two of them kept trying to convince me and I kept telling them to give it to someone else, but they insisted that they wanted me to do it. At one point they set up a meeting with Dianne Walker, the assistant choreographer. I walked in and said, "Even though you brought this beautiful young lady down here to convince me, I'm still not doing it."

After about a month of going back and forth, one of them suggested that I think of choreographing a day in the life of a dancer . . . and something about that clicked for me. Wheels started turning, and some ideas started to form in my head. I began picturing people getting ready to go to a dance, primping and preening. Then I saw them social dancing in a ballroom (not Lindy hopping, because that didn't work with the music), and interacting like people do at a dance.

At the same time, I was listening to "Black and Tan Fantasy" over and over. I would go to sleep with it playing. Finally, I realized that I could deal with the music by working with the steady under-beat, and use the solo work of the musicians as inspiration for the movements of the dancers.

Between the two breakthroughs, I decided to accept the job, but told Héctor and Claudio that if I got halfway through and wasn't happy with it, they would have to get someone else. I made sure they knew that I wasn't kidding.

Once I had a clear concept for the piece, I was able to move forward and complete the routine, which ended up being a bluesy, swing number composed of funky, low-down jazz movements. I looked back to all of the

REVIVAL

dances and steps that I'd seen in the past, slowed them down to fit the music, and in some cases adapted them to fit the abilities of the dancers. Choreographing this number was a huge challenge, and there were some tough moments. It was always on my mind. In fact, this was when I first began writing down my choreographic ideas. Something might come to me while I was lying in bed or driving, and I didn't want to lose it, so I would write it in a notebook. When the routine was finally finished, I was never so relieved in my life. I was so happy I fell out on the floor and hollered, "IT'S OVER! Now I can go home and get me some sleep."

Black and Blue opened on January 26, 1989 at the Minskoff Theatre, and it was a fabulous show. I mean, look at who was in it: Ruth Brown, Linda Hopkins, Carrie Smith, Bunny Briggs, Ralph Brown, Lon Chaney, Jimmy Slyde, Dianne Walker, Savion Glover (who was just a kid then), Grady Tate, Sir Roland Hanna, and Virgil Jones, just to name a few. Everybody in it was top-notch, and it was a real thrill to share the bill with the three other choreographers, Cholly Atkins, Henry LeTang, and Fayard Nicholas, all chosen for the expertise they brought to their dance specialties. When we won the 1989 Tony Award for Best Choreography, I was so happy to have had a hand in achieving this honor for all of us. I remember standing up on the stage at the Lunt-Fontanne Theater in front of all these show people, with Angela Lansbury as the host, and being told that we were the best of Broadway for that year. Then, the great Jerome Robbins handed us the statues. It was so gratifying.[12]

After *Black and Blue,* so much stuff began happening that I can't even tell you about all of it. It's hard to say how much winning the Tony affected my career, but I did get quite a bit of work in the next few years. I don't know if it was from the award or just that swing dancing was getting more popular. There started to be a lot of articles in newspapers and magazines about swing dancing coming back, including quite a few about this turkey named Frankie Manning. One of the biggest stories was produced for ABC's *20/20* by Alice Pifer, a young swing dance enthusiast. This was major because so many people watch the show, and you had Barbara Walters saying, "Do you remember the Lindy hop?" Some folks started recognizing me on the street after that, and I think it helped quite a few people who were interested in swing dancing realize it was still around.[13]

X

Just before I went to Sweden in 1991, I got a call asking if I was available to work on Spike Lee's new movie about the life of Malcolm X.[14] Since I was going away for a month, I declined, but when I came back in August, the choreographer for the movie, Otis Sallid, still wanted me to come in. I spent a couple of hours working with them, and right away, Otis said to Spike, "This guy knows what he's doing. This is the one we need."

There was one big dance scene in the movie, which was to be filmed at the Diplomat Hotel ballroom. We held an audition and hired mostly professional dancers, but we also picked quite a few social dancers I knew from the NYSDS dances at the Cat Club, including Dawn Hampton, Sonny Allen, Debbie Elkins, John Festa, John Elejalde, and Eddie Sanabria.

When Otis asked if there was anyone I wanted to recommend, I told him about Ryan Francois, who I'd first met in 1986 when he was working with the Jiving Lindy Hoppers. He couldn't make the audition, but he was going to be in New York when they shot the scene, so they hired him because I said he was so talented. (Steven Mitchell was living in Germany at the time, and I didn't have any idea how to get in touch with him.) I also had them bring in Norma Miller as my partner, since they had asked me to appear in the dance number. My son Chazz and his partner, Debbie Williams, were also hired. They were vital to the production because they could take my steps and teach them to other dancers. By this time, Chazz's career had also started to take off again. He had danced in Francis Ford Coppola's *The Cotton Club*, and had begun performing with some of the older tap dancers in the Copasetics.

Spike was searching for music for the ballroom scene, so I brought in a few tunes, including "Flying Home," which I told him I thought was the most exciting, and he agreed. Once that was decided, I began working a couple of hours a day with Denzel Washington and Theresa Randle on their solo in the Lindy scene, and did the same with Spike and his partner, Cynthia Thomas, for their special comic moment. No matter how busy he was, Spike always made those rehearsals. And I showed Otis and the other dancers the right way to do the steps he wanted to use for the group choreography.

One afternoon, I showed the whole company some of the old films, like *Hellzapoppin'* and *Day at the Races,* and these cats were like, "I want to learn that!" and "I want to do that!" Denzel wanted to do the snatch with Theresa. I tried to talk them out of it, but they insisted, so I taught it to them, and I must say they did a very good job.

Personally, when I saw the movie (which came out in 1992), I was a little disappointed because the dance scene didn't capture the social aspect of swing dancing. It was more like a performance with a lot of air steps that wouldn't have been done in a ballroom. But the whole experience of working with all these great actors and filmmakers was just wonderful.

Almost as soon as we finished making *Malcolm X*, Norma was hired by Debbie Allen as the choreographer for a made-for-TV movie she was about to direct called *Stompin' at the Savoy*.[15] Norma brought me in as her assistant, and we went right out to California to audition dancers.

One very interesting thing happened at the tryouts: This famous gymnast who had won a gold medal at the Olympics came. Now, here's someone who was a perfect ten in the top athletic competition in the world, but it was difficult for her to get the air steps. Debbie's husband, Norm Nixon, who had been a point guard for the Los Angeles Lakers, was at the audition, and he tried to help her. He had the strength to get her through the air, but she just couldn't get the hang of the timing, which just shows that it's the rhythm of the air steps that makes them so difficult.

We rehearsed for a few weeks in California, before the whole company went down to North Carolina for about a month because it was more economical to shoot the movie there. We also picked up a few hometown dancers, but they weren't in the big Lindy scene that I helped Norma choreograph, which was supposed to take place at the Savoy Ballroom.

Besides teaching all of the dancers, we had to work with the main characters: Lynn Whitfield, Mario Van Peebles, Vanessa Bell Calloway, Jasmine Guy, Vanessa Williams, and of course Debbie Allen, who, besides directing, also helped with the choreography. These are big-time stars, but they were so regular. We gave each one a little routine. They wanted to try everything, including the air steps, but I talked them out of it because I didn't want to take a chance on anybody getting hurt. I thought the scene turned out quite well because you can see the dancing, and I was very happy that Norma got an Emmy Award nomination for her choreography in *Stompin' at the Savoy*.

Throughout 1992, I continued to do quite a bit of choreography. I created a routine for Pat Canon's Foot & Fiddle Dance Company and choreographed a number called "Swing" for American Ballroom Theater, which was the company of Pierre Dulaine and Yvonne Marceau, the two dancers who later started the school program that's shown in the movie *Mad Hot Ballroom*. I worked on Broadway again in 1997 as a consultant for Mercedes Ellington's show, *Play On!*.

The dancers in these shows were terrific, top-notch at what they were used to doing. But just like with all the other professional groups I'd been working with (except the ones that already knew how to Lindy hop), the challenge was to get them to change from an upright position to dancing down.

The other issue that kept coming up on all these jobs was that the dancers wanted to learn to fly because that's where the excitement is. My feeling is that it's difficult for anyone to learn routines with air steps in them without mastering the basics. I tell *all* my students that they should learn how to dance socially first, but swing was getting so popular that all these companies wanted a Lindy sequence in their repertoire. Despite the challenges, I enjoyed every one of these professional gigs because it involved working with fantastic dancers. It was also a great way to get Lindy hop out there for people to see.

In early 1993, I was commissioned to travel to England to choreograph a couple of routines for Zoots and Spangles Authentic Jazz Dance Company, which Ryan Francois and Julie Oram had started in 1987. This was a group of professional dancers who did Lindy hop, tap, and jazz, and it was a pleasure to work with them. Ryan had impressed everybody so much on the set of *Malcolm X* that Otis Sallid hired him as his assistant choreographer for *Swing Kids*,[16] a movie about swing dancing in Germany under the Nazis. He and his partner of the last twelve years, a very talented tap dancer named Jenny Thomas who is also his wife, were featured in the Broadway play *Swing!* which opened in late 1999. Ryan was also associate choreographer. They did a heck of a job in all the numbers they were in, but especially in a Lindy hop routine that they choreographed. They've also done quite a bit of film and television work, including a professional demonstration on *Dancing with Stars*, and Ryan was just in *Idlewild*.[17]

I consider Ryan and Steven to be almost like my sons. In some respects, they remind me of myself when I was a young man. Once they get their minds set on learning something, they keep at it until they do it well. They and their partners (now Virginie Jensen for Steven) are terrific talents, some of the best teachers around, and they're so dedicated to the Lindy hop that long after I'm gone, I know they're going to be taking the dance forward.

It's All Swing

By the late 1990s, swing dancing's popularity had climbed to a whole new level. There had always been a younger crowd in Europe, mostly kids in their teens and twenties, but in America swing dancing had been attracting more people in their thirties and on up. Suddenly, there were all these kids in the States coming out for my classes—for everybody's classes—and the workshops and dances were filling up! People say it was from that Gap commercial that showed kids swing dancing in khakis, but I kind of think the Gap ad got made *because* there were all these kids who were *already* into swing dancing.[18] This is also around the time that Web sites, like

Savoystyle.com and Yehoodi.com, started springing up, and I really think they helped get the word out and brought people closer together.[19]

Swing dancing exploded in America, and all these different styles—Savoy-style, shag, Balboa, Carolina shag, steppin', hand dancing, Hollywood, and West Coast—became popular in different parts of the country. It's all swing dancing to me, which is a name that covers all the different kinds of dances done to swing music. Back in the '30s, once the Lindy hop got very popular, many people started using the term "jitterbug" instead, although the entertainers and dancers I was around always said "Lindy." When I got back into circulation, I started asking my students who had heard of the Lindy hop. Only a few hands would go up. When I asked about the jitterbug, almost every hand went up. Most of the people who knew both terms thought I was talking about two different dances. It became my mission to let swing dancers know that jitterbug is just a nickname for the Lindy hop, and I think a lot more people realize that now.

During all these years, I've kept up *my* social dancing by Lindy hopping all over the world. Wherever I go to teach, there's usually a party in the evenings, and I get to see how people dance in different places. It's also become very important to me to go out dancing in Harlem whenever I can. There's a tradition in Harlem of entertainers going to clubs for their own enjoyment on Mondays, because that's the night theaters and nightclubs were dark. Quite a few Monday night swing places have opened and closed during the last twenty years—Smalls' Paradise, Northern Lights, Willy's, Well's Restaurant (which was getting busloads of tourists some nights), and Luci's—but there's almost always been something going on, and the Cotton Club (not the original) and Swing 46 (a Midtown club) are still happening.

Birthday Boy

Looking back on my life, as I have in this book, has been an incredible experience. I have to say that in just the last twenty years, there have been so many highlights that I can't even tell you about all of them. One of my greatest joys has been my close relationship with Chazz. We have such a wonderful time together, always joking around and cutting up. I choreographed a specialty for the two of us—a comic version of the shim sham to "'Tain't What You Do" where we really ham it up—that's pure fun for us to perform and has been a real hit with the swing crowd. Chazz teaches in Herräng every year, and at lots of other swing and tap dance weekends and camps. Things have really picked up for him as well as for me, and I couldn't be happier about that.

Another thing I've got to mention is the many birthday parties that swing dancers have thrown for me. I really love these celebrations because they're a great opportunity for people to get together. I am so honored each time one is arranged.

The first was put on by the NYSDS at the Cat Club for my seventy-fifth birthday. A lot of the old Lindy hoppers were still around then, and they were all invited. I hadn't seen some of them for years. When I blew out all of the candles on the cake, with a little help from Norma, I said, "Twenty-five years from now, I'll see you back here at the same place." I think about that quite often.

The next big birthday party, when I was eighty, was even more elaborate. Three swing dancers, Karen Goldstein, Odella Schattin, and Bruce Nelligan, produced this huge celebration, which they called "CAN'T TOP THE LINDY HOP!" (It was also presented by the NYSDS and several local ballroom dance studios.) The party went on for an entire weekend and included Lindy hop workshops taught by the best teachers from around the world during the day, and social dances with performances at night. There were swingin' big bands, including the Harlem Renaissance Orchestra and the Clark Eno Band; a lecture; a panel discussion; and a film program by Ernie Smith. On the last night, there was dinner and dancing in Harlem. More than 750 people from 8 different countries attended the birthday party. As far as I know, it was the first event of this size dedicated to the Lindy hop. Imagine that many people out on the floor doing the shim sham! We must have set some kind of record.

There's a custom that when a swing dancer has a birthday, he or she celebrates by dancing with all of the women or men who want to dance with him or her. It's kind of like a jam circle. I had done this for several birthdays, but this time I decided to dance with one woman for every year of my life. I asked eighty women to line up, and said, "I'm gonna dance with all eighty of you," and I've been doing it ever since. Every year, I do a few bars with each woman while somebody keeps count. Sometimes, just to make it go faster (and because it's entertaining), I dance with two ladies at a time, and if there's more women than years, which there usually is, I just keep going until everybody who wants a turn has had one. It's a real crowd pleaser.

At my eightieth, just before they brought the cake out, they sat me down for what I thought was going to be a special performance that one of the dance groups had cooked up. Instead, they began running this film on a giant video screen that showed dance teachers, friends, and students of mine from all over the world Lindy hopping to my favorite song, "Shiny Stockings."

•

Stuart Math and Kathy LaCommare, two filmmakers and swing dancers, had asked all these people to film themselves dancing to the song and edited the clips together. It was a *wonderful* surprise. I mean, it went straight to my heart, the whole weekend did. When they sang "Happy Birthday," I told the crowd, "I think this is the greatest day in my life since I was born."

My eighty-fifth birthday party was held at Roseland Ballroom. It was a one-night affair with fantastic performances and two bands, George Gee and His Make Believe Ballroom Orchestra, and the Count Basie Orchestra under the direction of Grover Mitchell. Alan Sugarman produced this evening along with Karen Goldstein and Laura Jeffers, and it was fabulous! This time there were more than 1,800 people, and about 250 dancers performed the Lindy chorus, which is a routine I choreographed and teach all over the world.

If you recall, Roseland was the place that wouldn't allow me and the other Lindy hoppers to enter in 1935 when we wanted to see Fletcher Henderson. Well, this time it was a little bit different. A spokesperson for the ballroom read a letter from the management that said, "We wish we could rewrite the history of that time, but we cannot. . . . Now in 1999, on your 85th birthday, we are delighted to have . . . you on our dance floor with your thousands of friends and admirers."

For many years, Roseland had a glass case in the lobby where they displayed the shoes of famous dancers, including Gregory Hines, Fred Astaire, and Savion Glover. As a surprise, Alan arranged for them to put a pair of my shoes in there too. Someone tricked me by asking for a signed pair for a charity auction, and when I got to Roseland, they were in the case! What a thrill and an honor it was to have my shoes sharing a home with shoes from all these other *great* dancers. Roseland was also the site of my eighty-eighth birthday party, which was produced by Larry Kang with a birthday film by Manu Smith.

My favorite way to spend a vacation is on a cruise ship. In fact, my girl-friend, Judy Pritchett, and I go on a jazz cruise every October. I met Judy at Northern Lights in the mid-1980s, and we became very friendly because she loves to dance, and loves the same jazz and big band music that I do. In fact, she introduced me to some very good swing bands. Judy is now a very important part of my life. She's done a lot to promote swing dancing and help get the word out about me through her Web site. She's my advisor, my translator, my friend, and my lover. She wears many hats, all of them well.

When Christine Sampson from Seattle asked if I'd like to celebrate my eighty-ninth birthday on a Caribbean cruise, I said, "Well, all right!" To be with a whole gang of swing dancers, family, and friends *and* to be on a cruise was one of my greatest desires come to fruition. Christine worked hard, with help from Jodi Fleischman, to put together a fabulous affair. We did the whole thing again for my ninetieth birthday, with Christine, Jodi, and Elliott Donnelly (from San Francisco) producing it and, baby, it was just as spectacular, even better.

I had felt for a long time that there should be some kind of marker where the Savoy Ballroom once stood. It closed in 1958, and was torn down to make way for a housing development. Whole generations of Harlem residents didn't even know that this great institution had existed in their neighborhood. Dancers Yvonne Marceau and Jun Maruta decided to remedy the situation, and I could not have been happier when, in 2002, they held a ceremony on my birthday to unveil a plaque that stands right where the entrance to the Savoy once was.

In between all these big birthdays, there are often smaller ones in many of the different places where I go to teach, and people have been so creative about them. Of course, some years it seems as if I've danced with about a thousand women . . . but I've enjoyed every single step.

Looking Back to the Future

People ask me all the time how I've managed to live such a long, healthy life. As Eubie Blake said: "If I'd known I was going to live this long, I would have taken better care of myself." Seriously, I think it's due to a lot of things. Although I'm not a health nut, I've always lived a pretty healthy life. I've never been a person that overindulges in food or alcohol, and I've never smoked a cigarette in my whole life. When I was a kid, my mother said that if I wanted to be an athlete I shouldn't smoke because it would hamper my breathing.

I also never got into doing drugs. It just wasn't interesting to me, and I could never see the benefit of it. Once, when I was in the Congaroos, I was at a party at Dizzy's apartment at 122nd Street and Seventh Avenue, and there were so many cats smoking weed that I got a contact high. When I left with some friends and we got to a corner, it looked to me like I was about to step off the curb into a deep canyon. I kept refusing to step down, and my buddies could not get me to cross that street. They thought it was hilarious.

Even though some people have tried to get me into drugs, I've never felt the need to keep up with my peers. They'd say, "It'll make you feel good," but I'd tell them, "I feel good already." I was generally pretty happy, and still am. Whenever I did feel a little bit down in spirits, I'd go to the Savoy, and before you'd know it, I'd forget about everything else. I get high from Lindy hopping. To me, swing music and dancing is the best therapy in the world. That's why, even though we've been through so many dances in the last seventy years, the Lindy is still going strong.

I've always exercised, although I'm not strict about doing it every day. I've tried lots of different things, lifting weights, doing push-ups, jogging, stretching, Pilates, and all kinds of sports. And, of course, I've danced since I was a kid. I can only remember one time when I got injured while performing (other than with Dottimae). I pulled a muscle in the back of my leg doing a split in the Congaroos' tap number. A doctor told me I shouldn't dance for six weeks. I stopped for three days.

Not that I haven't had my problems. I've had a hip replacement, knee surgery, a hernia operation, two cataract surgeries, my prostate was removed, and I have to wear a hearing aid. But I'm still kicking, and I think it's partly because I built my body up from the time I was a youngster. That made me strong and gave me stamina, so it's been a little harder to break it down. The Lord's been so good to me, and I get down on my knees every night and thank him.

For me, this whole revival has been as if a door opened and I walked into a place where the sun is always shining and the flowers are always blooming. It makes me feel so light, so exhilarated. I've had such a wonderful life—I know it—and I feel like I owe it all to Lindy hoppers around the world. That's where I get my energy. More than anything else, that's what's kept me going.

When I reflect back on all my years, and I'm older than dirt, I'm kind of proud of the contributions I made to the Lindy hop, like the air step, ensemble dancing, and bending forward. I feel very good about having been a member of Whitey's Lindy Hoppers and the Congaroos, and about my choreography in *Hellzapoppin'*, *Radio City Revels*, *Hot Chocolate*, and *Killer Diller*, which I think has inspired quite a few people. But I have to say that the thing I'm happiest about is my role in helping to get the Lindy hop going again.

The last time I was in Herräng, while I was giving a talk with Dawn Hampton and Chazz, I told the audience, "They should have politicians from all of the different governments come and dig this wonderful scene to see how well everybody gets along on the dance floor."

When Whitey first started getting Whitey's Lindy Hoppers together, I think he had the idea to spread the dance everywhere. He didn't have a way to really do that like we do now, but if he was alive today, I think he would be very, very happy. This is what he dreamed of, and I guess I got that from him. When I travel to all these different swing dance events, I'm finally seeing what I've wanted to see my whole life—people from all over the world, with smiles on their faces, getting together to dance.

APPENDIXES

FRANKIE MANNING TIMELINE

1914 • Born on May 26 in Jacksonville, Florida.

1917 • Sails to New York City with his mother and aunt to live in Harlem.

1926 • Savoy Ballroom opens at Lenox Avenue and 140th Street in Harlem.

1927 • Charles Lindbergh completes first solo transatlantic flight from New York to Paris.

1928 • Shorty Snowden coins the name Lindy hop.

1932 • First son, Chazz Young, is born to FM and Dorothy Young.

1933 • First ventures to Savoy Ballroom.

1934 • Invited by Herbert "Whitey" White to join elite group of Savoy Lindy hoppers.
 • Introduces more horizontal style of Lindy hopping.
 • Wins Lindy contest with Hilda Morris at the Apollo Theatre and performs with Duke Ellington.

1935 • Wins second place in Lindy competition with Maggie McMillan at first Harvest Moon Ball.
 • Introduces the first Lindy air step, over-the-back.
 • Introduces stops and synchronized ensemble dancing.

1936 • Whyte's Hopping Maniacs appear in downtown reopening of the Cotton Club.
 • Wins third place in Lindy competition with Naomi Waller at Harvest Moon Ball.

1937 • Whitey's Lindy Hoppers appear in *A Day at the Races* (uncredited).
 • Whyte's Hopping Maniacs tour France and England with *Le Cotton Club de New York*.

1938 • Whitey's Hopping Maniacs appear in *Radio City Revels* (uncredited).
 • 8 Big Apple Dancers commence year-long tour of New Zealand and Australia.

1939 • Whitey's Jitterbugs perform on Broadway in *Swingin' the Dream*.
 • Arthur White's Lindy Hoppers appear in *Keep Punching*.

1940 • Wins second place in Lindy competition with Ann Johnson at Harvest Moon Ball.

1941 • Congeroo Dancers appear in *Hellzapoppin'*.
 • Whitey's Lindy Hoppers appear in *Hot Chocolate ("Cottontail")* with Duke Ellington.
 • Whitey Congeroo Dancers sail to Rio for Brazilian tour.

1943 • Inducted into Army. Serves in New Guinea, the Philippines, and Japan.

1946 • Returns to civilian life.

1947 • FM's new group, the Congaroo Dancers, debuts at Roxy Theatre.

1948 • Four Congaroos appear in *Killer Diller*.

1950 • Mura Dehn produces and directs documentary, *The Spirit Moves* (circa).

1954 • Marries Gloria Holloway (two children: Marion and Frank Jr.).

1955	• Disbands the Congaroo Dancers.
	• Goes to work for the U.S. Postal Service.
1958	• Savoy Ballroom closes.
1968	• *Jazz Dance* by Marshall and Jean Stearns is published.
1976	• Separates from Gloria Manning (they are divorced in 1989).
1984	• Smalls' Paradise in Harlem begins holding swing dances on Monday nights.
1985	• New York Swing Dance Society holds first "Savoy Sunday" big band dance at Cat Club in New York City.
1986	• Meets longtime companion, Judy Pritchett.
	• Begins teaching career by agreeing to work with Erin Stevens and Steven Mitchell.
1987	• First travels to Sweden to work with The Rhythm Hot Shots.
	• Retires from the post office.
1988	• Choreographs section of "Opus McShann" with Norma Miller for Alvin Ailey American Dance Theater.
1989	• Artist Richard Yarde creates mural depicting Savoy Lindy hoppers, including FM, for the Joseph P. Addabo Federal Building in Jamaica, New York.
	• Featured in a *20/20* profile on ABC.
	• Wins the Tony Award for Best Choreography for *Black and Blue* with Cholly Atkins, Henry LeTang, and Fayard Nicholas.
1992	• Serves as consultant/performer in Spike Lee's film *Malcolm X.*
	• Serves as assistant choreographer/performer with Norma Miller in Debbie Allen's *Stompin' at the Savoy.*
1993	• Inducted into City Lore People's Hall of Fame at Museum of the City of New York.
	• Receives New York City Arts in Education Roundtable Award.
1994	• Eightieth birthday is celebrated in New York City at "CAN'T TOP THE LINDY HOP."
	• Receives NEA Choreographers' Fellowship.
1996	• Norma Miller's memoir, *Swingin' at the Savoy*, is published.
1997	• Serves as consultant to Mercedes Ellington for *Play On!* on Broadway.
1999	• Performs in PBS special *Swinging' with Duke,* featuring the Lincoln Center Jazz Orchestra with Wynton Marsalis.
	• Eighty-fifth birthday is celebrated at Roseland Ballroom.
2000	• Receives NEA National Heritage Fellowship.
	• Appears in Ken Burns's documentary, *Jazz.*
2004	• Celebrates ninetieth birthday on Caribbean cruise.
	• Receives Flo-Bert Award for Lifetime Achievement in Tap Artistry in New York City.
	• Receives Yehoodi Legacy Award in New York City.
2005	• Inducted into Hall of Fame at the National Museum of Dance in Saratoga Springs, New York.

BIOGRAPHICAL SKETCHES OF LINDY HOPPERS

Below is a list of early Savoy dancers and members of Whitey's Lindy Hoppers who Frankie remembers, or whose names appear in programs, articles, and film credits. Although more information is available about some than others, by listing all of these dancers, most of whom have passed on, we hope they will be remembered for having been a part of swing dance history. **—C.M.**

The First Generation of Savoy Dancers

BLACKJACK was one of the standout dancers Frankie noticed when he first began going to the Savoy, although he never turned professional.

BEATRICE "LITTLE BEA" ELAM, one of the top dancers at the Savoy, danced with **LEROY "STRETCH" JONES** in Shorty Snowden's professional dance troupe during the 1930s. Frankie characterizes him as a tall, elegant, and smooth dancer. Her short stature paired with Leroy's height contrasted with Shorty and Big Bea's physical configuration. Little Bea and Leroy later performed briefly with Whitey's Lindy Hoppers in *Swingin' the Dream.*

"TWIST MOUTH" GEORGE GANAWAY, a.k.a. **"SUSQUEHANNA,"** impressed Frankie with his extravagant dress and entertaining bravado regarding his dance abilities. A standout when Frankie began going to the Savoy, Ganaway performed solo for most of his professional dancing career. In mid-1935, he and Edith Matthews introduced the ladies' twist.

FREDDIE LEWIS and **MADELINE LEWIS,** a brother-sister team in Shorty Snowden's professional dance group during the 1930s, danced in a flash style, according to Frankie.

PAULINE MORSE became Shorty Snowden's partner after Mattie Purnell. In fall 1928, the two performed at various Harlem venues, including the Lincoln Theatre and Rockland Palace, in conjunction with advertised Lindy hop contests.

MATTIE PURNELL, Shorty Snowden's first known partner, competed with him at a 1928 dance marathon in Harlem, where he reportedly coined the term "Lindy hop."

THE SHEIK, a regular at the Savoy when Frankie first began going there, distinguished himself by imitating Rudolph Valentino in physical appearance, facial expression, and dance style. Frankie never knew his name or that of his partner (she may have been his sister), but says she was also a fine ballroom dancer who did not Lindy hop. Although they entered the ballroom preliminaries at the Savoy for the 1935 Harvest Moon Ball, along with a team named **DIANNE** and **AUSTIN,** neither couple reached the finals. They were African American, and Frankie points out that all the ballroom finalists were white.

SHOEBRUSH was one of the Savoy dancers under Whitey's auspices when Frankie was invited to join the group, and an excellent ballroom dancer.

GEORGE "SHORTY" SNOWDEN (July 1904–1982) was born in Lower Manhattan, but moved to Harlem by 1910. After breaking both ankles ice-skating, he recovered and went on to become a star at the Savoy Ballroom. Shorty is widely credited with naming the Lindy hop, and is considered to have been the first Lindy hopper to turn professional. His group of six couples performed during the 1930s, notably at Smalls' Paradise, and with Paul Whiteman at the Paradise Restaurant. He danced in *After Seben* and, with his main partner, **BEATRICE "BIG BEA" GAY**, in the 1937 short subject, *Ask Uncle Sol*. Snowden exploited the comic possibilities of his short stature through his partnership with Big Bea, a top Savoy dancer who towered over him. Their signature step, in which Big Bea carried Shorty off the stage on her back, inspired Frankie to create the first Lindy air step. Snowden is immortalized in the Shorty George, a step of his own creation. He retired from professional dancing in 1938 due to poor health, although he continued to dance socially and later operated a dance studio in Harlem for a time.

SPEEDY, one of the dancers who most impressed Frankie on his first visit to the Savoy Ballroom circa 1933, was known for his fast footwork. He never became a professional Lindy hopper.

ROBERT "RABBIT" TAYLOR (April 16, 1904–circa 1997) was part of the Savoy dancers under Whitey's auspices when Frankie was invited to join the group. Frankie says Rabbit shined at fast footwork, but never went on to dance professionally. Rabbit claimed to have won the first dance contest at the Savoy Ballroom.

HERBERT "WHITEY" WHITE (unknown–September 30, 1950), born in Portsmouth, Virginia, and a veteran of World War I, was reportedly a dancing waiter before becoming a bouncer at the Savoy Ballroom. In the late 1920s or early 1930s, he began organizing exceptionally talented dancers at the Savoy into an informal club. This group grew, and spawned the earliest professional Lindy hoppers, first under the aegis of Shorty Snowden, with later groups directly under Whitey's management. Generally known as Whitey's Lindy Hoppers by the mid-1930s, his dancers dominated competitions, toured the world's stages and nightclubs, and appeared in numerous films. Renowned as the greatest practitioners of Lindy, Whitey's protégés epitomized the high rhythmic energy and athleticism of the dance. Although some of his disciples complained that Whitey underpaid and mistreated them, many admired his abilities as a promoter of Lindy hop. Most spoke highly of the sense of pride he instilled in them. In the early 1940s, Whitey relocated to Oswego, New York to open a restaurant/bar for African American soldiers. A decade later, he died of a heart attack.

Early Whitey's Lindy Hoppers

PETTIS DOTSON "SNOOKIE" BEASLEY (July 7, 1918–August 1970), a wonderful dancer, according to Frankie, known for doing a step called "the lock," toured with Ethel Waters in 1936, danced in *A Day at the Races*, and was part of the 8 Big Apple Dancers' Australian tour. He and Frankie remained friends until his death.

CLYDE "BROWNIE" BROWN, one of Whitey's dancers when Frankie arrived at the Savoy, for a time served as Whitey's right-hand man, assuming the role of manager when Whitey was absent. Brownie performed as one of the Lindy hoppers with the Lucky Millinder revue at the Alhambra Theatre in early 1936.

JOHN "TINY" BUNCH was one of Whitey's most memorable dancers, for both his ability to step lively despite his size and the entertaining interplay with his petite partner, **DOROTHY "DOT" MOSES**, an excellent dancer in her own right. Tiny Bunch and the Original Lindy Hoppers, one of Whitey's groups, appeared at the Harlem Uproar House in 1937. Tiny and Dot danced in *Radio City Revels* and *Manhattan Merry-Go-Round*. The pair was immortalized by Aaron Siskind in his photograph, "At the Savoy," in *Harlem Document: Photographs 1932–40*.

HELEN BUNDY danced with George Greenidge in the Savoy Lindy Hoppers March 1936 engagement at the Roxy Theatre, and with Billy Ricker at the Harlem Uproar House, appearing with Tiny Bunch and the Original Lindy Hoppers.

CHICK danced with **GERTIE** in the Savoy Lindy Hoppers March 1936 engagement at the Roxy Theatre.

WILDA CRAWFORD (February 13, 1921–December 15, 1989) was born in Harlem and began hanging out at the Savoy as a teenager, where Frankie reports she was affectionately called Quack-Quack, for her wacky behavior. She danced with **ERNEST "CHAMP" HARRISON** at the Harlem Uproar House in 1937, and appeared in *Swingin' the Dream*. She won the 1940 Harvest Moon Ball Lindy hop championship and danced in *Keep Punching* with Thomas "Tops" Lee. Tops and Wilda continued to perform together for about ten years after they left Whitey's Lindy Hoppers in the early 1940s. She worked for Sunshine Biscuits until retiring around 1988.

MILDRED CRUSE (1916–after May 1989) was raised in the Bronx, started frequenting the Savoy in 1935, and began dancing for Whitey after **BILLY WILLIAMS** asked her to be his regular partner. The pair were in the Savoy contest between Whitey's and Shorty's groups, won the 1936 Harvest Moon Ball Lindy hop division, and performed with Whyte's Hopping Maniacs from 1936 to 1937. Cruse quit Lindy hopping soon after, moved to Detroit in 1938, and married William Martin, a tap dancer, with whom she performed as a dance act until 1950. After raising a family, husband and wife began performing together again in 1985. Billy Williams went on to perform in *Swingin' the Dream*.

WILLIAM DOWNES started dancing with Whitey just before Frankie did. He appeared in *Swingin' the Dream* and danced with Mickey Jones in *Keep Punching, Hellzapoppin',* and *Hot Chocolate*. Downes and Mickey continued to perform after Whitey's Lindy Hoppers disbanded. Upon returning from World War II, he became a New York City policeman, and lived in Harlem.

RED ELAN danced as part of the Lindy hoppers with the Lucky Millinder revue at the Alhambra Theatre, and with Tiny Bunch and the Original Lindy Hoppers at the Harlem Uproar House.

ELLA GIBSON appeared in *A Day at the Races*.

"LONG-LEGGED GEORGE," a.k.a. **"LONG GEORGE" GREENIDGE** was part of the group with whom Frankie first ventured to the Savoy. Frankie considers him one of the top Lindy hoppers because of his excellent dancing and many contributions to the dance's vocabulary, including the turnover Charleston and long-legged Charleston. He was featured with Willamae Ricker in a 1936 photo essay on the Lindy in *Life*. Greenidge appeared in *A Day at the Races, Radio City Revels,* and *Keep Punching*. He apparently left show business around 1940.

"STOMPIN' BILLY" HILL won third place with Norma Miller in the Lindy division of the first Harvest Moon Ball. The couple toured Europe as winners with Leon James and Edith Matthews, becoming the first Lindy hoppers to perform overseas.

JOHN "JOHNNY" INNIS served as a driver for Whitey's Lindy Hoppers on their Ethel Waters tour, and danced in *A Day at the Races*.

LEON JAMES (April 27, 1913–July 30, 1970) was born in New York City, lived in New Jersey from about 1924 to 1929, then moved back to Manhattan. He began dancing at the Savoy shortly before Frankie, who says James was a charismatic performer who added highlights to his dynamic dancing through the expressive use of his face and hands. James won the first Harvest Moon Ball Lindy hop championship with Edith Matthews, toured with Ethel Waters, appeared in *A Day at the Races* and *Hot Mikado,* and was featured with Willamae Ricker in a 1943 *Life* magazine spread on the Lindy. He continued to perform during the war (he had a medical deferment), then worked in a factory before returning to dancing in an act with Al Minns, appearing in *The Spirit Moves* and *Jazz Dance.* In the early 1950s the pair began giving presentations on the history of jazz dance that were organized and narrated by Marshall Stearns, who relied on them as the main sources for the Lindy chapters in *Jazz Dance.* Upon Stearns's death in 1966, James's dance career came to a halt, after which he worked for a time with the Neighborhood Youth Corps.

WILLIE JONES (1910–date unknown) was born in St. Kitts, and began going to the Savoy when he moved to New York City in 1929. Although he never considered himself one of Whitey's stars, he did perform with the group in *Knickerbocker Holiday,* a musical that toured New England and Washington, D.C. before opening on Broadway on October 19, 1938. Jones continued to perform as a professional dancer after the demise of Whitey's Lindy Hoppers, eventually moving to Philadelphia.

EDITH MATTHEWS, along with Twist Mouth George, was responsible for introducing a twisting motion into the ladies' basic swing-out in mid-1935. She and Leon James were the first winners of the Harvest Moon Ball Lindy hop division, which was followed by a European tour. Frankie considered her to be one of the best female dancers during his early years at the Savoy.

MAGGIE MCMILLAN won second place with Frankie in the Lindy competition at the first Harvest Moon Ball. He considered her one of the top female dancers during his early days at the Savoy. After Frankie refused an opportunity for the champion couple to go on tour to Europe, she continued to perform with him for a short period (including at the Alhambra Theatre Cotton Club Revue in early 1936) before quitting to work as a fill-in for Shorty Snowden's troupe.

LUCILLE MIDDLETON grew up in Harlem, and started dancing at the Savoy around the same time as Frankie. She danced with Jerome Williams in the 1935 Savoy contest during which Frankie introduced the Lindy air step, for the first stage performances by Whitey's dancers in early 1936, and in Whyte's Hopping Maniacs' Cotton Club engagement. Upon returning from the Cotton Club European tour in mid-1937, she partnered Frankie until mid-1939, appearing in *Radio City Revels* and *Keep Punching,* and touring Australia. Frankie says Lucille was known for her twist, had comic abilities, and was very good at air steps. Lucille married Thomas "Tops" Lee around 1940, and worked at Whitey's establishment in Oswego for a time.

DOROTHY "DOT" MILLER (March 7, 1918–August 13, 2001), Norma Miller's older sister, grew up in Harlem. She danced briefly with Whitey's Lindy Hoppers, appearing in *A Day at the Races.* Dot later became a nurse's aide at Harlem Hospital and was an active member of Union Congregational Church.

NORMA MILLER (December 2, 1919–present) was recruited by Whitey after winning a Savoy contest as a teenager. She soon became one of his top dancers, displaying comic talents and acrobatic abilities. As a member of Whitey's Lindy Hoppers, she toured with Ethel Waters and appeared in *A Day at the Races, Swingin' the Dream, Keep Punching, Hellzapoppin'* (also in the play), and *Hot Chocolate.* After Whitey's group dissolved, Norma ran her own jazz dance company and worked as a comedian, often appearing with Redd Foxx. In recent years, she choreographed for the Alvin Ailey American Dance

Theater, appeared in *Malcolm X,* and was nominated for an Emmy for her choreography in *Stompin' at the Savoy.* Norma's autobiography, *Swingin' at the Savoy,* and a children's book based on her life by Alan Govenar, tell her story.

HILDA MORRIS won the late 1934 Lindy hop contest at the Apollo Theatre with Frankie, for which the prize was a week of performances with Duke Ellington. At the end of this engagement, the couple appeared in a variety show in West Virginia, becoming the first Lindy hop team sent on the road by Whitey. After they returned, Frankie rarely saw her at the Savoy.

BILLY RICKER (1914–September 1, 1988) first went to the Savoy and began dancing for Whitey at the same time as Frankie. He married Willamae Briggs in 1934, performed at the Harlem Uproar with Tiny Bunch, toured extensively, and is known for having devised the "mutiny" routine. He formed a strong dance bond with Norma Miller, whom he partnered in *Hellzapoppin'* and *Hot Chocolate.* After serving in the Army during World War II, Ricker performed with the Norma Miller Dancers for two decades, then worked in the post office.

WILLAMAE BRIGGS (RICKER) (unknown–June 1978) first went to the Savoy and began dancing for Whitey at the same time as Frankie, who considers her to have been one of the most versatile female Lindy hoppers. As a member of Whitey's Lindy Hoppers, Willamae toured extensively, and appeared in *A Day at the Races, Hellzapoppin',* and *Hot Chocolate.* Thanks to her managerial abilities, Willamae often served as group captain. She was featured in two *Life* photo essays on the Lindy hop: in 1936 with George Greenidge and in 1943 with Leon James. She continued to perform during World War II, and subsequently joined the Congaroo Dancers, dancing in *Killer Diller* and *The Spirit Moves.* Known for her stylishness and business savvy, Willamae went on to a successful career in fashion after the Congaroos disbanded.

NAOMI WALLER (GAY) (September 21, 1919–August 12, 2000) was recruited by Whitey after she won a Lindy hop contest at the Apollo Theatre in 1935. Whitey teamed her with Frankie, with whom she won many Savoy contests, thanks in part, says Frankie, to her wild style of dancing, which pleased the crowd. Beginning in early 1936, the pair performed together, including at the Cotton Club, making her Frankie's first professional partner and one of his two favorites. Upon returning to the States from the Cotton Club European tour in mid-1937, Naomi left Lindy hopping to become a chorus girl. She appeared at the Savannah Club, in *Swingin' the Dream,* and in USO shows before moving to Philadelphia with her husband. She later returned to New York, where she worked in her mother's hardware store in the Bronx and became a community activist.

SARAH WARD and **WILLIAM WARD** were a brother-sister team who danced briefly with Whitey's Lindy Hoppers.

FRIEDA WASHINGTON was Frankie's partner in the 1935 Savoy Ballroom contest for which he devised the first Lindy air step. Frankie worked with her for two weeks before the event to perfect the move. Shortly after their triumph over Shorty Snowden and his dancers, Frankie and Frieda lost contact when she and her family moved back down South.

JEROME WILLIAMS, whom Frankie first noticed soon after joining Whitey's Savoy dancers, was one of the most comical dancers in Lindy hopping. Jerome danced with Lucille Middleton in the 1935 Savoy contest against Shorty Snowden's dancers. The team performed together in the first stage performances by Whitey's dancers from early 1936 through mid-1937, including at the Cotton Club and on the subsequent European tour. He toured Australia with the 8 Big Apple Dancers, and danced in *Sugar Hill Masquerade.*

Later Whitey's Lindy Hoppers

LOUISE "PAL" ANDREWS (February 13, 1924–date unknown) was born in Newark, New Jersey, grew up in Harlem, and was recruited into Whitey's Lindy Hoppers in 1939. Her first gig was at the Savoy pavilion at the 1939 World's Fair. In 1940, Andrews and Snookie Beasley went on a Midwest tour as part of a revamped *Hollywood Hotel Revue* with two other couples. She danced with Pepsi Bethel in *Born Happy*, starring Bill Robinson, and continued to work with Whitey as his gal Friday after his move to Oswego until his death in 1950. She then worked at the Savoy until it closed in 1958, and thereafter in various stores.

FRANK BELL danced briefly with Whitey's Lindy Hoppers.

HILDA BESS and **RICHARD BESS**, a husband-and-wife team, appeared in *Swingin' the Dream*.

ALFRED "PEPSI" BETHEL (August 31, 1918–August 30, 2002) was born in Greensboro, North Carolina. Eunice Callen coached Pepsi on his Lindy hop at the Savoy in the early 1940s. He also trained with Whitey in Oswego. In the 1950s, Bethel worked with Mura Dehn and danced in *The Spirit Moves*. He went on to a long professional dance career, directing several dance groups in the 1960s and 1970s, including the American Authentic Jazz Dance Company. He later taught jazz dance in New York City.

JOYCE BOYD appeared in *Swingin' the Dream*. She later moved to Staten Island.

EUNICE CALLEN (January 7, 1921–August 1, 2003) grew up in Harlem, took dance lessons as a child, and started working for Whitey in 1936. Self-described as a fast learner, a low twister, and a wild dancer, Eunice performed around New York State before touring Australia with the 8 Big Apple Dancers, during which she was featured in a jazz routine singing "A-Tisket, A-Tasket." Eunice helped train a new generation of Savoy dancers in the early 1940s and continued to perform until 1949, dancing in *Sugar Hill Masquerade*. She retired from working for the Department of Health in the Bronx in the late 1980s.

PAUL CHADWELL performed at the Roxy Theatre in 1945.

SAMUEL CLARKE appeared in *Knickerbocker Holiday*.

GLADYS CROWDER won the Lindy hop title at the 1937 Harvest Moon Ball with **EDDIE "SHORTY" DAVIS**. The two performed together in *Hot Mikado*. Davis also appeared in *Radio City Revels*.

HELEN DANIELS (DABNEY) (September 11, 1928–present) performed briefly with Frankie at the Roxy Theatre in 1943. She joined the Congaroo Dancers after the war, at first substituting for Willamae Ricker, then replacing Ann Johnson. After the Congaroos disbanded, she married, helped manage various eating establishments, and owned a liquor store. Now retired, she lives in Pennsylvania with her second husband, Clyde Dabney.

JOE "BIG STUPE" DANIELS and **JOYCE "LITTLE STUPE" JAMES (DANIELS)** began dancing at the Savoy in 1937. Frankie remembers the pair, who married, as being two of the wildest dancers. Both appeared in *Swingin' the Dream* and *Keep Punching*. Joe eventually worked in the post office. Frankie thinks Joyce was employed by the city.

GENEVA DAVIS appeared in *Hot Mikado* with fellow Lindy hopper **LEE LYONS**, whom she married.

ELNORA DYSON (March 9, 1920–present) was born in Beaufort, South Carolina, but moved to Hyannis, Massachusetts at age two, where she began dancing as a child at the ballroom owned by her aunt. She moved to New York in 1938, shortly after hearing about Whitey's Lindy Hoppers from Willie Jones while he was performing in Boston. Whitey invited Dyson to join the Lindy hoppers on her first visit to the Savoy. She performed at the Savoy pavilion during the 1939 World's Fair, and on and off at other local venues until 1943. During the war, she worked as a riveter at a New Jersey defense plant; she later became a beautician, retiring in 1980.

ARLYNE EVANS appeared in *Hot Mikado.*

FOSTER "THE DANCING MAN" HICKSON (March 4, 1917–December 23, 2000) was born and raised in South Carolina. After moving to New York City and frequenting the Savoy Ballroom, he performed with Whitey's Lindy Hoppers for several years during the early 1940s.

BELLE HILL appeared in *Hot Mikado.* She later moved to Chicago.

CORNELIA "CONNIE" HILL won the 1939 Harvest Moon Ball Lindy division with Russell Williams, with whom she also danced in a 1943 Cootie Williams short. Frankie attributes the head snatch to Russell and Connie. She appeared in *Hot Mikado* and *Swingin' the Dream,* and later became a chorus girl.

SONNY JENKINS appeared in *Swingin' the Dream* (credited in the program as Lonnie Jenkins) and *Keep Punching.*

ANN JOHNSON was one of Frankie's two favorite partners because she was willing to try any movement, learned quickly, and could do all of the air steps. She began working for Whitey around 1938, appearing in *Swingin' the Dream* and *Keep Punching.* She danced with Frankie in *Hellzapoppin', Hot Chocolate,* and during the Brazilian tour. The duo was featured in a 1940 photo essay in *Life,* and in a picture-to-the-editor, also in *Life,* in 1941. Ann was Frankie's first partner in the Congaroos, and appeared with him in *Killer Diller.*

DOTTIEMAE JOHNSON danced with Frankie in *Swingin' the Dream,* and with Leon James in a 1943 Cootie Williams short.

WALTER "COUNT" a.k.a. "LEFTY" JOHNSON appeared in *Hot Mikado.*

FRANCES "MICKEY" PARRIS (JONES) (January 25, 1919–May 9, 1982) was born and raised in Harlem. Frankie remembers her as a wonderful dancer, who was exceptionally quick to catch on to new steps. She performed at the 1939 World's Fair and danced in *Keep Punching, Hellzapoppin',* and *Hot Chocolate* with partner William Downes. After Whitey's Lindy Hoppers disbanded, for a time the pair continued performing locally as a tap act. Mickey also performed in a tap duet with her sister, Sales, but eventually went solo.

THOMAS "TOPS" LEE appeared in *Keep Punching* and *Swingin' the Dream,* and won the 1940 Harvest Moon Ball Lindy hop division with Wilda Crawford, with whom Whitey had paired him. Known for a movement called the wrap-around, they continued to perform together professionally after Whitey's Lindy Hoppers disbanded. Frankie says his nickname was a play on his high opinion of himself.

JOHNNY MCAFEE performed at the Roxy Theatre in 1945.

EMILY MCCLOUD appeared in *Swingin' the Dream.*

MAE MILLER appeared in *Hot Mikado.*

AL MINNS (January 1, 1920–April 24, 1985) hailed from Newport News, Virginia, was raised in Harlem, and started attending dances at the Savoy in 1937. He won the 1938 Harvest Moon Ball with Mildred Pollard soon after he began dancing with Whitey's Lindy Hoppers. Known for his crazy-legs style, Minns toured extensively, performed in *Hot Mikado, Hellzapoppin'* (also in the play), and *Hot Chocolate.* Minns and Leon James had a second-wind career during the 1950s and 1960s presenting vernacular jazz dance with narration by Marshall Stearns on concert stages and television. He served as one of Stearns's main sources for the Lindy chapters in *Jazz Dance,* and is featured in *The Spirit Moves* and *Jazz Dance.* After retiring from dancing, Minns began sharing his expertise with a new generation of swing dancers in the early 1980s. He taught at the Sandra Cameron Dance Center until shortly before his death.

WILHELMINA "PEEWEE" MOORE appeared in *Swingin' the Dream.*

JAMES "BLUE" OUTLAW appeared in *Swingin' the Dream,* and at the Roxy Theatre in 1945.

CONSUELLA "SALES" PARRIS (October 21, 1921–late 1970s), Mickey Jones's sister, danced briefly with Whitey's Lindy Hoppers and had a tap act with Sidney J. "Jazz" Richardson.

SAMUEL PIERCE appeared in *Swingin' the Dream* and *Knickerbocker Holiday.*

MILDRED POLLARD (later known as **SANDRA GIBSON**) (1919–date unknown) was born in Atlanta, moved to New York at age five, and began going to the Savoy in 1937. She won the 1938 Lindy title at the Harvest Moon Ball with Al Minns. Nicknamed "Boogie," Mildred was known for her sensual dance style, as demonstrated in *The Spirit Moves,* and was strong enough to have engineered a movement in which she flipped Minns. She danced in *Radio City Revels* and *Hot Mikado* before leaving the Lindy hoppers, but continued in show business as an exotic dancer, singer, and comedian under the name Sandra. After she married entertainer Albert Gibson in 1966, the couple formed their own act.

RUTHIE RHEINGOLD (ETTIN) (September 30, 1916–present) grew up in Manhattan, moved to the Bronx at age thirteen, and started going to the Savoy at nineteen. She soon partnered with **HARRY ROSENBERG** (name later changed to **ROWE**) (1919–date unknown), who had started Lindy hopping in the Bronx, where he was born and bred, before making his way to the Savoy around the same time as Ruthie. Within months, Whitey approached Harry and invited him to perform in a group with Ruthie, the only white couple to do so. Frankie admired their dancing tremendously. Ruthie worked with the group for about a year, performing at two Apollo engagements. She later taught ballroom dancing at a studio in Manhattan. Harry continued with the Lindy Hoppers until he joined the military in 1941. After the war, he became a dentist.

SYDNEY J. "JAZZ" RICHARDSON danced with Elnora Dyson at the Savoy pavilion at the 1939 World's Fair.

"JITTERBUG JOE" RIDDICK (September 10, 1920–November 17, 1978) appeared in *Swingin' the Dream.* After serving in World War II, he lived in Corona, New York and worked as a baggage handler for Braniff Airlines. He later became a boxer, competing in the Golden Gloves.

BLANCHE SHAVERS performed at the Roxy Theatre in 1945. She was married to trumpeter/arranger Charlie Shavers.

JIMMY VALENTINE (born **PAUL PERRONE**) (September 5, 1915–February 1, 1999) grew up in the New York City area, learned to Lindy hop at the Savoy, and went on to perform with Whitey's Lindy Hoppers for two years in the late 1930s. Despite being one of the group's few white dancers, and the only one-legged member, Valentine was highly regarded as a superb dancer by Savoy regulars, including Frankie. He performed on the *Ed Sullivan* show many times and, in the late 1950s, often teamed up with tap dancer Peg Leg Bates. His latter years were spent in Las Vegas.

ESTHER WASHINGTON entered the Savoy dance scene around 1937 or 1938. According to Frankie, she was a good all-around dancer who could Lindy well with anyone. She had many partners, including Jerome Williams during the 8 Big Apple Dancers' Australian tour, and Leon James in *The Spirit Moves*. In subsequent years, she became active in New York City politics.

OLIVER "BUCKLES" WASHINGTON, Esther's brother, danced with Elnora Dyson in an Ella Fitzgerald show in New Jersey, and at the Roxy Theatre in 1943.

THOMAS WASHINGTON appeared in *Swingin' the Dream*.

ELEANOR "STUMPY" ATKINSON (WATSON) (unknown–present), who is 4'11", earned her nickname, given by Whitey, from Lindy hopping with Long-Legged George Greenidge. She grew up in Brooklyn, began dancing as a young teen, and first went to the Savoy around 1937, where she was asked to join Whitey's Lindy Hoppers while watching the group rehearse at the ballroom. Frankie says she had very good footwork. Eleanor danced in *Radio City Revels* with George, with whom she says she created down-the-back and improved on other air steps. She is also in *Keep Punching*.

RUSSELL WILLIAMS began dancing with Whitey's Lindy Hoppers around 1937 or 1938. He won the 1939 Harvest Moon Ball Lindy hop championship with Connie Hill, appeared in *Hot Mikado*, and performed with the Congaroo Dancers during the group's entire run, dancing in *Killer Diller*. In the early 1950s, he changed his name to Rasul Ali Ibm Aleem. Frankie, who stayed in touch with Russell for a time, later heard that he was killed trying to break up a fight between two men.

Congaroo Dancers

HELEN DANIELS

ANN JOHNSON

FRANKIE MANNING

WILLAMAE RICKER

RUSSELL WILLIAMS

Many thanks to the following sources:

Bethel, Pepsi. *Authentic Jazz Dance: A Retrospective*. New York: American Authentic Jazz Dance Theatre, 1990.

Callen, Eunice. Personal interviews, 21 July 1997, 23 July 1997.

Crease, Robert P. "James, Leon and Albert Minns." *American National Biography*. New York: Oxford University Press, 1999.

———. "Profiles of Original Lindy Hoppers," series in *The New York Swing Dance Society Footnotes*. "Pal Andrews" (Spring 1991):2; "Eunice Callen" (November–December 1989):1–2; "Wilda Crawford" (November–December 1988):1; "Mildred Cruse" (January–March 1988):1; "Elnora Dyson" (January–March 1989):1; "Sandra Gibson" (April–June 1987):1; "Willie Jones" (Spring 1990):5; "Norma Miller" (April–June 1986):1; "Naomi Waller Gay" (Winter 1991):3–4; "Billy Ricker" (July–September 1987):1; "Harry Rowe" (July– September 1989):1–2.

Dyson, Elnora. Telephone interviews, 13 October 2002, 3 June 2006.

Gabay, Malikia. Telephone interview and e-mail, 8 May 2006.

"Herbert W. White, Restaurateur, Dies." *Syracuse Herald-American*, 1 October 1950, 47.

Hickson, Martha. Telephone interview, 4 June 2006.

Loggins, Peter. *California Historical Jazz Dance Foundation*. "Jimmy Valentine." http://www.caljazzdance.com/jimmy.htm.

Manning, Frankie. Personal and telephone interviews. 1993–2006.

MGM film contract for *A Day at the Races,* 23 March 1937.

MGM film contract for "musical photoplay," 9 September 1935.

Miller, Norma. Telephone interview, 18 June 2006.

———. *Swingin' at the Savoy: The Memoir of a Jazz Dancer.* Philadelphia: Temple University Press, 1996.

Monaghan, Terry. Telephone interviews and e-mails. 2006.

———. "Remembering 'Shorty': A Few Thoughts on the Beginnings of Jive and Lindy Hop on George Snowden's Centenary." *The Dancing Times,* July 2004, 49, 51.

———. *Savoy Ballroom: Dancers Profiles.* "George Snowden," "Naomi Waller." http://www.savoyballroom.com.

Pritchett, Judy. Telephone interviews and e-mails, 2006.

———. *Archives of Early Lindy Hop: Biographies of the Original Swing Dancers.* "Tiny Bunch," " 'Twist Mouth George' Ganaway," "Sandra Gibson," "George Greenidge," "Leon James," "Ann Johnson," "Dorothy Johnson," "Leroy 'Stretch' Jones," "Norma Miller," "Al Minns," "Mildred Pollard," "Billy Ricker," "Willa Mae Ricker," "Naomi Waller," "Russell Williams." http://www.savoystyle.com.

Rayno, Don. Telephone interviews and e-mails, 2004–2005.

Rheingold, Ruthie. Telephone interviews, 26 October 2002, 3 June 2006.

Riddick, Hazel. Telephone interview, 4 June 2006.

Schaap, Phil. Personal and telephone interviews, and e-mails, 2006.

Schulz, Larry. Telephone interviews, 2006.

Watson, Eleanor "Stumpy." Personal interview, 18 June 1997.

Libraries and Archives

New York Public Library for the Performing Arts, 40 Lincoln Center Plaza, New York, NY 10023-7498, (212) 870-1630, www.nypl.org/research

Institute of Jazz Studies, John Cotton Dana Library, Rutgers, The State University of New Jersey, 185 University Avenue, Newark, NJ 07102, (973) 353-5595, www.libraries.rutgers.edu/rul/libs/jazz/jazz.shtml

Schomburg Center for Research in Black Culture, 515 Malcolm X Boulevard, New York, NY 10037-1801, (212) 491-2200, www.nypl.org/research

Archives Center, National Museum of American History, Smithsonian Institution, 14th Street and Constitution Avenue, NW, Washington, DC 20013-7012, (202) 633-3270 (Ernie Smith Jazz Film Collection, 1894–1979), www.americanhistory. si.edu/archives/d4491-1.htm

Web Sites

Archives of Early Lindy Hop (history): www.savoystyle.com
Mark the Savoy (history): www.savoyplaque.org
Savoy Ballroom, 1926–1958 (history, news): www.savoyballroom.com
SavoyStyle Swing Dance Shop (videos, DVDs, CDs, shoes, posters): www.swingdanceshop.com
Yehoodi (news, links, chat): www.Yehoodi.com

Frankie's List of Swing Dance on Film/TV
(* means Frankie appears in film)

Pre–1955
FEATURE FILMS
A Day at the Races. MGM, 1937.
Manhattan Merry-Go-Round. Republic Pictures, 1937.
Radio City Revels. RKO Radio Pictures, 1938.*
Keep Punching. M. C. Pictures, 1939.*
Hellzapoppin'. Universal Pictures, 1941.*
Cabin in the Sky. MGM, 1943.
Killer Diller. All-American News, 1948.*

SHORT SUBJECTS
After Seben. Paramount, 1929.
Ask Uncle Sol. Twentieth Century-Fox, 1937.
Jittering Jitterbugs. Sack Amusement Enterprises, 1943.*
"Lindy Hoppers." *Cootie Williams and His Orchestra.* Official Films, 1943 or 1944.
Jammin' the Blues. Warner Bros., 1944.

NEWSREELS
It Takes "Hot Dogs" to Win the Lindy Hop. Pathe, 1931.
New Dance Sweeping Up from the South. Paramount, 1937.

Jitterbugs Jive at Swingeroo. Paramount, 1938.
"World Series" Dance has N.Y. Swinging. Paramount, 1938.
Pick Dance Champs. Paramount, 1941.

SOUNDIES

Air Mail Special. Soundies Distributing Corp. of America, 1941.
Hot Chocolate ("Cottontail"). R.C.M. Productions, 1941.♦
Outline of Jitterbug History. R.C.M. Productions, 1942.♦
Sugar Hill Masquerade. Minoco Productions, 1942.

DOCUMENTARIES

The Spirit Moves. Mura Dehn, 1950s.♦
Jazz Dance. Roger Tilton, 1954.

Post–1955

FEATURE FILMS

Malcolm X. Warner Bros., 1992.♦
Swing Kids. Buena Vista, 1993.

DOCUMENTARIES

Watch Me Move. KCET Production, 1986.♦
Call of the Jitterbug. Green Room Production, 1988.♦
Jitterbug. National Geographic Society Explorer, 1990.♦
Dancing: New Worlds, New Forms, 5. Thirteen/WNET, 1993.♦
Swingin' at the Savoy: Frankie Manning's Story. Living Traditions, 1995.♦
Swingin' with Duke. Storyville Films, 1998.♦
Jazz: A Film by Ken Burns. Florentine Films, 2000.♦

TELEVISION

"American Jazz Dances." *American Musical Theater.* WCBS-TV, 1960.
Chicago and All That Jazz (The DuPont Show of the Month). NBC-TV, 1961.
"Back into Swing." *20/20.* ABC News, 1989.♦
Stompin' at the Savoy. WCBS-TV, 1992.♦

Swing Dancing Around the World
(partial list of organizations/individuals for which Frankie taught between 2000 and 2006)
American Lindy Hop Championships, Stamford, CT. artspectrum.org/alhc.htm
Apollo Swing, Brussels, Belgium. lindyhop.be
Arizona Lindy Hop Society, Phoenix, AZ. savethearts.org/swing
Atlanta Swing Era Dance Association, Atlanta, GA. aseda.org
Atomic Ballroom, Irvine, CA. atomicballroom.com
Audrey Wilson, Irvine, CA. audreydancing.com
Avalon Dance, Catonsville, MD. avalondance.com
Baarder Institute of Dance, Oslo, Norway. baardar.no
BarSwingOna, Barcelona, Spain. barswingona.org

Bill Borgida, Ithaca, NY. billborgida.com

Boogie-Bären, Munich, Germany. boogie-baeren.de

Century Ballroom, Seattle, WA. centuryballroom.com

Coal Country Traditions, Pittsburgh, PA. coalcountry.org

Crazy Legs, Western MA. crazylegs.org

Chris Lee's Savoy Swing Club, Sacramento, CA. sacramentoswing.com

Dance Flurry, Saratoga Springs, NY. danceflurry.org

Dance Manhattan, New York, NY. dancemanhattan.com

Dance New Orleans, New Orleans, LA. danceneworleans.com

Disc'n'Roll, Lyon, France. disc-nroll.com

Emily Belt, San Diego, CA. swingorama.com

FEET with Heat 4dance, Wellington, New Zealand. feetwithheat.co.nz

Festival de Lindy Hop, Strasbourg, France. afrolatino.net

Fonzies, Darwin/Adelaide, Australia. fonzies.net

Foundation Lindyhop.nl, Amsterdam, Netherlands. lindyhop.nl

Got2Lindy, Hudson Valley, NY. got2lindy.com

Gottaswing, DC, MD, VA. gottaswing.com

Grimaldi Danse, Grenoble, France. grimaldidanse.com

Herräng Dance Camp, Herräng, Sweden. herrang.com/en

Historic Columbia Foundation, Columbia, SC. historiccolumbia.org

Hop to the Beat, Boston, MA. hoptothebeat.com

Houston Swing Dance Society, Houston, TX. hsds.org

Jitterbugs Swingapore, Singapore. jitterbugs.com

Jiving Lindy Hoppers, London, England. jivinglindyhoppers.com

Jonathan and Sylvia, Santa Barbara, CA. jonathanandsylvia.com

Jules Klapper, New York, NY. cutcat.com

Jumpers TSKE, Budapest, Hungary. jumpers.uw.hu

Jumpin at the Woodside, Gloucester, England. jazzjiveswing.com

Karen Lee Dance Theatre, Denver, CO. karenleedance.com

Les Fous du Swing, Paris, France. lesfousduswing.net

Live2Jive, London, England. live2jive.co.uk

Louis & Company Dance Studio, Overland Park, KS. funwithstyle.com

Lynn Miller & Company, Syracuse, NY. swinginsyracuse.com

Midsummer Night Swing, New York, NY. lincolncenter.org

Northern CA Lindy Society, Bay Area, CA. ncls.com

Northwest Dance Network, Seattle, WA. nwdance.net

Pasadena Ballroom Dance Association, Pasadena, CA. pasadenaballroomdance.com

Philadelphia Swing Dance Society, Philadelphia, PA. swingdance.org

Piedmont Swing Dance Society, Piedmont Triad, NC. piedmontswingdance.org

Pittsburgh Swing, Pittsburgh, PA. pittsburghswing.com

San Diego Lindy Hop Instructors, San Diego, CA. swingorama.com

Sandra Cameron Dance Center, New York, NY. sandracameron.com

Saratoga SAVOY Center of Dance, Saratoga Springs, NY. saratogasavoy.com

Savoy South "Make Believe" Dance Hall, St. Petersburg, FL. savoysouth.com

Savoy Swing Club, Seattle, WA. savoyswing.com

Some Like It Hot!, Vienna, Austria. somelikeithot.at

Swing Cat Cie, Montpellier, France. swingcatcie.com

Swing Dance Genova, Genova, Italy. swingdancegenova.net

Swing Dance Heritage Club, Fayetteville, NC. swingmasterproductions.com

Swing Devils of the Palouse, Moscow, ID. swingdevils.org

SwingKatz, Sydney, Australia. swingkatz.com

Swing Patrol, Melbourne/Sydney, Australia. swingpatrol.com.au

Swingout Northwest, Port Townsend, WA. savoyswing.com

Swingsation, Dallas, TX. swingsation.net

Suzie-Q Swing Productions, CT, RI. havetodance.com/suzie-q

Tapit/new works, Madison, WI. tapitnewworks.org

TC Swing, Twin Cities, MN. tcswing.com

The Joint is Jumpin! Dance Studios, OR. thejointisjumpin.com

Tokyo Swing Dance Society, Tokyo, Japan. impetus.ne.jp

Toronto Swing Dance Society, Toronto, Canada. dancing.org/tsds

Toulouse Swing Festival, Toulouse, France. 144danceavenue.com

Triangle Swing Dance Society, Durham, Raleigh, NC. triangleswingdance.org

Upper Valley Swing Dance Network, VT, NH. uvswingdance.net

USA Grand National Dance Championships, Atlanta, GA. usagrandnationals.com

Virginia State Open Swing Dance Championships, Herndon, VA. vsoswing.com

Windy City Lindy Exchange, Chicago. chicagoswingmusicfestival.org

NOTES

An Appreciation

1. Cynthia R. Millman, "Swing Dancing Glides Into Style," *The West Side Spirit,* 29 June 1987, 19.
2. Archer Winston, "Wake of the News," *New York Post,* 7 May 1936, 21.
3. Ernie Smith, jazz dance historian, in conversation, circa 1994.
4. Tobi Tobias, "Soft Touch," *New York,* 15 May 1989, 115.

Prologue

1. For a detailed description of house rent parties, see Willie the Lion Smith with George Hoefer, *Music on My Mind: The Memoirs of an American Pianist* (1964; reprint, New York: Da Capo Press, 1978).

PART I

Chapter 1

1. The Lincoln Theatre presented virtually all of the great African American vaudeville stars during its two decades of operation, and was known as the home of Fats Waller's (born May 21, 1904) first professional engagement while still a teenager. After opening in 1909, it became especially popular with Harlem's working-class Southern immigrants by virtue of its appealing entertainment bill. See Lisa Clayton Robinson, "Lincoln Theatre," in *Africana: The Encyclopedia of the African.American Experience,* ed. Kwame Anthony Appiah and Henry Louis Gates Jr. (New York: Civitas Books, 1999).
2. This architectural arrangement inspired Duke Ellington's "Harlem Air Shaft."

Chapter 2

1. According to Hopkins's biography, the pianist/band leader moved to New York just after Labor Day, 1927. There is no mention of his performing at the Alhambra Ballroom at this time, but he was playing in the city, so it's possible that Frankie did, in fact, hear him at the Alhambra. See Warren W. Vaché Sr., *Crazy Fingers: Claude Hopkins' Life in Jazz* (Washington, DC: Smithsonian Institution Press, 1992), 27–29.
2. Occupying most of the top floor, the dance hall crowned the stately building whose architectural detail derived from the Italian Renaissance style popular from 1890 to 1935. Linda Micale (architect), telephone interview with Cynthia R. Millman, 8 August 2002.

3. Marshall Stearns and Jean Stearns, *Jazz Dance: The Story of American Vernacular Dance* (1968; reprint, New York: Da Capo Press, 1994), 12.

4. Melville J. Herskovits, *The Myth of the Negro Past* (New York: Harper & Brothers, 1941), 146; quoted in Stearns, *Jazz Dance*, 13.

5. A. N. Tucker, *Tribal Music and Dancing in the Southern Sudan* (London: Wm. Reeves, Ltd, n.d.), 36; quoted in Stearns, *Jazz Dance*, 13.

6. Roark Bradford, "New Orleans Negro Declared Not Guilty of the Charleston" (no publication given), January 3, 1926, Dance Clipping File, Dance Collection, Lincoln Library of the Performing Arts, Lincoln Center, New York, n.p.; quoted in Lynne Fauley Emery, *Black Dance From 1619 to Today* (Princeton, NJ: Princeton Book Company, 1988), 226.

7. Thaddeus Drayton, from numerous interviews, New York: 1962–1965; quoted in Stearns, *Jazz Dance*, 112.

8. Willie the Lion Smith with George Hoefer, *Music on My Mind: The Memoirs of an American Pianist* (1964; reprint, New York: Da Capo Press, 1978), 66, 97.

9. Stearns, *Jazz Dance*, 112.

10. Jacqui Malone, *Steppin' on the Blues: The Visible Rhythms of African American Dance* (Urbana: University of Illinois Press, 1996), 77.

11. Stearns, *Jazz Dance*, 112.

12. Paul Colin, *Josephine Baker and La Revue Négre: Paul Colin's Lithographs of Le Tumulte Noir in Paris, 1927* (New York: Abrams, 1998), 9.

13. *Our Dancing Daughters*, MGM, 1928.

14. Stearns, *Jazz Dance*, 112.

15. Abel Green and Joe Laurie Jr., *Show Biz* (New York: Henry Holt, 1951), 228; quoted in Stearns, *Jazz Dance*, 112.

16. Stearns, *Jazz Dance*, 112.

17. Mervyn Cook, *The Chronicle of Jazz* (New York: Abbeville Press, 1997), 9.

18. The concept of jazz music as a democratic, pluralistic art form is discussed at length in Lewis A. Erenberg's *Swingin' the Dream: Big Band Jazz and the Rebirth of American Culture* (Chicago: University of Chicago Press, 1998).

19. *How to Dance the Shag*, Skibo Productions, 1937.

20. This might explain why, although the Alhambra Ballroom reportedly had an official opening date of September 13, 1929 (some years after the Alhambra Theatre opened), Frankie recalls dancing there as early as 1927. The 1929 date may actually have been for the reopening of the ballroom. Another possible explanation is suggested by Janice Wilson, director of the now defunct American Institute of Vernacular Jazz Dance. Her research with elderly Harlem residents has led her to believe that the large hall atop the Alhambra Theatre may have operated as a private social club prior to its grand opening, hosting various events, including dances. Janice Wilson, telephone interview with Cynthia R. Millman, 9 July 2001.

21. By 1930, the phrase had made enough of an impression on Duke Ellington for him to record Andy Razaf and Eubie Blake's composition "That Lindy Hop."

22. Mimi Shaw Hayes, *Watch Me Move,* KCET Production, 1986.

23. *After Seben,* Paramount, 1929.

24. After African American Jack Johnson's domination of heavyweight boxing from 1908 to 1915, the white sports establishment was so anxious to recapture and retain the world title that many white boxers refused to risk fighting black contenders. When heavyweight champion Jack Dempsey was ordered to fight Wills (known as the "Brown Panther") by the New York State Athletic Association in 1923, he forfeited $50,000 rather than risk his title. See Andrew S. Dolkart and Gretchen S. Sorin, *Touring Historic Harlem: Four Walks in Northern Manhattan* (New York: New York Landmarks Conservancy, 1977), 77.

PART II
Chapter 3

1. The Savoy was advertised as "The World's Finest Ballroom." David Watkins, Dan Burley, and Ben Murray, *The Savoy Story* (New York: Savoy Ballroom, 1951), n.p.

2. Likely due to references to the Cats' Corner in Marshall and Jean Stearns, *Jazz Dance: The Story of American Vernacular Dance* (1968; reprint, New York: Da Capo Press, 1994), 322, 326–327.

3. Stearns, *Jazz Dance,* 322. *The New Cab Calloway's Cat-ologue: A Hepsters Dictionary,* rev. ed. (New York: 1939), 2, defines "cat" as a "musician in a swing band." "It was [Louis] Armstrong who started musicians referring to themselves as cats," Albert Murray, *Stomping the Blues* (1976; reprint, New York: Da Capo Press, 2000), 238.

4. Archer Winsten, "Wake of the News," *New York Post,* 7 May 1936, 21.

5. Martha Hickson, personal interview with Cynthia R. Millman, 2 March 2003.

6. Stearns, *Jazz Dance,* 322.

7. Stearns, *Jazz Dance,* 326–327.

8. Watkins, *Savoy Story,* n.p.

9. Don McDonagh, "Twentieth-Century Social Dance Before 1960," *International Encyclopedia of Dance,* ed. Selma Jean Cohen (New York: Oxford University Press, 1998).

10. Irving Lewis Allen, "Slang," *The Encyclopedia of New York City,* ed. Kenneth T. Jackson (New Haven: Yale University Press for the New York Historical Society, 1995).

11. Louis Seymour (Historian and Musical Director of Astors' Beechwood Mansion in Newport, RI), telephone interview with Cynthia R. Millman, 29 March 2003.

12. This is confirmed in an article about the 1943 closing of the Savoy Ballroom: "Before closing, the Savoy was owned by a corporation in which Buchanan had a thirty-five percent interest." Russell Gold, "Guilty of Syncopation, Joy, and Animation: The Closing of Harlem's Savoy Ballroom," *Studies in Dance History* 5 (Spring 1994): 59.

13. Frankie says a jam circle is "when a crowd forms around a dancing couple in order to watch them. Then, one couple after another goes into the circle to perform, each trying to outdo the others."

14. See Rusty E. Frank, *TAP! The Greatest Tap Dance Stars and Their Stories, 1900–1955,* rev. ed. (New York: Da Capo Press, 1994), 38, 43. See also Stearns, *Jazz Dance,* 195–196, 272.

15. Roseland Ballroom opened on New Year's Eve, 1919.

16. In a 7 June 1990 panel discussion about the Savoy Ballroom sponsored by the New York Swing Dance Society, musician Panama Francis indicates that Saturday was the most integrated night at the Savoy: "Saturday was like salt and pepper, with as many white kids as black." "The Savoy Ballroom Remembered," *The New York Swing Dance Society* 5 (Fall 1990): n.p.

17. Regarding the treatment of celebrities, Charles Buchanan commented: "As long as they behave, we ignore them. That is our policy." Leonard Q. Ross, *The Strangest Places* (New York: Harcourt, Brace, 1939), 187.

18. "On 16 January 1938 Goodman brought a new level of recognition to jazz with a concert in Carnegie Hall, presenting Harry James, Ziggy Elman, Jess Stacy, [Lionel] Hampton, [Gene] Krupa, and [Teddy] Wilson from his own entourage as well as guest soloists from the bands of Duke Ellington and Count Basie." Richard Wang, "Benny Goodman," *The New Grove Dictionary of Jazz,* ed. Barry Kernfeld (1988; reprint, New York: St. Martin's Press, 2000).

19. Norma Miller with Evette Jensen, *Swingin' at the Savoy: The Memoir of a Jazz Dancer* (Philadelphia: Temple University Press, 1996), 102–106.

Chapter 4

1. "Twenty years ago [White] was the first dancing waiter at Baron Wilkins at 134th and Seventh Avenue. Later he trained dancing waiters at Smalls' [Paradise] when it was on upper Fifth Avenue." Archer Winsten, "Wake of the News," *New York Post,* 7 May 1936, 21.

2. Frankie can't confirm this, and it is not clear from Norma Miller's autobiography, *Swingin' at the Savoy: The Memoir of a Jazz Dancer* (Philadelphia: Temple University Press, 1996).

3. A list of 105 "Famed Organizations that entertain at Savoy" includes: Century Social Club, Cosmopolitan Social Club, Flamingoes Social Club, Gentlemen's Social Club, Modern Ladies Social Club, Mystery Girls Social Club, Progressive Social Club, and the Seven Star Social Club. David Watkins, Dan Burley, and Ben Murray, *The Savoy Story* (New York: Savoy Ballroom, 1951), n.p.

4. See also Marshall and Jean Stearns, *Jazz Dance: The Story of American Vernacular Dance* (1968; reprint, New York: Da Capo Press, 1994), 315–316, 323–324 for a corresponding version of Snowden's story.

5. "Herbert White, the man who created and made an international profession out of the Lindy Hop back in 1927 directly after Colonel Charles A. Lindbergh flew the Atlantic Ocean, pulled out his dancing shoes again last week with an eye and

mind set on the making and popularizing of a dance to honor the great Joe Louis."
"To Create Joe Louis Shuffle," *Pittsburgh Courier,* 28 September 1940, 20.

6. Frankie only knew of the cakewalk as a dance from the past that had been incorporated into the Lindy. He never saw it done in its original context.

7. For a superb explanation of the evolution of swing music and its relationship to the dance, see "Portrait of the Swing Era," Ernie Smith's preface in Norma Miller, *Swingin' at the Savoy,* x–xxxvii.

8. For a consummate example of this stylistic element, see Frankie and Ann Johnson's solo (the fourth couple) in *Hellzapoppin'*, Universal Pictures, 1941.

Chapter 5

1. For a history of the famed amateur contest, see Ted Fox, *Showtime at the Apollo* (1983; reprint, New York: Da Capo Press, 1993), 61–66.

2. Frankie defines legomania as "a style of eccentric dance in which a dancer uses his or her legs to do all sorts of crazy, wild movements. Legs are generally in the air, may have a rubbery feel, and can include twisting motions."

3. Various companies, including Paramount, Pathe, and MGM, produced newsreels (short subjects highlighting news of the week) that were shown in movie theaters before the feature film.

4. The sailor step evokes a hornpipe. Holding hands the entire time, partners maneuver into a back-to-back position with their bodies leaning diagonally right, arms held out to the side at shoulder height. Thus locked together, they pivot clockwise in a hopping movement.

5. Henderson had been dealing for some time with an unstable roster of band personnel (as well as legal and financial troubles), which might explain Frankie's disappointment with his music at the 1935 Harvest Moon Ball. See Walter C. Allen, *Hendersonia: The Music of Fletcher Henderson and His Musicians,* Jazz Monographs (Highland Park, NJ: Walter C. Allen, 1973), 273–329.

Chapter 6

1. There is evidence that Snowden had done some performing on Harlem stages since fall 1928. "The 'Lindy Hop Revue' which is underlined for next week will introduce Lottie Brown, Cy Williams, Brother Albert, Wade and Wade and will feature George (Shorty) Snowden and Pauline." In "Dance Revue Contest at Lincoln Theatre," *New York Age,* 15 September 1928, 6. And "'Bojangles' will present his Surprise Revue, with a group of performers who have won distinction on Broadway. The revue will include Altha Leagus, Bertha Vanderbilt, Morgan Spencer, Eloise Parham, Francis Jacobs, Beatrice Winston, George Snowden and Pauline Morse." In "Great Interest Shown in Annual Monarch Concert," *New York Age,* 8 November 1928, 7.

2. This short subject, with music by the Chick Webb and His Orchestra, contains a scene that features three pairs of dancers performing early Lindy hop (which was still similar to the breakaway), shows many Charleston steps, and ends with a

cakewalk. Shorty Snowden is the male partner in the third couple. We do not know the identities of the other five dancers.

3. Frankie is describing a jump turn, a movement in which the man jumps high enough for his left arm to clear his partner's head as he spins her around in an over-the-head turn.

4. The jig walk is a six-count movement featuring two touch-steps or kicks, followed by a rock step. It is done in place with partners in ballroom stance, and is essentially the same as the basic step in East Coast swing.

5. This describes the typical AABA pattern of a 32-bar chorus.

6. It is difficult to definitively date this event, but there are some clues. Whiteman's orchestra opened at the Paradise Restaurant for an extended run in April 1935. See Philip R. Evans and Larry F. Kiner with William Trumbauer, *Tram: The Frank Trumbauer Story* (Newark: Institute of Jazz Studies, Rutgers—The State University of New Jersey; Metuchen, NJ: Scarecrow Press, 1994), 176–179, 622. Snowden's group may have left New York sometime during the latter half of 1935 to appear in an MGM film, although we have been unable to confirm this. A contract dated 9 September 1935 that names all six dancers states: "We hereby employ the act consisting of six (6) negro dancers (three men and three women), known as the 'Lindy Hoppers', who have recently appeared with Paul Whiteman's Band, to appear and perform for us in a musical photoplay, such services to commence not later than December 1, 1935."

7. Standing in a ballroom hold, partners jockey by simply shifting their weight forward and backward with a step-touch, repeating as desired. Although the jockey can be a resting step, it allows dancers to gather their energy before bursting into motion.

8. In the fall-off jig walk, the woman drapes herself over her partner in an exaggerated ballroom position. As he walks backward, dragging her along with her legs lunging out behind her, he pivots her away from him and back.

9. The third couple in *Hellzapoppin'*, Willamae Ricker and Al Minns, do down-the-back in the waterfall (lineup) at the end.

10. Over-the-shoulder starts with the woman standing in front of and slightly to the right of her partner, his right arm around her waist. As she simultaneously jumps up and arches her back, he scoops her up into a backward somersault over his right shoulder. Frances "Mickey" Jones and William Downes, the first couple to perform in *Hellzapoppin'*, do over-the-shoulder for their second air step.

11. In the side-flip, the woman somersaults backward using her partner's right arm as a fulcrum while his left arm assists her. The side-flip is the first air step Jones and Downes do in *Hellzapoppin'*.

12. Frankie doesn't really consider ace-in-the-hole to be an air step, but rather a lift, because the woman is never released to fly through the air, and it is not always tightly timed to the music. Facing her partner, arms around his shoulders, the woman initially jumps up to straddle his waist with her legs. (In the original version, her legs go between his on the floor.) He then thrusts his hips forward

with enough force to rock her legs back up behind her toward the ceiling. After hanging upside down for an instant, her feet swing down to the floor. Norma Miller and Billy Ricker, the second couple in *Hellzapoppin'*, do ace-in-the-hole for their first air step.

13. In handspring-front-flip, the woman dives into a handstand in front of her partner, who then hoists her upward as she simultaneously jackknifes her torso up, thus flipping into a somersault. She lands facing her partner, and briefly hangs onto his shoulders for support before dashing into the next step. Willamae Ricker and Al Minns do handspring-front-flip for their second air step in *Hellzapoppin'*.

14. In handspring-down-the-back, both partners perform the initial moves of handspring-front-flip, but with more exertion, which lobs the woman over the man and into a head-first slide down his back. The move concludes as in down-the-back. Handspring-down-the-back is Miller and Ricker's third air step in *Hellzapoppin'*.

15. Steven Mitchell, telephone interview with Cynthia R. Millman, 25 April 2004.

16. Wynton Marsalis, *Marsalis on Music* (New York: Norton, 1995), 115.

17. Albert Murray, *Stomping the Blues* (1976; reprint, New York: Da Capo Press, 2000), 99.

18. John F. Szwed, *Jazz 101: A Complete Guide to Learning and Loving Jazz* (New York: Hyperion, 2000), 30.

19. See Brenda Bufalino and Jane Goldberg, *By Word of Foot,* Changing Times Tap Dancing Co., c. 1980.

20. Szwed, *Jazz 101*, 104.

21. Barry Kernfeld, "Break," *The New Grove Dictionary of Jazz*, ed. Barry Kernfeld (1988; reprint, New York: St. Martin's Press, 2000).

PART III

Chapter 7

1. The original Cotton Club, open since 1920, closed on February 16, 1936 to relocate to Broadway and 48th Street. The move was initially a failure, and the Cotton Club owners found themselves temporarily without a home. After sorting things out, they reopened with great fanfare and success on September 24, 1936. See Jim Haskins, *The Cotton Club* (1977; reprint, New York: New American Library, 1984), 112–116.

2. "In Trucking, the shoulders are often hunched up, one above the other, the hips sway in Congo fashion, and the feet execute a variety of shuffles." Marshall and Jean Stearns, *Jazz Dance: The Story of American Vernacular Dance* (1968; reprint, New York: Da Capo Press, 1994), 41.

3. "We didn't know what to expect. We heard the music start and Boom! the three teams came out. Not only had their routines changed, but, unbelievably, they were all dancing together! While we were gone, the Lindy Hop had changed." Norma Miller with Evette Jensen, *Swingin' at the Savoy: The Memoir of a Jazz Dancer* (Philadelphia: Temple University Press, 1996), 97.

4. Frankie remembers that performers featured peckin' on stage and social dancers inserted it into the Lindy. The step was popularized by The Chocolateers in the mid-1930s. "Then a trio, *The Chocolateers,* arrived from the West Coast with a barnyard novelty called Pecking that became a ballroom sensation." Stearns, *Jazz Dance,* 246.

5. Doubling was a relatively common practice for vaudeville performers when they could get the work.

Chapter 8

1. Dot Moses and Tiny Bunch perform their specialty during the Lindy hop scene in the film *Radio City Revels* to "Swinging in the Corn." *Radio City Revels,* RKO Radio Pictures, 1938.

2. *A Day at the Races,* MGM, 1937. Whitey's Lindy Hoppers dance to "All God's Chillun Got Rhythm," with vocal by Ivy Anderson.

3. "Herbert White, creator of the famous Lindy Hop, will give the country a new dance some time this year, when he unveils his Joe Louis Shuffle. He's shown here taking a few of his dancers through the paces, getting them in the mood for things to come. Dance is named in honor of the Brown Bomber." In "Developing New Dance in Honor of Joe Louis," *Pittsburgh Courier,* 28 September 1940, 21.

4. The MGM contract for the appearance of Whitey's dancers in *Day at the Races* is dated 23 March 1937. An interoffice communication on MGM letterhead cites 18 March 1937 as the date the dancers were to begin working on the film. According to a Harlem Uproar House program, Tiny Bunch and the Original Lindy Hoppers premiered on 28 March 1937 in a show headlined by Erskine Hawkins' 'Bama State Collegians.

5. An advertisement for the Hollywood Theatre engagement bills the group as "Cab Calloway's Lindy Hoppers" to take advantage of Calloway's fame and popularity. Unidentified newspaper clipping from Frankie's scrapbook, circa 1937.

6. "Clarence Robinson's Cotton Club show opened at the London Palladium Theatre last Tuesday for a four week stay." "Cotton Club Show Opens At London Palladium," *New York Age,* 7 August 1937, 9.

Chapter 9

1. Developed during vaudeville's heyday, theater circuits were chains of theaters that provided a touring route for traveling performers or packaged shows. Each circuit consisted of theaters grouped by geographic region such as the South, Northeast, or Mid-Atlantic. Tivoli Circuit, Pantages, T.O.B.A. (Theatre Owners Booking Association), Orpheum Circuit, and Loews Circuit are examples. See also Rusty Frank, *TAP!: The Greatest Tap Dance Stars and Their Stories,* rev. ed. (New York: Da Capo Press, 1994).

2. *Everybody Sing,* MGM, 1938. The film was released on February 4, 1938.

3. Pollard and Davis perform the cradle at the end of the first solo during the Lindy scene in *Radio City Revels.*

4. "'Head arrangements' are often developed in the playing, made up night after night, with some parts being added as they go along, and others dropped." John F. Szwed, *Jazz 101: A Complete Guide to Learning and Loving Jazz* (New York: Hyperion, 2000), 47.

5. See Robert Farris Thompson, *African Art in Motion: Icon and Act in the Collection of Katherine Coryton White* (Los Angeles: University of California Press, 1974) for a superb study of African dance.

6. This paragraph incorporates information from Terry Monaghan. Terry Monaghan, e-mails to Cynthia R. Millman, 16 February 2006, 17 February 2006.

7. Katrina Hazzard-Gordon, *Jookin': The Rise of Social Dance Formations in African-American Culture* (Philadelphia: Temple University Press, 1990), 81. See also Lynne Fauley Emery, *Black Dance From 1619 to Today* (1972; reprint, Princeton, NJ: Princeton Book Company, 1988).

8. Based on telephone discussions and e-mails between Judy Pritchett and Cynthia R. Millman, 2006. See also Art Rosenbaum, *Shout Because You're Free: The African American Ring Shout Tradition in Coastal Georgia* (Athens: University of Georgia Press, 1998).

9. At a 2001 event commemorating the big apple in Columbia, South Carolina, Frankie met a woman who had done the dance at the Big Apple Club in the 1930s and told him that blacks did not have a specific name for it.

10. Dexter and Anita Peters-Wright, *The Big Apple* (New York: Peters-Wright Studio, 1938), 4.

11. Catherine A. Rudenick, "Big Applers Still Truckin' in the Southeast," *Dancing USA* (September/October 1992), 18.

12. Ibid.

13. Jeff Wilkinson, "'You Just Got in a Group and Followed Along': Teens Took Big Apple to the Beach, and from There It Swept the Nation," *TheState.com*, 25 August 2003, http://www.thestate.com/mld/thestate/news/local/6612112.htm.

14. "1937 Closes with Big Apple," *Life*, 20 December 1937, 29–32.

15. Thomas E. Parson, "The Ballroom Observer: A Forum of the Social Dance," *The American Dancer* (March 1938):28.

16. Bosley Crowther, "From the Turkey Trot to the Big Apple," *New York Times Magazine*, 7 November 1937, 14–15, 18.

17. "On a street set built as a replica of 33 and 7th avenue in front of Whitey's dance school the eight dancers led by 350 pound Tiny bunch put on a variation of the big apple. . . . The adagio stunts kept the stars Allan Jones, Judith Garland and others gasping in fear of the four girls getting their neck broken in case they fell on the hard street pavement." Unidentified newspaper clipping from Frankie's scrapbook, circa fall 1937.

18. "Meanwhile 47 atmosphere dancers kept time in a circle surrounding the Big Applers as represented passersby on Harlem's lively street." Ibid.

19. *Keep Punching*, M. C. Pictures, 1939. This feature film includes two dance scenes: a big apple first, and a Lindy hop routine.

20. Frankie stylized the movements he had seen as a child in revival church meetings into a jazz step when he choreographed the big apple. In his version of shouts, the arms swing out to the side, then back in like a pendulum to cross in front of the chest, as the knees bounce rhythmically and the feet do small, alternating kicks. The feeling is expansive and exuberant. The movement is repeated over and over, usually for eight bars.

21. London Bridge starts with one couple standing face to face, holding hands (or one hand) overhead to form an arch. Each successive pair dances under the bridge, then joins the line, until all are forming the bridge. (This first half of London Bridge can be seen in *Keep Punching*.) To conclude, the first couple then lowers their arms, releases one hand, and dances through the fully formed archway, followed by one pair at a time until the bridge is disbanded.

22. Break-a-leg is the exit step in the big apple routine in *Keep Punching*.

23. Clark Gable (who was under contract to MGM from 1931 to 1954), Myrna Loy, and Spencer Tracy were probably filming *Test Pilot*, released in 1938.

24. Professional swing dancer Jack Carey came up with the idea for the Jack & Jill contest in order to encourage dancers who were not training with regular partners to enter swing competitions. He devised the format in California during the mid-1950s, whereby dancers compete with whomever they are paired with in a random drawing of names.

25. *Manhattan Merry-Go-Round,* Republic Pictures, 1937. Release date for this feature film was November 13, 1937.

26. One reviewer disagreed with Frankie's assessment: "In the barbecue scene for 'Swingin' in the Corn,' a highlight is developed through the shagging routines of four colored couples in character. They stand out strongly." Roy Chartier, "Radio City Revels," *Variety (Weekly),* 2 February 1938, 15.

27. "Unlike the musical, the revue has no real story; unlike the vaudeville show, it has a specific theme." Rudiger Bering, *Musicals* (Hauppage, NY: Barron's, 1998), 29.

28. "Hot Rhythm," *Teleradio* (Melbourne), 3 December 1938, n.p.

29. F.K.M., "Hollywood Hotel Revue," *Table Talk* (Melbourne) 29 December 1938, n.p.

30. Marshall and Jean Stearns, *Jazz Dance: The Story of American Vernacular Dance* (1968; reprint, New York: Da Capo Press, 1994), 232.

Chapter 10

1. Todd's Broadway production of *Hot Mikado* opened on 23 March 1939 at the Broadhurst Theatre and ran for eighty-five performances.

2. Dancers listed in a program for *Hot Mikado* (no exact date given): "Gladys Crowder, Geneva Davis, Belle Hill, Connie Hill, May [Mae] Miller, Mildred Pollard, Eddie Davis, Leon James, Walter Johnson, Lee Lyons, Albert Minne [Minns], Russell Williams."

3. Born 10 February 1909, Chick Webb died of tuberculosis on 16 June 1939.

4. The five couples who perform the big apple in *Keep Punching* are: Lucille Middleton and Frankie Manning, Norma Miller and George Greenidge, Wilda Crawford and Thomas "Tops" Lee, Joyce James and Joe Daniels, and Frances "Mickey" Jones and William Downes. The six couples who solo in the Lindy scene are (in order): Ann Johnson and Billy Williams, Joyce James and Joe Daniels, Eleanor "Stumpy" Watson and Sonny Jenkins, Lucille Middleton and Frankie Manning, Wilda Crawford and Thomas "Tops" Lee, and Norma Miller and George Greenidge.

5. *Swingin' the Dream* opened 29 November 1939 at the Center Theatre, which is now the New York City Center.

6. The program says, "Scenery after cartoons by Walt Disney."

7. A *Swingin' the Dream* program from the week beginning Monday, 4 December 1939 lists the following: "Jitterbugs: Dottiemae Johnson and Frank Manning, Beatrice Elam and George Greenidge, Wilda Crawford and William Downes, Joyce Boyd and Joseph Daniels, Wilhelmina Moore and Billy Williams, Anne [Ann] Johnson and Thomas Lee, Norma Miller and Thomas Washington, Lucille Middleton and Joe Riddick, Emily McCloud and Samuel Pierce, Frances Jones and James Outlaw, Hilda Bess and Richard Bess, Joyce James and Leroy Jones, Arlyne Evans and Lonnie Jenkins." Frankie claims the program incorrectly pairs several couples. He remembers the following partnerships: Beatrice Elam and Leroy Jones, Norma Miller and George Greenidge, Frances "Mickey" Jones and William Downes, Ann Johnson and Billy Williams, and Wilda Crawford and Thomas "Tops" Lee. Additionally, he says Lonnie Jenkins was really Sonny Jenkins.

8. The couples that were featured most often were Norma Miller and George Greenidge, Ann Johnson and Billy Williams, Wilda Crawford and Thomas "Tops" Lee, Frances "Mickey" Jones and William Downes, and Dottiemae Johnson and Frankie.

9. According to the program for *Swingin' the Dream*, the song was probably "Peace Brother," sung by the Deep River Boys and the Ensemble.

10. *Swingin' the Dream* ran for thirteen performances.

11. Bundles for Britain was an American volunteer organization that donated supplies to the British war relief effort before the United States entered World War II.

12. Norma Miller and Billy Ricker, the second couple to solo in *Hellzapoppin'*, do the shake-around right after their first air step.

13. In cradle-round-the-back, the man scoops the woman into his arms and rocks her in front, from one side to the other, before guiding her around his back and returning her to standing. The entire group does this movement in *Hellzapoppin'*.

14. Tops and Wilda perform the wrap-around in their solo during the Lindy hop scene in *Keep Punching*.

15. Beasley does the lock in *A Day at the Races*. Eddie Davis does it in *Radio City Revels*.

16. Frankie recalls: "Rubberlegs performed with most of the big bands in many nightclubs and theaters in Harlem, including Smalls' Paradise and the Apollo. Basie, who he worked with quite a bit, came up with a head tune about Rubberlegs, who was gay, called 'Miss Thing.' He didn't have any special music that he danced to, so Basie and the band would just play this song whenever Rubberlegs performed with them. Eventually, Basie had it arranged and recorded it. You can see Rubberlegs in the short subject *Smash Your Baggage*." *Smash Your Baggage*, Vitaphone Corp., 22 April 1933.

17. See Minns's solo in *Hellzapoppin'* for a marvelous demonstration of his style of dancing.

18. *Hellzapoppin'*, Universal Pictures, 1941.

19. *Hellzapoppin'* opened on Broadway on 22 September 1938 for a run of 1,404 performances.

20. See Norma Miller with Evette Jensen, *Swingin' at the Savoy: The Memoir of a Jazz Dancer* (Philadelphia: Temple University Press, 1996), 146–147.

21. Norma Miller and George Greenidge perform this step in their solo during the Lindy hop scene in *Keep Punching*.

22. Photographs of some of the steps that Frankie and Ann used in their solo appear in a two-page *Life* spread taken at a special photo shoot at the Savoy Ballroom. See W. Eugene Smith, "Harlem's New 'Congeroo' Gives Girls a Workout," *Life* (16 June 1941):49–50.

23. Connie Hill and Russell Williams do the head snatch in a short subject featuring the Cootie Williams Orchestra. Their dancing references some of Frankie's choreography from *Hellzapoppin'*. "Lindy Hoppers," *Cootie Williams and His Orchestra*, Official Films, 1943 or 1944. Dottimae Johnson and Leon James also appear.

Chapter 11

1. Popular in the early 1940s, soundies were brief musical movies shown on a juke-box called a Panaram. See Maurice Terenzio, Scott MacGillivray, and Ted Okuda, *The Soundies Distributing Corporation of America: A History and Filmography of Their "Jukebox" Musical Films of the 1940s* (Jefferson, NC: McFarland & Co., 1991), vii.

2. *Hot Chocolate ("Cottontail")*, R.C.M. Productions, 1941.

3. According to an article by James J. Cummings in the Oswego County Historical Society annual journal, 1,800 African American inductees were stationed at Fort Ontario beginning 13 January 1941 to train for active duty. The author, who explores racial relations between the citizens of Oswego and the newly installed Army population, devotes a page to the role Whitey's establishment played during this period. In addition to his restaurant being a social center for the soldiers, Cummings reports that Whitey was an important link to New York City, and "could be relied upon to help in rough times for he often lent money to the men when it was needed." Whitey also served as a decrier of intolerance when,

in an impassioned letter to the local *Palladium-Times,* he implored the upstate community to treat the soldiers respectfully and without discrimination. See John J. Cummings, "The Black 369th in Oswego (1941)," *Oswego County Historical Society Journal* 33 (1972): 55–69.

4. See W. Eugene Smith, "Harlem's New 'Congeroo' Gives Girls a Workout," *Life* (16 June 1941):49–50.

5. *Stormy Weather* premiered on Wednesday, 21 July 1943 at the Roxy Theatre.

PART IV

Chapter 12

1. Stump and Stumpy were an African American comedy/tap team who appear in the film *This Is the Army,* a 1943 musical sponsored by the War Department.

2. William H. Smith and Ellen Ternes, *Invisible Soldiers: Unheard Voices,* ComTel Productions, 2000. See also A. Russell Buchanan, *Black Americans in World War II* (Santa Barbara, CA: Clio Books, 1977) and Neil A. Wynn, *The Afro-American and the Second World War,* rev. ed. (New York: Holmes & Meier, 1993).

3. David W. Stowe, *Swing Changes: Big-Band Jazz in New Deal America* (Cambridge: Harvard University Press, 1994), 157.

4. See Cholly Atkins and Jacqui Malone, *Class Act: The Jazz Life of Choreographer Cholly Atkins* (New York: Columbia University Press, 2001), 61–64, 66–71; Constance Valis Hill, *Brotherhood in Rhythm: The Jazz Tap Dancing of the Nicholas Brothers* (New York: Oxford University Press, 2000), 215.

Chapter 13

1. This is the first routine the Congaroos do in *Killer Diller* (All-American News, 1948).

2. Whaley worked as Duke Ellington's copyist.

3. The Lindy hop is the Congaroos' second routine in *Killer Diller.*

4. "Bradley, Clarence 'Buddy': Early 1920s–1960s. Tap teacher. Created dance routines for many Broadway musicals in the late twenties and early thirties. Coached some of the tap greats, including Pat Rooney, Jessie Matthews, Ann Pennington, Eddie Foy, Ruby Keeler, Jack Donahue, Adele and Fred Astaire, Tom Patricola, Eleanor Powell, Paul Draper. Choreographed in Europe during 1920s–30s." Rusty Frank, *TAP!: The Greatest Tap Dance Stars and Their Stories,* rev. ed. (New York: Da Capo Press, 1994), 284.

5. Marshall and Jean Stearns, *Jazz Dance: The Story of American Vernacular Dance* (1968; reprint, New York: Da Capo Press, 1994), 317–319.

6. Terry Monaghan, e-mail to Cynthia R. Millman, 3 March 2006.

7. Judy Pritchett, e-mail to Cynthia R. Millman, 8 March 2006.

PART V

Chapter 14

1. Smalls' Paradise held swing dances to live big bands on Monday nights from January 1984 through spring 1985.

2. Frankie recalls, "Al Minns, Norma Miller, Billy Ricker, Eunice Callen, William Downes, Pepsi Bethel, and Pal Andrews from Whitey's Lindy Hoppers were all there, as well as some of those who started dancing a little later like, among others, Sugar Sullivan, Sonny Allen, Harry Connor, and Ruby Reeves. So was Buster Brown (the tap dancer), Ernie Smith, and Paul Grecki, a teacher at the studio, and his wife, Carol."

3. Norma's dancers included Chazz Young, Debbie Williams, Clyde Wilder, Darlene Gist, and Stoney Martini.

4. The first dance given by the NYSDS was held on 5 May 1985. Their mission statement, as printed on a schedule announcing upcoming dances from 1 September 1991 through 9 February 1992, states, "The New York Swing Dance Society is a nonprofit organization dedicated to preserving the Lindy Hop (aka swing or jitterbug), the expressive and improvisational jazz dance that developed in Harlem nightclubs and ballrooms of the late 1920s. The Society serves to promote the artists, the music and the musicians of Swing as well as the dance itself."

5. Bryant Dupré's dance parties started in early spring 1986 and continued until October of that year, at which point the Swing Now Trio (Dupré, Anthony DiGregorio, and John DeCesare) initiated a weekly swing night at the North River Bar. These continued until December 1988. Bryant DuPré, telephone interview by Cynthia R. Millman, 11 January 2006.

6. Minns died on 24 April 1985.

7. This event was organized by NYSDS board member Bob Crease and the Jiving Lindy Hoppers' manager, Terry Monaghan, on behalf of the NYSDS.

8. The Savoy Swingers included Norma and Frankie, Chazz Young and Debbie Williams, and Mickey Davidson and Clyde Wilder.

9. Lennart Westerlund, Anders Lind, and Henning Sörensen. Lennart Westerlund, e-mail to Cynthia R. Millman, 23 December 2005.

10. The Rhythm Hot Shots wasn't formed until 1985, but some members of the group had begun working together as early as 1983. Ibid.

11. Jitterbugs was produced by Simon Erland.

12. *Black and Blue* received ten nominations for the 1989 Tony Award, more than any other play that year. Ruth Brown won the Tony for Best Performance by a Leading Actress in a Musical. Claudio Segovia and Héctor Orezolli won the Tony for Best Costume Design.

13. "Back into Swing," *20/20*, ABC News, 1989, aired on 6 June.

14. *Malcolm X*, Warner Bros., 1992.

15. *Stompin' at the Savoy*, CBS, 1992.

16. *Swing Kids*, Buena Vista, 1993.

17. *Idlewild*, HBO Films, 2006.

18. The Gap's "Khakis Swing" commercial first aired in April 1998.

19. Savoystyle.com was launched in 1995; Yehoodi.com in 1998.

SOURCES

Books

Allen, Debbie. *Brothers of the Knight.* New York: Dial Books for Young Readers, 1999.

Allen, Irving Lewis. "Slang." In *The Encyclopedia of New York City,* ed. Kenneth T. Jackson. New Haven: Yale University Press for the New York Historical Society, 1995.

Allen, Walter C. *Hendersonia: The Music of Fletcher Henderson and His Musicians.* Jazz Monographs. Highland Park, NJ: Walter C. Allen, 1973.

Atkins, Cholly and Jacqui Malone. *Class Act: The Jazz Life of Choreographer Cholly Atkins.* New York: Columbia University Press, 2001.

Bering, Rudiger. *Musicals.* Hauppage, NY: Barron's, 1998.

Bordman, Gerald. *The Oxford Companion to American Theatre.* 2nd ed. New York: Oxford University Press, 1992.

Buchanan, Russell A. *Black Americans in World War II.* Santa Barbara, CA: Clio Books, 1977.

Calloway, Cab. *The New Cab Calloway's Cat-ologue: A Hepsters Dictionary.* Rev. ed. New York: 1939.

Castle, Mr. and Mrs Vernon. *Modern Dancing.* New York: Harper & Brothers, 1914.

Charters, Samuel B. and Leonard Kunstadt. *Jazz: A History of the New York Scene.* 1962; reprint, New York: Da Capo Press, 1984.

Chilton, John. *Who's Who of Jazz: Storyville to Swing Street.* Rev. ed. New York: Da Capo Press, 1985.

Colin, Paul. *Josephine Baker and La Revue Négre: Paul Colin's Lithographs of Le Tumulte Noir in Paris, 1927.* New York: Abrams, 1998.

Cook, Mervyn. *The Chronicle of Jazz.* New York: Abbeville Press, 1997.

Crease, Robert P. "Divine Frivolity: Hollywood Representations of the Lindy Hop, 1937–1942." In *Representing Jazz,* ed. Krin Gabbard, 207-228. Durham, NC: Duke University Press, 1995.

Dance, Stanley. *The World of Swing: An Oral History of Big Band Jazz.* New York: Da Capo Press, 1974.

Dolkart, Andrew S. and Gretchen S. Sorin. *Touring Historic Harlem: Four Walks in Northern Manhattan.* New York: New York Landmarks Conservancy, 1997.

Driggs, Frank and Harris Lewine. *Black Beauty, White Heat: A Pictorial History of Classic Jazz, 1920–1950.* 1982; reprint, New York: Da Capo Press, 1996.

●

Emery, Lynne Fauley. *Black Dance From 1619 to Today.* 1972; reprint, Princeton, NJ: Princeton Book Company, 1988.

Erenberg, Lewis A. *Swingin' the Dream: Big Band Jazz and the Rebirth of American Culture.* Chicago: University of Chicago Press, 1998.

Evans, Philip R. and Larry F. Kiner with William Trumbauer. *Tram: The Frank Trumbauer Story.* Newark: Institute of Jazz Studies, Rutgers—The State University of New Jersey; Metuchen, NJ: Scarecrow Press, 1994.

Ferrett, Gene. *Swing Out: Great Negro Dance Bands.* 1970; reprint, New York: Da Capo Press, 1993.

Fox, Ted. *Showtime at the Apollo.* 1983; reprint, New York: Da Capo Press, 1993.

Frank, Rusty. *TAP!: The Greatest Tap Dance Stars and their Stories.* Rev. ed. New York: Da Capo Press, 1994.

Gillerlain, Gayle. *The Reverend Thomas's False Teeth.* Mahwah, NJ: Troll Associates, Bridgewater Books, 1995.

Govenar, Alan. *Stompin' at the Savoy: The Story of Norma Miller.* Cambridge: Candlewick Press, 2006.

Hasse, John Edward. *Jazz: The First Century.* New York: HarperCollins, 2000.

Haskins, Jim. *The Cotton Club.* 1977; reprint, New York: New American Library, 1984.

Hazzard-Gordon, Katrina. *Jookin': The Rise of Social Dance Formations in African-American Culture.* Philadelphia: Temple University Press, 1990.

Hill, Constance Valis. *Brotherhood in Rhythm: The Jazz Tap Dancing of the Nicholas Brothers.* New York: Oxford University Press, 2000.

Jonas, Gerald. *Dancing: The Pleasure, Power, and Art of Movement.* New York: Abrams in association with Thirteen/WNET, 1992.

Kernfeld, Barry. "Break." In *The New Grove Dictionary of Jazz,* ed. Barry Kernfeld. 1988; reprint, New York: St. Martin's Press, 2000.

Leiter, Samuel L. *The Encyclopedia of the New York Stage, 1930–1940.* New York: Greenwood Press, 1989.

Malcolm X with Alex Haley. *The Autobiography of Malcolm X.* New York: Ballantine, 1964.

Malone, Jacqui. *Steppin' on the Blues: The Visible Rhythms of African American Dance.* Urbana: University of Illinois Press, 1996.

Marsalis, Wynton. *Marsalis on Music.* New York: Norton, 1995.

McDonagh, Don. "Twentieth-Century Social Dance Before 1960." In *International Encyclopedia of Dance,* ed. Selma Jean Cohen. New York: Oxford University Press, 1998.

McKissack, Patricia C. *A Million Fish . . . More or Less.* New York: Knopf, 1992.

Michelson, Richard. *Happy Feet: The Savoy Ballroom Lindy Hoppers and Me.* San Diego: Gulliver Books, 2005.

Miller, Norma with Evette Jensen. *Swingin' at the Savoy: The Memoir of a Jazz Dancer.* Philadelphia: Temple University Press, 1996.

Millman, Cynthia R. "Big Apple." In *International Encyclopedia of Dance,* ed. Selma Jean Cohen. New York: Oxford University Press, 1998.

Millman, Cynthia R. "Frankie Manning." In *International Encyclopedia of Dance,* ed. Selma Jean Cohen. New York: Oxford University Press, 1998.

———. "Lindy Hop." In *International Encyclopedia of Dance,* ed. Selma Jean Cohen. New York: Oxford University Press, 1998.

Monaghan, Terry. "The Legacy of Jazz Dance." In *Annual Review of Jazz Studies 9, 1997–98,* ed. Edward Berger, David Cayer, Henry Martin, Dan Morgenstern, 295–338. Newark: Institute of Jazz Studies, Rutgers—The State University of New Jersey; Lanham, MD: Scarecrow Press, 2000.

Murray, Albert. *Stomping the Blues.* 1976; reprint, New York: Da Capo Press, 2000.

O'Meally, Robert G., ed. *The Jazz Cadence of American Culture.* New York: Columbia University Press, 1998.

Peters-Wright, Dexter and Anita. *The Big Apple.* New York: Peters-Wright Studio, 1938.

Robinson, Lisa Clayton. "Lincoln Theatre." In *Africana: The Encyclopedia of the African American Experience,* ed. Kwame Anthony Appiah and Henry Louis Gates Jr. New York: Civitas Books, 1999.

Ross, Leonard Q. *The Strangest Places.* New York: Harcourt, Brace, 1939.

Schoener, Allon, ed. *Harlem on My Mind: Cultural Capital of Black America, 1900–1978.* New York: Dell, 1978.

Schuller, Gunther. *The Swing Era: The Development of Jazz, 1930–1945.* New York: Oxford University Press, 1989.

Sellman, James Clyde. "World War II and African Americans." In *Africana: The Encyclopedia of the African American Experience,* ed. Kwame Anthony Appiah and Henry Louis Gates, Jr. New York: Civitas Books, 1999.

Smith, Ernie. "A Selected List of Films and Kinescopes." In Marshall and Jean Stearns, *Jazz Dance: The Story of American Vernacular Dance,* 403–427. 1968; reprint, New York: Da Capo Press, 1994.

Smith, Morgan and Marvin. *Harlem: The Vision of Morgan and Marvin Smith.* Lexington: University Press of Kentucky, 1998.

Smith, Willie the Lion with George Hoefer. *Music on My Mind: The Memoirs of an American Pianist.* 1964; reprint, New York: Da Capo Press, 1978.

Stearns, Marshall and Jean. *Jazz Dance: The Story of American Vernacular Dance.* 1968; reprint, New York: Da Capo Press, 1994.

Stowe, David W. *Swing Changes: Big-Band Jazz in New Deal America.* Cambridge: Harvard University Press, 1994.

Szwed, John F. *Jazz 101: A Complete Guide to Learning and Loving Jazz.* New York: Hyperion, 2000.

Terenzio, Maurice, Scott MacGillivray, and Ted Okuda. *The Soundies Distributing Corporation of America: A History and Filmography of Their "Jukebox" Musical Films of the 1940s.* Jefferson, NC: McFarland, 1991.

Thompson, Robert Farris. *African Art in Motion: Icon and Act in the Collection of Katherine Coryton White.* Los Angeles: University of California Press, 1974.

Vaché, Warren W. Sr. *Crazy Fingers: Claude Hopkins' Life in Jazz.* Washington, DC: Smithsonian Institution, 1992.

Wang, Richard. "Benny Goodman." In *The New Grove Dictionary of Jazz,* ed. Barry Kernfeld. 1988; reprint, New York: St. Martin's Press, 2000.

Ward, Geoffrey C. and Ken Burns. *Jazz: A History of America's Music.* New York: Knopf, 2000.

Watkins, David, Dan Burley, and Ben Murray. *The Savoy Story.* New York: Savoy Ballroom, 1951.

Wilmeth, Don and Tice L. Miller, eds. *Cambridge Guide to American Theatre.* Cambridge: Cambridge University Press, 1993.

Wynn, Neil A. *The Afro-American and the Second World War.* Rev. ed. New York: Holmes & Meier, 1993.

Articles

"A L'ill Yalla Basket." *Teleradio* (Brisbane), circa late November or early December 1938, n.p.

Chartier, Roy. "Radio City Revels." *Variety (Weekly),* 2 February 1938, 15.

"Cotton Club Show Opens at London Palladium." *New York Age,* 7 August 1937, 9.

Crease, Robert P. "Swing Story." *Atlantic* (February 1988):77–82.

———. "Last of the Lindy Hoppers." *Village Voice,* 25 August 1987, 27–32.

Crowther, Bosley. "From the Turkey Trot to the Big Apple." *New York Times Magazine,* 7 November 1937, 14–15, 18.

Cummings, John J. "The Black 369th in Oswego (1941)." *Oswego County Historical Society Journal* 33 (1972): 55–69.

"Dance Revue Contest at Lincoln Theatre." *New York Age,* 15 September 1928, 6.

"Developing New Dance in Honor of Joe Louis." *Pittsburgh Courier,* 28 September 1940, 21.

"Dixie's New Dance Craze 'Big Apple,' Terped Barefoot." *Variety,* 27 July 1937, 28.

Engelbrecht, Barbara. "Swinging at the Savoy." *Dance Research Journal* 15 (Spring 1983): 3–10.

F. K. M. "Hollywood Hotel Revue." *Table Talk* (Melbourne), 29 December 1938, n.p.

Gold, Russell. "Guilty of Syncopation, Joy, and Animation: The Closing of Harlem's Savoy Ballroom." *Studies in Dance History* 5 (Spring 1994): 50–64.

"Great Interest Shown in Annual Monarch Concert." *New York Age,* 8 November 1928, 7.

"Hot Rhythm." *Teleradio* (Melbourne), 3 December 1938, n.p.

"Life Goes to a Party: At the Savoy with the Boys and Girls of Harlem." *Life,* 14 December 1936, 64–68.

"Lindy Hoppers." *Life,* 28 December 1936, 30–31.

Millman, Cynthia R. "Swing Dancing Glides Into Style." *The West Side Spirit,* 29 June 1987, 19, 25.

"1937 Closes with Big Apple." *Life,* 20 December 1937, 29–32.

Parson, Thomas E. "The Ballroom Observer: A Forum of the Social Dance." *The American Dancer* (March 1938):28.

Rudenick, Catherine A. "Big Applers Still Truckin' in the Southeast." *Dancing USA* (September/October 1992):18.

Smith, Ernie. "Recollections and Reflections of a Jazz Dance Film Collector." *Dance Research Journal* 15 (Spring 1983): 46–48.

Smith, W. Eugene. "Harlem's New 'Congeroo' Gives Girls a Workout." *Life,* 16 June 1941, 49–50.

Smith, Morgan S. "Pictures to the Editor." *Life,* 8 July 1940, 84.

"The Lindy Hop." *Life,* 23 August 1943, 95–103.

"The Savoy Ballroom Remembered." *The New York Swing Dance Society Footnotes* 5 (Fall 1990): n.p.

"To Create Joe Louis Shuffle." *Pittsburgh Courier,* 28 September 1940, 20.

Tobias, Tobi. "Soft Touch." *New York Magazine,* 15 May 1989, 115.

Wilkinson, Jeff. "'You Just Got in a Group and Followed Along': Teens Took Big Apple to the Beach, and from There It Swept the Nation." *TheState.com,* 25 August 2003, http://www.thestate.com/mld/thestate/news/local/6612112.htm.

Winsten, Archer. "Wake of the News." *New York Post,* 7 May 1936, 21.

Published Interviews

Manning, Frankie. "The Swing Era." Interview by Robert P. Crease (New York, 22–23 July 1992). *Jazz Oral History Project.* Washington, DC: Smithsonian Institution, 1992.

Young, Chazz. "All That Chazz." Interview by Cindy Geiger (Herräng, Sweden, July 1998). *Strutters Quarterly* (Autumn 1998).

Conference Papers and Theses

Batiuchok, Margaret. "The Lindy." M.A. thesis, New York University, 1988.

Crease, Robert P. "The Lindy Hop." *Research Forum Papers: Proceedings of the 1988 International Early Dance Institute.* Towson, MD: Goucher College, 1988.

Documentaries

Bufalino, Brenda and Jane Goldberg. *By Word of Foot.* Changing Times Tap Dancing Co., c. 1980.

Hayes, Mimi Shaw. *Watch Me Move.* KCET Production, 1986.

Smith, William H. and Ellen Ternes. *Invisible Soldiers: Unheard Voices.* ComTel Productions, 2000.

INDEX

I N D E X

Frankie Manning won a 1989 Tony Award for his choreography in *Black and Blue*, and was honored by the National Endowment for the Arts with a National Heritage Fellowship. He served as a consultant for and danced in Spike Lee's *Malcolm X* and Debbie Allen's *Stompin' at the Savoy*. Now in his nineties, Frankie continues to travel the world teaching the Lindy hop and sharing his riveting stories culled from a lifetime of dancing.

Cynthia R. Millman performed with the Big Apple Lindy Hoppers, and has studied, partnered, and lectured with Frankie Manning. A librarian at The Town School in Manhattan, Cynthia has contributed articles to *Dance Magazine* and *The International Encyclopedia of Dance*.